Spaces and Places in Western India

This book studies places and spaces in Western India both as geographical locations and as imagined constructs. It uncovers the rich history of the region from the perspective of places of pilgrimage, commerce, community, expression and indigeneity.

The volume examines how spaces are intrinsically connected to the lived experiences of people. It explores how spaces in Western India have been constructed over time and how these are reflected in both historical and contemporary settings – in the art, architecture, political movements and in identity formation. The rich examples explored in this volume include sites of Bhakti and Sufi literature, Maharashtrian-Sikh identity, Mahanubhav pilgrimage, monetary practices of the Peshwas and the internet as an emancipatory space for the Dalit youth in Maharashtra. The chapters in this book establish and affirm the forever evolving cultural topography of Western India.

Taking a multidimensional approach, this book widens the scope of academic discussions on the theme of space and place. It will be useful for scholars and researchers of history, cultural studies, geography, the humanities, city studies and sociology.

Bina Sengar is an Assistant Professor in Department of History and Ancient Indian Culture, Dr. Babasaheb Ambedkar Marathwada University, Aurangabad, and was a Fulbright Fellow for the year 2018–2019 at Florida International University, Miami. She has published on various themes related to state policy and tribal studies in India. Her recent articles on tribal communities in Western India are: 'Policies for Ethnic Communities' Assimilation in India: A Gandhian Perspective' (2018), 'Trade Routes and Commercial Networks in Deccan-Marathwada during Seventeenth and Eighteenth Centuries' (2017) and 'Prospects for Sustainability in Human–Environment Patterns: Dynamic Management of Common Resources' (2017).

Laurie Hovell McMillin is a Professor of Rhetoric and Composition at Oberlin College, USA. An interest in the construction of place animates her work: *English in Tibet, Tibet in English: Self-Presentation in Tibet and the Diaspora* (2001) and *Buried Indians: Digging up the Past in a Midwestern Town* (2006). More recently, her travel writing has appeared in *The Lonely Planet Travel Anthology* (2016), *Travel Writing: Theory and Practice* (2013) and in other publications. She has researched and travelled in Maharashtra for many years.

Spaces and Places in Western India

Formations and Delineations

Edited by
Bina Sengar and
Laurie Hovell McMillin

Routledge
Taylor & Francis Group
LONDON AND NEW YORK

First published 2020
by Routledge
2 Park Square, Milton Park, Abingdon, Oxon OX14 4RN

and by Routledge
52 Vanderbilt Avenue, New York, NY 10017

Routledge is an imprint of the Taylor & Francis Group, an informa business

British Library Cataloguing-in-Publication Data
A catalogue record for this book is available from the British Library

Library of Congress Cataloging-in-Publication Data
A catalog record has been requested for this book

ISBN: 978-0-8153-9258-3 (hbk)
ISBN: 978-0-429-34369-8 (ebk)

Typeset in Sabon
by codeMantra

This volume is dedicated to the memory of
Meera Kosambi (1939–2015)
and
Eleanor Zelliot (1926–2016)

Contents

List of figures ix
List of contributors xi
Foreword xiii
Acknowledgements xv

Introduction: location, expositions and synthesis in the region 1
BINA SENGAR AND LAURIE HOVELL McMILLIN

PART I
Urban, rural and indigenous spaces in Maharashtrian politics and environment 13

1 **The aftermath of placeless space: mapped, delimited, bifurcated, merged: a phenomenon of Dewas S. and Dewas J.** 15
IRINA GLUSHKOVA

2 **The spatial analysis of the transition of the land revenue system in Western India (1761–1836), with special reference to Indapur Pargana** 35
MICHIHIRO OGAWA

3 **Creating spaces for indigeneity from Nizam's Hyderabad state to Maharashtra** 51
BINA SENGAR

4 **Internet as an emancipatory space: case study of Dalits in Maharashtra** 77
SHRADDHA KUMBHOJKAR

PART II
Constructing space and place: material culture and public spaces 85

5 Place, space and money in Maharashtra, c. 1750–1850: some insights 87
SHAILENDRA BHANDARE

6 Architectural continuity across political ruptures: early Marathas and the Deccan sultanates 107
PUSHKAR SOHONI

7 Blurred lines: historical knowledge and the politics of statues 115
DANIEL JASPER

8 Karle/Ekvira: many places over time, and at once 126
LAURIE HOVELL McMILLIN

PART III
Religious spaces and places in Western India 145

9 The significance of place in early Mahānubhāv literature 147
ANNE FELDHAUS

10 Seven Sufi brothers: *dargah* vernacular narratives and Konkani Sufi-Muslims 161
DEEPRA DANDEKAR

11 Emplacing holiness: the local religiosity between Vaishnavas, Sufis and demons 181
DUŠAN DEÁK

12 Dakhani Sikh identity and the religious space(s) in Nanded (Maharashtra) 204
BIRINDER PAL SINGH

Appendices 221
Index 225

Figures

1.1	Location of contemporary Dewas	16
1.2	Mr. Vijay Pandit, a resident of present-day Dhar, next to a photo of his grandfather, a dewan of Dewas Senior during the times of Tukojirao III	17
1.3	The goddess Chamunda, the famous devi of the hill	25
1.4	Sign for the two goddess temples divided between two families of Dhar S. and Dhar J.	25
1.5	The goddess Tulja-Bhavani	26
1.6	Clock tower at the Subhash Square (in former Dewas J.)	28
1.7	A view of the desolated palace at Dewas S., now a residential building	29
2.1	The location of Pune District and Indapur Pargana in Bombay Presidency	38
2.2	The arrangement of villages in Indapur Pargana in the period of 1768–1822	38
2.3	The structure of administrative place under the Maratha rule	42
2.4	Location of *jagir* villages in Indapur Pargana in the late eighteenth century	45
2.5	Location of *jagir* villages in Indapur Pargana in the early nineteenth century	47
3.1	The Gond region in the Central Provinces of British India	57
3.2	Gond territories of Hyderabad state	64
5.1	The 'Hali Sikka' rupee, struck at Pune	93
5.2	The 'Ankushi' rupee, struck at Pune	93
5.3	The rupee of Chinchwad with the symbol of a battleaxe or *Furshee*	94
5.4	The Chakan rupee with the letter 'Shri' impressed on it	94
5.5	The Nasik rupee the symbol of the Maratha pennant or *Jaripatka*	94
5.6	The 'Ankushi' rupee struck at Phulgaon with an additional symbol of a *Hibiscus* flower	97
5.7	The 'Ankushi' rupee struck at Janjira, known as the 'Hubshee' rupee	98

8.1 The entrance to Karle caves next to the Ekvira temple 127
8.2 Inside the Karle *chaitya*, in view of the main *stupa*, 2004 130
8.3 Photo of poster at Karle, with an image of Ekvira superimposed on the site, January 2016 132
11.1 A picture of Sheikh Muhammad near his shrine 184
11.2 Vaishnava performers in front of Sheikh's dargah-samadhi 187
11.3 Devotees during the first day of Sheikh's utsava 190
11.4 Paying respect to Yogasangram 192
11.5 Devotees encircling Sheikh Muhammad's grave in Vahira 193
11.6 Khaki Buva's dargah 195

Contributors

Shailendra Bhandare is a Senior Assistant Keeper at the South Asian and Far-eastern Numismatics and Paper Money Collections, and a member of the Faculty of Oriental Studies at Oxford University. He has been curator in the Ashmolean Museum since 2002.

Deepra Dandekar is a researcher at the Center for the History of Emotions, Max Planck Institute for Human Development, Berlin. A historian and anthropologist, Deepra has written on religion and minority experiences in India.

Dušan Deák is an associate professor at the Department of Comparative Religion at Comenius University in Bratislava, Slovakia. His research focuses on the social history of religious communities in the Deccan.

Anne Feldhaus is a foundation professor of Religious Studies at Arizona State University. She has written extensively on the religious traditions of the Maharashtra.

Irina Glushkova, Ph.D., D.Litt., works with the Center for Indian Studies, Institute of Oriental Studies of Russian Academy of Sciences (Moscow). Her field of interests ranges from religion and politics of Indian regions (primarily Maharashtra and Hindi belt) to dynamics of cultural integration and new methodological 'turns' in humanities.

Daniel Jasper is an associate professor of Sociology, and co-director of the Peace and Justice Studies program, at Moravian College, Pennsylvania, USA.

Shraddha Kumbhojkar teaches History at the Savitribai Phule Pune University, India. She is interested in historiography, memory studies, dalit studies, digital humanities and the history of modern India.

Laurie Hovell McMillin is a professor of Rhetoric and Composition at Oberlin College, Ohio, USA. Her interests include travel writing, South Asian culture and Tibetan studies.

Michihiro Ogawa is an associate professor at the Kanazawa University, Japan. He studies socio-economic transition in Western India (Maharashtra) from the eighteenth century to the nineteenth century.

Bina Sengar is an assistant professor of History at the Dr. Babasaheb Ambedkar Marathwada University of Aurangabad, India. She works on indigenous people's history in context to environment, health and nation state policies.

Birinder Pal Singh is a professor of eminence at the Department of Sociology and Social Anthropology, Punjabi University, Patiala, India. His research areas include tribal, peasant and community studies and the sociology of violence.

Pushkar Sohoni teaches in the Humanities and Social Sciences programme at the Indian Institute of Science (IISER) Pune. He trained as a conservation architect and received his doctorate on the sultanate architecture of the Deccan.

Foreword

By Jim Masselos
The International Conference on
Maharashtra: Culture and Society

It is a delight to welcome this impressive collection of essays. All are distinguished by high standards of scholarship and by keen insights directed towards understanding a common theme in a common region – that of spaces and places in Maharashtra. There is considerable variety in the coverage of what is in the volume: some contributors, for instance, are interested in early Maharashtra; others are concerned with developments in more recent times. Whichever, a shared thematic concern helps bring the volume together into a coherent whole. Whatever the chronology or time frame, the interest is in how the themes play out against the background of Maharashtra in past and recent times.

The result is that the volume gives us an agreeable range of topics and presents a lot of rich material that is in itself fascinating. That the collection has an overall coherence is an added virtue, one that derives from the shared exploration of location and locality and one that enables comparison between the different parts. A lot of fresh analysis and unfamiliar subject matter come together in this collection.

The volume is the product of the co-operative efforts of a number of scholars, Maharashtrian as well as foreign, who come together with their research to help build new ways of looking at Maharashtra through the prism of space and place. They move towards giving us new understandings and important insights into aspects of Maharashtra's society and culture. Just how relevant the scholarship is and how fine its quality becomes evident as we read through the various chapters. They contain many insights and much new research.

Specifically, the volume derives from a gathering of scholars and the research papers they presented at a conference concerned with Maharashtra held at Dr. Babasaheb Ambedkar Marathwada University in Aurangabad in 2016. It is one of the more recent conferences promoted by this group of scholars. They are an informal gathering who meet irregularly but approximately every two years or so. There is no specific organization, no secretariat or any continued institutional base to maintain the conferences or manage their affairs. Instead, the conference works through the commitment of individual scholars who in turn over the years have taken responsibility for organizing the conference in their own home bases. It is their commitment that has enabled the conference to survive as an institution.

The usual convention for setting up the conferences is that they meet in alternate years in alternate locations – if one year the conference meets at a university in Maharashtra or India, then the next one is held at an international location sometime within the next two years. So, in India, the conference has met in Mumbai, Pune, Aurangabad and Delhi and outside in Toronto, Phoenix, St. Paul, Heidelberg, Sydney, Bratislava, Moscow and Tokyo. It will be evident from the list that the conferences have been able over the years to tap into and interact with expertise scattered around the world – not in itself an easy feat to achieve.

If the lineage of the gatherings is impressive in terms of where they have been held, equally impressive is their duration. They go back to 1984 when the first gathering was convened at the University of Toronto. The second of these conferences followed at the University of Pune in 1987.

Another convention developed over the years – that each conference has a theme and that a selection of the papers be published in book form. Although not every conference has managed to result in a published volume – most have done so.[1]

The result is an impressive list of volumes concerned with Maharashtra and its history and culture, with most volumes usually devoted to a particular theme. They represent a major contribution to Marathi studies and to our understanding of what is and what has been Maharashtra. This volume is a worthy addition to that corpus of research and publication. Its essays make interesting reading in themselves and they also open up fresh approaches in understanding Maharashtra.

Note

1 For a list of the conferences and publications up to 2008, see Meera Kosambi, 'A Short History of the International Conference on Maharashtra: Culture and Society', Appendix to M. Naito, I. Shima, and H. Kotani eds., *Marga Ways of Liberations, Empowerment, and Social Change in Maharashtra*, Manohar, Delhi, 2008, pp. 471–474.

Acknowledgements

The volume *Spaces and Places in Western India: Formation and Delineations* owes a great deal to Prof. Anne Feldhaus, who initially and insightfully raised the problem inherent in notions of spaces and places when discussions about the making of this book first began. This book took almost three years to take its final shape. Most of the edited essays in it were presented during the 16th International Conference of Maharashtra held at Dr. Babasaheb Ambedkar Marathwada University, Aurangabad, in January 2016. During the conference, the scholars came from all parts of the world to the historic city of Aurangabad, which graciously hosted them. We gratefully acknowledge the generous financial support of the Indian Council of Historical Research, the Indian Council of Social Science Research, as well as administrative and financial aid from Prof. V.L. Dharurkar, Director School of Liberal Arts and Prof. B.A. Chopade, Hon. Vice Chancellor of Dr. Babasaheb Ambedkar Marathwada University, Aurangabad, Maharashtra, India.

During the conference, discussions among the scholars such as Prof. Jim Masselos, Prof. Jayant Lele, Prof. Suhas Palshikar, Prof. Sadanand More, Prof. Prachi Deshpande, Prof. Aruna Pendse, Dr. Mohan Agashe greatly benefitted the content and formulation of this book in the present format. After the conference, a number of scholars continued to brainstorm and discuss ideas for a book, including Anne Feldhaus, Irina Glushkova, Birinder Pal Singh, Dusan Deak, Deepra Dandekar, Daniel Jasper, Michihiro Ogawa, Pushkar Sohoni, Shailen Bhandare, Laurie McMillin and Bina Sengar.

We are sincerely indebted to Prof. Anne Feldhaus and Prof. Suhas Palshikar who went through the initial drafts of the volume and gave their valuable comments. We are also grateful to our reviewers who gave their comments to further improve the contents of the volume. The work is a product of the collaborative spirit and intellectual interests of the International Conference on Maharashtra, which takes place biannually in India and other parts of world. Within this group, scholars working in and around themes of Maharashtra and Western India share their ideas and research. Between 1984 and 2019, the International Conference on Maharashtra has met eighteen times in various settings, and from these meetings, twelve volumes related to the themes of Maharashtra and Western India have been published. The present volume aims to further contribute to this collection of essays and hopes to enrich the debates and discussions about the ideas of space and place.

The work of this edited volume would not have been possible without the institutional support given both the editors. Additionally, Bina Sengar would like to thank her students, colleagues and staff members in Dr. Babasaheb Ambedkar Marathwada University, Aurangabad, India; Laurie McMillin is grateful to supportive colleagues and students at Oberlin College.

We want to offer a special word of thanks to our families, who stood with us during our work for this book.

Bina Sengar and Laurie Hovell McMillin
Aurangabad, August 2019, and Oberlin, August 2019

Introduction

Location, expositions and synthesis in the region

Bina Sengar and Laurie Hovell McMillin

Historically, Western India has been a crossroads of connection; from north to south and east to west, by land and sea, people navigated and settled in its varied geographical places. At the same time, this territory has also been constructed in terms of the geographic/cultural regions of *ghat*, *desh* and *Konkan*, each with their own conceptual framework and history. In this way, this area – which includes what is bounded within the state of Maharashtra as well surrounding environs – has historically been dynamic and multiple. Brought together as a whole or in parts by language, rulers and pilgrimage routes, the many places and spaces within this region have been as likely to pull against each other as unite, and different places within this region revolved around numerous centres – some established by rulers, some by sacred sites and still others by lived experiences that define what is home.

Numerous cultural phenomena and historical moments in Western India, Maharashtra, and the Deccan offer rich sites for exploring constructions of space and place, both in historical and contemporary settings. Considering the role of space and place in the context of India requires a multidimensional approach: engagements from the social sciences, humanities, scientific studies pertaining to history and geography and other contemporary studies contribute to interdisciplinary and multidisciplinary approaches that widen the scope of academic discussions on the theme of space and place. The present volume takes up the study of the place and space of Western India in this multidimensional and interdisciplinary way. This multi-authored book explores the many ways that spaces and places in and around Maharashtra have been created over time as reflected in art and architecture, in religious texts and structures, in state formations and in notions of identity. Hence, this project grapples with the complexity of this region and widens the scope of academic discussions on the theme of space and place.

Space or place?

Although in the literature 'space' and 'place' have sometimes been used interchangeably to refer to imagined and constructed locations (as opposed to geographical ones), this book follows many social science scholars in using the terms in a more restricted manner. In simple terms, we treat 'place' as concrete, historical and discrete; it is a geographical-environmental concept. In contrast, 'space' is abstract, imagined and produced; space is a more elastic concept that refers to a construed identity. Place and space are deeply connected, nonetheless, because concrete, geographically given places are constructed as spaces with meanings (natural, political, religious, semiotic, commercial, capitalist, migratory, etc.), and cultural ideas of space and spatiality are necessarily anchored to geographical surroundings (Deshpande et al., 1997). Furthermore, in a world where movements of all types have intensified, geography has not been eliminated; on the contrary, globalization has accentuated the significance of a location/place (Ouslé & Varrel, 2012).

The concepts of space and place received a great deal of scholarly attention in the 1980s, when discussions of space and place extended beyond the field of geography, particularly with the interventions of LeFebvre and Foucault. Their work emphasized the multiplicity and layered formation of space, which is influenced not merely by geography but also by the intricate functions of society and its structures, social values, and cultural practices.[1] Following their work, Edward Soja's provocative work on 'space' and 'spatiality' radically altered the interpretive framework for studying regions and territories. Through Soja, 'space' became a new theoretical paradigm for exploring questions of region. For Soja, space is not a scientifically observable or pragmatic object removed from ideology or politics; space is always political and strategic. He argued that if the term 'space' had heretofore seemed neutral and formal, and 'spaces' seemed to exist irrespective of their contents, that is precisely because space has been occupied; it has already been the focus of past processes whose traces on the landscape were not always evident on the landscape. Soja's work emphasized that space is shaped and moulded from historical and natural elements, and that this is always a political and ideological process (Soja, 1980, 1985). Indeed, Lefebvre argued that space can be a difficult concept to grasp because of the ways in which power and knowledge conjoin within it (Lefebvre et al., 1999); for him, space is literally filled with ideologies. In contrast, place is often considered to be the smallest geographical unit where distance is abolished; it is, therefore, a specific loci where social relations take place and where spatial meanings are created (Bruslé & Varrel, 2012). Space can thus be seen as embracing a network of places, which include a combination of locations, locales and a sense of place. The dialogue between place and space engages socio-political discourses, which in turn transforms the ways in which they are theorized in the academy (Whitehead, 2002).

If we understand space as political and ideological (and not somehow neutral), it soon becomes apparent that different notions and identities are produced and constructed for spaces, separately or jointly. There are spaces of subservience and marginality and spaces of collective elitist identities; there are 'transnational social spaces' (Pries, 1999) where routine spatial practices, common concepts, mythic, philosophical and scientific interpretations of the human species create 'cultural space' and 'political landscape/places' (Randviir, 2002). Similarly, new approaches to space/place have suggested how multicultural-cosmopolitan spaces bring multiple identities together. This space/place dynamic can also be studied as multi-locality in a singular space, where mobility is inherent in the construction of space. There are also public and private spaces, where public spaces as a cosmos are not egalitarian and private spaces gain credence in an impromptu way. There are also those who 'resist spaces'; these include 'silent users of spaces' and others who feel marginalized or unrepresented by dominant spaces.

Space and place in the context of studies of India and South Asia

Previous works on space and place in South Asia have tended to focus on one or two aspects in the formation of space and place, focusing in turn on social identities, language, political polarizations, religious, cultural and economic dimensions. Religion has been a particular focus in studies of space and place. Surinder Bhardwaj (1983), for example, explored the effects of *tirtha-yatra* for conceptions of space, discussing how pilgrimage to sacred places creates a circulation mechanism in which all social strata of Hinduism participate.[2] The liberal distribution of sacred places throughout India has created an essentially continuous religious space where the otherwise great regional cultural diversity becomes less significant. Similarly, in *India: A Sacred Geography*, Diana Eck discussed the formations of networks of pilgrimage places, which led to the formation of India's very sense of region and later as a nation.[3] Joanne Punzo Waghorne's *Place/No-Place in Urban Asian Religiosity* (2016) ranged even more widely, as it explored spaces constructed for everyday religious practice in sites across Asia.[4] Also in this vein, Yoginder Sikand's *Sacred Spaces: Exploring Traditions of Shared Faith in India* (2003) examined twelve sites across modern India where people from different religious communities gather to worship. His ethnographic study suggested the ways that shared religious traditions challenge communalist tendencies in modern India.

In the context of Maharashtra and Western India, Israel and Wagle's collection *Religion and Society in Maharashtra* (1987) examined different dynamics of religion, folklore and traditions in the region. Their seminal work further accentuated the problematic inherent in spatial dynamics in Western India and Maharashtra per se.[5] Verma and Ray (2016) focused on shrines in Western India during a period of significant historical and religious development.[6] Their work centred on the shrine as a multivalent site that communicates to a wide-ranging audience and helps to integrate them into a larger cultural context. In this volume, the work of Feldhaus, Dandekar, Deák, McMillin and Singh extend the study of sacred spaces in new directions; collectively, their work adds new dimensions to the study of religious life.

Powerful though they are, sacred sites offer only part of the story of how spaces are constructed. Space when not seen in religious contexts has layers of representations, which vary from media, architectural, political, colonial, post-colonial, modernist, post-modernist and with many similar diverse facets. In a study focused on a particular region of South Asia, a volume edited by Martha Ann Selby and Indira Viswanathan examined the construction of space in Tamil texts over a long historical period. *Tamil Geographies: Cultural Constructions of Space and Place in South India* (2008) focused specifically on geography and considered how textual descriptions of land and space were further elaborated into aesthetic shapes and social realities over time. Akhil Gupta's work of 1995 paired a study of bureaucracy in a small north Indian town with representations of the state in mass media; his work aimed to raise questions about the state as a 'trans-local institution'.[7] Gupta's work accentuates the necessity of visualizing and comprehending notions of state, public culture, fieldwork and discourse in India through the space of media. In the present volume, the importance of media – including the press, social media and other public forums – are fully acknowledged by many of the studies, which include the consideration of media alongside other factors in the formation of spaces.

Another significant dynamic in the creation of space are people and their behaviour towards a given space, such as settlers, migrants, cohabiting members and so on. Allison Blunt (1999) took the feminine and family aspects of settlers and evaluated the problematic of and disruptions within filial systems.[8] As she wrote, 'Many feminists and post-colonial critics traced the spatiality of identities and the importance of destabilizing binaries between public and private spheres and between "self" and "other". And yet, many studies of imperial domesticity continue to posit the links between space and identity in fixed and polarized terms by reproducing imaginative geographies of "self" and "other" on a household scale and delimiting gendered and racially inflicted identities'.[9]

In her work, Anne Feldhaus (1998) further probed identities using historical documents from the eighteenth and nineteenth centuries, where she constructed the images of the conditions of women's lives in the modern state and traditional region of Maharashtra. Her work[10] is an important foundation for reflecting upon identity formations in the localized spaces by probing oral and vernacular textual references.

The essays in *Intersections: Socio-Cultural Trends in Maharashtra*, edited by Meera Kosambi (2000), investigated spatial continuity in which identities, folk beliefs and social constructions gradually developed due to colonial influence.[11] In *Producing India: From Colonial Economy to National Space* (2004), Manu Goswami used the concept of space to probe the origin of and contradictions within Indian nationalism. Her work challenged the conception of India as a bounded political and economic entity and emphasized the complex relationships between political-economic and socio-cultural processes on multiple spatial scales.[12]

Another recent work related to space formation in Western India is *Narratives, Routes and Intersections in Pre-Modern Asia*, edited by Radhika Seshan (2016). Taking a multidisciplinary approach, this volume examined connections in pre-modern Asia and considered how regions were connected by people, families, trade and politics and how these intersections were maintained and remembered. The chapters in this book began with the premise that an intersection is 'a meeting in a variety of ways: historical, geographical, economic, social, cultural, mythical, imaginary or conceptual'.[13] Thus, the book argued that trade and trade routes are not merely the outcome of economic and financial systems. Collectively, the twelve chapters in *Spaces and Places in Western India* try to go a step further by looking at place and space formation through an intersection of political, cultural, economic, material culture and religious frameworks. The present volume considers the construction of place and space in an interdisciplinary manner and thus presents a complex and layered view of 'Western India' over time. This book builds upon and extends recent insights into the constitutive and multiple projects of place- and space-making. The changeable nature of place and space is revealed through close readings of environs, populations, the political nexus, monetary and land holding systems and even through the contemporary viewpoints presented on virtual spaces.

'Maharashtra' and 'Western India'

Before we can further explore the contributions in this volume, we must attend to the concepts of 'Western India' and 'Maharashtra' that orient this volume. In the late nineteenth century, the area of 'Western India' included the provinces of Gujarat and Maharashtra, with parts of what are now Madhya Pradesh, Chhattisgarh, Telangana State and Karnataka of the Indian Union.[14] Today, one aspect which remains at the core of Western India is that of the State of Maharashtra. Whether we engage in an historical-geographical understanding of the Deccan, Western India or Central India, Maharashtra remains central to all these regions. Ideas about Maharashtra and Maharashtrian culture not only extended its geographical core and niche spaces to the regions of Western India, Central India and Deccan; the spatial influence of their political and cultural praxis is apparent in those respective places of India. The power structures of regional places within Western India shaped the patterns of interaction among people, places and material cultures. Thus, as posited by McLeod,[15] the place determined the space within it, which makes it apparent how people and places and their relationship were shaped by power owners among pre-colonial and colonial authorities.[16]

As we have noted, over time the place of Maharashtra has also often been constructed through the geographic/cultural regions of *ghat*, *desh* and *Konkan*.[17] The people of these areas, who may have migrated within or beyond the peripheries of Maharashtra, inevitably 'mobilize' their spaces as they occupy and inhabit new territories. At the same time, while creating these spaces, they acquire transnational identities and simultaneously create their spaces in a global arena. Historically, the five major regions of Maharashtra— Konkan, Western Maharashtra, Khandesh, Marathwada and Vidarbha— allowed migrant cultures to either create niches for their cultural spaces with unique identities within the larger space of Maharashtra or become silent users of dominant/dominated spaces. In this way, trans-local spaces within Maharashtra have connected regional identities with international spatial peripheries.

For centuries, the place that Maharashtra now occupies has been at the crossroads of cultural connections.[18] This part of Western India was shaped by the interactions of warriors, rulers, commercial entrepreneurs, artisans/artists and people with various ways of construing what was good and right. The patronage of these actors and others helped to create a wealth of sacred spaces and religious ideologies. These religious forms included Buddhism, Jainism, and Sikhism as well as Shakta, Nath, Varkari, Shiite and Sufi groups; their fates were all tied to the dynasties of the Satvahanas, Chalukyas, Rashtrakutas, and Yadavas and later to those of the Bahmanis and their progeny the Shahis in Bidar, Bijapur, Ahmadnagar, Berar and Golconda. Religious and cultural change continued apace under the Sultanate and later Mughal Maratha and Nizam's rule, which are highlighted in shared sacred spaces and places of heritage. The colonial and post-colonial histories of Maharashtra include histories of social reforms, which not only affected regional cultural spheres but also contributed to the making and unmaking of pan-Maharashtrian identities in India.[19] Colonial connections across social religious reforms and interactions among those of different beliefs helped in many cases to create shared religious and secular spaces. Indeed, this cosmos of shared spaces remains part of the social weave of rural and urban cultures of Maharashtra.

This volume organizes the discussion of space and place in Western India through three broad themes: urban, rural, indigenous spaces and virtual spaces and places; material culture and architectural spaces and places; the spaces and places of religious and folk beliefs.

Urban, rural and indigenous spaces and virtual spaces and places

Soja has emphasized that space is not limited to geography; instead, it is construed through an ensemble of factors. The mapping of land powerfully shapes spaces; in mapping, language gives birth to a space.[20]

Further, the mapping of space is shaped by politics and the associated socio-economic parameters of resource ownership. The first section of this book examines the making of spaces as inscribed on the land, on maps and in virtual locations, and teases out the power dynamics that are play in the formation of these spaces. In 'The Aftermath of Placeless Space: Mapped, Delimited, Bifurcated, Merged: A Phenomenon of Dewas S. and Dewas J.', Irina Glushkova explores the strange situation of a space that has been both singular and plural. The space and place formation of Dewas S. (Senior) and Dewas J. (Junior) are the creation of Maratha kingdoms in colonial times, and they continue to inherit the legacy of spatial identity in the post-colonial era. Both towns had a unique and anomalous configuration through subordination to the British and became an 'odd' place by bifurcation into two tiny kingdoms or 'territorial states' without real statehood. The article examines space as understood and created within these two territories and how ideas of power and space that identified them in the colonial times still influence them.

In the second chapter 'The Spatial Analysis of the Transition of the Land Revenue System in Western India (1761–1836), with Special Reference to Indapur Pargana', Michihiro Ogawa investigates patterns of land settlement and ownership laws that constructed the spaces within the Maratha-Peshwa territorial regime. Taking into account the case study of Indapur *pargana*, Ogawa discusses how proprietary rights became key to the way the land was governed. The Peshwas' assignment of *parganas* to commanders shaped the nature of space in the Maratha state, which helped to make possible a shift in the land-governing policies of the British Empire in Western India. The British policy of *ryotwari* drew on land systems developed by the Peshwa and instantiated their notions of place and space. While the predominant perception is that the colonial regime introduced land ownership laws that ran counter to the existing order in Western India, Ogawa's argument challenges this idea. For him, the case of Indapur suggests a pre-colonial policy on space that was continued by the colonial regime.

In the third chapter, 'Creating Spaces for Indigeneity from Nizam's Hyderabad State to Maharashtra', Bina Sengar discusses the transition in the Gond space from pre-colonial times to the post-colonial era. She shows how pre-colonial power equations among Mughals, Nizams of Hyderabad and the Maratha state exploited the Gond state and shared it among themselves. With the coming of the Britishers, the exploitation of the Gond space and place continued. Simultaneously, another major rupture that occurred in the Gond society and state was the creation of multiple binaries in their own cultural structures due to their scaffolding within the Maratha, British and Hyderabad states during the colonial era. These ruptured identities were spatially distributed into the language identities of the Marathi-speaking state of Maharashtra, the Hindi-speaking states of Chhattisgarh and Madhya Pradesh and the Telugu-speaking states of Telangana. In the changing historical trajectories, this multiplicity of spaces and places erased the Gonds' spatial and language identity of Gondwana and Gondi.

The last chapter of the first section takes up the powerful role of virtual spaces in the making of communities and the development of their discourses. In 'Internet as an Emancipatory Space: Case Study of Dalits in Maharashtra', Shraddha Kumbhojkar considers the role of virtual spaces in empowering marginalized communities of Indian society and bringing them together on a common platform of virtual spaces.

Material culture and architectural spaces and places

In the next section, we explore material culture and spaces and places in the built environment through a look at coins and coinage, architecture, statuary and contested religious and historical spaces. In 'Place, Space and Money in Maharashtra, c. 1750–1850: Some Insights', Shailendra Bhandare discusses money exchanged as tributes, levies, ransoms and other such transactions between Maratha and other polities during the eighteenth and nineteenth centuries. He argues that these monetary transactions helped to create a 'geography' of money. Because money can be both a form of payment and something that circulates as a medium of exchange, monetary objects such as coins can travel and create their own 'spaces'. In eighteenth- to nineteenth-century Maharashtra, the complexities involved in the circulation of money meant that 'uniformity' was not a virtue of currency. Money created spaces that were unifying as well as fragmenting – a situation that British colonial powers sought to rectify by enforcing uniformity and in this way asserting dominion.

In his chapter 'Architectural Continuity across Political Ruptures: Early Marathas and the Deccan Sultanates', Pushkar Sohoni examines how the architectural styles of the Nizamshahi and Bahmani sultans helped to shape the building practices of the early Maratha state. Sohoni examines three structures produced by the early Marathas in order to explore their continuities with works constructed by the Deccan sultanates.

Turning next to the contemporary scene, Daniel Jasper considers the construction of statues honouring Shivaji Maharaj. In 'Blurred Lines: Historical Knowledge and the Politics of Statues', Jasper considers statues as spaces of knowledge. What makes memorials meaningful spaces for making sense of the past? How do such sites create and demarcate spaces, and how do such spaces shape the membership of social groups? Jasper's thoughtful project considers that ways that statues 'sit within and between two realms of history', the popular and the cloistered.

In a similar vein, Laurie McMillin's 'Karle/Ekvira: Many Places Over Time, and at Once' considers the space she refers to as Karle/Ekvira, the site where a millennia-old Buddhist cave at Karle and a temple to the goddess

Ekvira sit side by side. Rather than trying to settle whose claim to the site should have precedence, McMillin develops a framework that attempts to do justice to the multiple perspectives on the place over time. Her concept of 'the one and the two' offers a way to move beyond dualistic approaches to this and other contested sites.

Religious spaces and places in Western India

As we have seen, religion in South Asia has contributed liberally to the construction of spaces, and studies of space in South Asia have frequently considered sacred spaces and the networks of connection created by pilgrims. The third section of this book examines various spaces as construed by religious adherents and religious texts. These studies offer a uniquely rich view of the construction of sacred spaces by considering both how particular places and spaces were formed in historical and sociological trajectories and how localized places in all their complexity and diversity contributed to their emergence. The four distinct and well-researched articles in this section explore the intricate connections of space and place in several regions of Maharashtrian and Western India.

In the first chapter of this section, 'The Significance of Place in Early Mahānubhāv Literature', Anne Feldhaus explores how early Mahānubhāv literature attends deeply to geography. Acknowledging that Mahānubhāv literature also has much to say about the formation of a broader regional consciousness, in this project, Feldhaus considers textual evidence for Mahānubhāv fascination with smaller places – with villages, houses, fields and tanks – and goes on to explore why such places are meaningful in Mahānubhāv theology. Her work suggests that not only has Mahānubhāv literature been involved in a dialectical process of interaction with the places it describes, the identities and meanings of these places have been involved in 'a fluid and on-going process of change'.

Following this, Deepra Dandekar's 'Seven Sufi Brothers: *Dargahs* Vernacular Narratives and Konkani Sufi-Muslims', uses locally assembled Sufi oral hagiographies to outline relationships between Sufi-Islam and present-day worship at Sufi *dargah*s in the Konkan. Dandekar explores the institution of Sufi-Muslim 'brotherhoods' in its vernacular Konkani version and argues that universalizing ideas about Sufi-Islam do not do justice to local and vernacular forms. Indeed, in this way, her project clears space for different conceptions of Islam and how to conceive local lived religions.

The penultimate chapter in this volume, Dušan Deák's 'Emplacing Holiness: The Local Religiosity between Vaishnavas, Sufis and Demons', examines the community surrounding a holy man, Sheikh Muhammad Baba from Shrigonda (ca. 1560–1660), whose worshippers are drawn from across castes and modern religious labels. Given that the places associated with a sheikh's life and death are especially important to his followers,

Deák's project considers how the different narratives his followers produce about the sheikh shape their veneration of him. Deák's subtle treatment of this topic, based on extensive fieldwork, challenges received ideas about religious identity in favour of a nuanced consideration of the way places help worshippers construe different sacred worlds.

The last chapter of this volume takes up one of the least studied and yet most fascinating aspects of religious space in Western India, that of the Deccani Sikhs. In 'Dakhani Sikh Identity and the Religious Space(s) in Nanded (Maharashtra)', Birinder Pal Singh considers the historical creation and present situation of this Sikh community. Over time, the Dakhani Sikhs have become fully entrenched in their social space and have carved a niche for themselves with a distinct identity. This process is deeply tied to narratives about places in the Deccan, and the sacred space of the Hazoor Sahib at Nanded continues to orient this community.

Thus, the present book aims to re-examine notions of space and place in Western India. Focusing on the wider region of Western India, the selected twelve chapters extend work on space and place into broader contexts of time and space. In thematically arranging the selected chapters, the project attempts to create a synergy that allows readers to consider each chapter on its own and also within larger questions about history, heritage, power and social and religious life. Altogether, the research in this book is designed to highlight connections and bring out dissonances among spaces and places in Western India.

Notes

1 Michel Foucault and Jay Miskowiec, 'Of Other Spaces', *Diacritics*, Spring 1986, 16 (1): 22–27 Also see (Another version): Jay Miskowiec (Translated from the French), 'Of Other Spaces: Utopias and Heterotopias' "Des Espace Autres: From: Architecture /Mouvement/ Continuité" October, 1984; March 1967, (Weblink: http://web.mit.edu/allanmc/www/foucault1.pdf) (Accessed on 8th February, 2018).
2 Surinder M. Bhardwaj, *Hindu Places of Pilgrimage in India: A Study in Cultural Geography*, Los Angeles: University of California Press, 1983.
3 Diana L. Eck, *India: A Sacred Geography*, New York: Harmony Books, 2012.
4 Joanne Punzo Waghorne (Ed.), *ARI-Springer Asia Series: Place/No-Place in Urban Asian Religiosity*, Singapore: Springer, 2016.
5 Milton Israel and Narendra K. Wagle, *Religion and Society in Maharashtra*, Toronto: University of Toronto, Centre for South Asian Studies, 1987.
6 Susan Verma Mishra and Himanshu Prabha Ray, *The Archaeology of Sacred Spaces: The Temple in Western India, 2nd Century BCE–8th Century CE*, London: Routledge, 2016.
7 Akhil Gupta, 'Blurred Boundaries: The Discourse of Corruption, the Culture of Politics, and the Imagines State', *American Ethnologist*, May 1995, 22 (2): 375–402.
8 Allison Blunt, 'Imperial Geographies of Home: British Domesticity in India, 1886–1925', *Transactions of the Institute of British Geographers (Royal Geographical Society)*, December 1999, 24 (4): 421–440.

9 Ibid., p. 439.
10 Anne Feldhaus, *Images of Women in Maharashtrian Society*, Albany, NY: SUNY Press, 1998.
11 Meera Kosambi, *Intersections: Socio-cultural Trends in Maharashtra*, New Delhi: Orient Blackswan, 2000.
12 Manu Goswami, *Producing, India: From Colonial Economy to National Space*, New Delhi: Orient Blackswan, 2004.
13 Radhika Seshan (Ed.), *Narratives, Routes and Intersections in Pre-Modern Asia*, New Delhi: Routledge, 2016, p. 2.
14 Katharine Blanche Guthrie, *Life in Western India*, Vols. 1 & 2, London: Hurst and Blackett, 1881.
15 John McLeod, *Sovereignty, Power, Control: Politics in the States of Western India*, 1916–1947, Leiden: Brill, 1999.
16 Ibid., p. 4.
17 Chandrashekhar Dhundiraj Deshpande, *Western India: A Regional Geography*, Mumbai: Students' Own Book Depot, 1948.
18 B.V. Bhanu, *People of India: Maharashtra*, Vol. II, Part-XXX, Mumbai: Popular Prakashan, 2004, pp. xxii–xxiii.
19 Arvind M. Deshpande, Shrikant Paranjpe, Raja Dixit, and C. R. Das, *Western India: History, Society, and Culture*, Pune: Itihas Shikshak Mahamandal, Maharashtra, 1997.
20 Michel Foucault (Trans: Gerald Moore), 'The Language of Space', in Jeremy W. Crampton and Stuart Elden (Eds.), *Space, Knowledge and Power: Foucault and Geography*, London: Ashgate, 2007.

References

Bhanu, B.V. *People of India: Maharashtra*, Vol. II, Part-XXX. Mumbai: Popular Prakashan, 2004.

Bhardwaj, Surinder M. *Hindu Places of Pilgrimage in India: A Study in Cultural Geography.* Los Angeles: University of California Press, 1983.

Blunt, Allison. 'Imperial Geographies of Home: British Domesticity in India, 1886–1925'. *Transactions of the Institute of British Geographers (Royal Geographical Society)*, December 1999, 24 (4): 421–440.

Buslé, Tristan and Aurélie Varrel. 'Introduction. Places on the Move: South Asian Migrations through a Spatial Lens'. *South Asia Multidisciplinary Academic Journal*, 2012, 6: 1–12.

Deshpande, Chandrashekhar Dhundiraj. *Western India: A Regional Geography.* Mumbai: Students' Own Book Depot, 1948.

Deshpande, Arvind M., Shrikant Paranjpe, Raja Dixit, and C. R. Das. *Western India: History, Society, and Culture.* Pune: Itihas Shikshak Mahamandal, Maharashtra, 1997.

Eck, Diana L. *India: A Sacred Geography.* New York: Harmony Books, 2012.

Feldhaus, Anne. *Images of Women in Maharashtrian Society.* Albany, NY: SUNY Press, 1998.

Foucault, Michel. Trans. Gerald Moore. 'The Language of Space'. In *Space, Knowledge and Power: Foucault and Geography.* Jeremy W. Crampton and Stuart Elden, Eds. London: Ashgate, 2007.

Foucault, Michel and Jay Miskowiec. 'Of Other Spaces'. *Diacritics*, Spring 1986, 16 (1): 22–27.

Goswami, Manu. *Producing, India: From Colonial Economy to National Space*. New Delhi: Orient Blackswan, 2004.

Gupta, Akhil. 'Blurred Boundaries: The Discourse of Corruption, the Culture of Politics, and the Imagines State'. *American Ethnologist*, May 1995, 22 (2): 375–402.

Guthrie, Katharine Blanche. *Life in Western India*, Vols. 1 & 2. London: Hurst and Blackett, 1881.

Henri, Lefebvre and Catherine Régulier. Trans. Mohamed Zayani. 'The Rhythmanalytical Project'. *Rethinking Marxism*, 1999, 11 (1): 5–13.

Israel, Milton and Narendra K. Wagle, Eds. *Religion and Society in Maharashtra*. Toronto: University of Toronto and Centre for South Asian Studies, 1987.

Kosambi, Meera. *Intersections: Socio-cultural Trends in Maharashtra*, New Delhi: Orient Blackswan, 2000.

McLeod, John. *Sovereignty, Power, Control: Politics in the States of Western India, 1916–1947*. Leiden: Brill, 1999.

Mishra, Susan Verma and Himanshu Prabha Ray. *The Archaeology of Sacred Spaces: The Temple in Western India, 2nd Century BCE–8th Century CE*. London: Routledge, 2016.

Miskowiec, Jay. Translated from French. 'Of Other Spaces: Utopias and Heterotopias'. ('Des Espace Autres'). From Architecture /Mouvement/ Continuité' October, 1984; March 1967, (Weblink: http://web.mit.edu/allanmc/www/foucault1.pdf) (Last accessed on 8th February, 2018).

Pries, Ludger, Ed. *Migration and Transnational Spaces*. Brookfield, VT: Ashgate, 1999.

Randviir, Anti. 'Space and Place as Substrates of Culture'. *Place and Location*, 2002, 2: 140–155.

Selby, Martha Ann and Indira Viswanathan Peterson. *Tamil Geographies: Cultural Constructions of Space and Place in South India*. Albany, NY: SUNY, 2008.

Seshan, Radhika, Ed. *Narratives, Routes and Intersections in Pre-Modern Asia*. New Delhi: Routledge, 2016, p. 2.

Sikand, Yoginder. *Sacred Spaces: Exploring Traditions of Shared Faith in India*. New Delhi: Penguin, 2003.

Soja, Edward. 'The Socio-Spatial Dialectic'. *Annals of the Association of American Geographers*, 1980, 70 (2): 207–225.

Soja, Edward. 'Regions in Context: Spatiality, Periodicity, and the Historical Geography of the Regional Question'. *Environment and Planning D: Society and Space*, 1985, 3: 175–190.

Waghorne, Joanne Punzo, Ed. *ARI-Springer Asia Series: Place/No-Place in Urban Asian Religiosity*, Singapore: Springer, 2016.

Whitehead, Ann. 'Tracking Livelihood Change: Theoretical, Methodological and Empirical Perspectives from North-East Ghana'. *Journal of Southern African Studies*, 2002, 28 (3): 575–598.

Part I

Urban, rural and indigenous spaces in Maharashtrian politics and environment

Chapter 1

The aftermath of placeless space: mapped, delimited, bifurcated, merged

A phenomenon of Dewas S. and Dewas J.

Irina Glushkova

Introduction

What was once the twin-states of Dewas is now a district, which takes its name from its headquarters at the city of Dewas. This city is now the home of 290,000 citizens and houses one of the largest bank note presses in Asia; it is also the known as the soya capital of India. It is easily found on the administrative map of modern Madhya Pradesh about 143 km southwest from Bhopal, the state capital, and 35 km northeast from Indore, its commercial hub. The popular etymology links the town's name to Chamunda, a local goddess, or *devīvāsinī*, whose abode is located in a rocky shrine on the top of a conical hill 300 feet high, a single salient geographical feature of the local landscape, now also occupied by a variety of deities. More than a century ago, Malcolm Darling, a colonial civil servant, in a letter to his friend Edward Morgan Forster, a British writer, described Dewas as the 'oddest corner of the world outside *Alice in Wonderland*'. In 1908, one year after his arrival here, Darling mentioned in another letter, 'How I loathed the place then! Now I could hardly wish for anything better'.[1] To this about thirteen years later in a letter comparing Dewas Senior with another tiny principality, Forster reinforced his friend's perception, 'How I wish that Dewas wasn't so meagre! Though I have no doubt as to which state I would choose to live in'.[2] It is because of Forster who managed to have finally shaped his otherwise abandoned novel – *The Passage to India*[3] – after his return from Dewas to England that this name still rings a bell outside India. Three decades later Forster's letters from India to his mother and kin were brought together under the title of *The Hill of Devi*, preceded by a note he supplemented at the time of their publication his faithful dues to Dewas' 'fineness' and 'strangeness', 'It was the great opportunity of my life'.[4] He sums up in one of his letters his impression of the place: 'Here, indeed, was a very dull India, except for Devi, the sacred acropolis with the rakish cap, half a mile away … She concludes the curiosities of Dewas. Nothing detained the tourist there, and the surrounding domain was equally unspectacular. No antiquities, no picturesque scenery, no large rivers or mountains or forests, no large wild animals, "usual birds and fishes," according to the gazetteer, no factories, no railway station. Only agriculture ... Amidst these surroundings, I was to pass six months of 1921 in the capacity of a Private Secretary [to Maharaja Tukojirao Pawar III]'. (Figures 1.1 and 1.2)[5]

Since then, the colonial government built the Agra–Bombay road, now known as the National Highway 3, running through Dewas; in 1952, the railway came here. It has also become an object of my focused interest, and for the last few years, I have kept tracking its past glory and collecting my own set of impressions of the span and structure of the eighteenth-century Maratha Confederacy and of the princely state(s) which had been once jointly owned by the renowned Maratha generals Puar/Ponwars/Pawar brothers and then divided by their descendants into Dewas Senior and

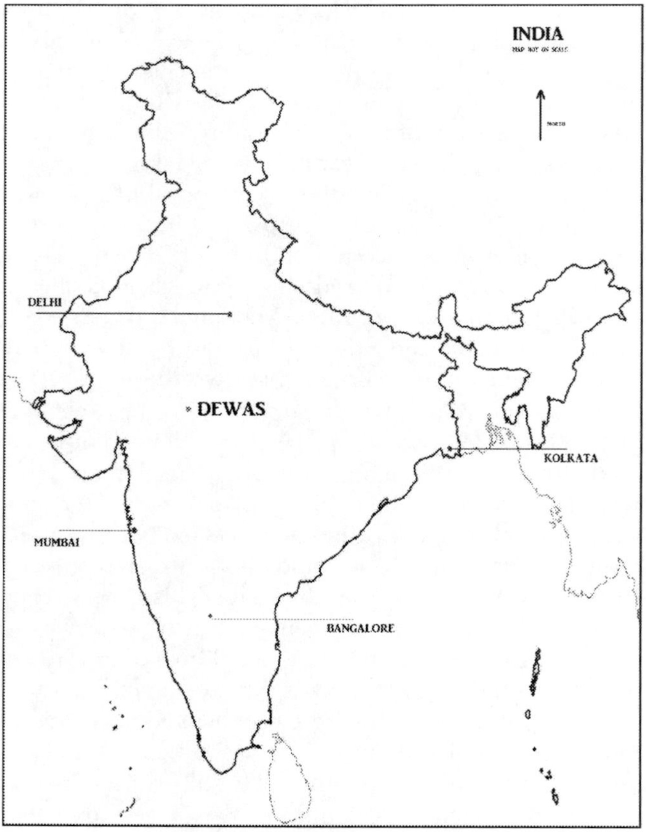

Figure 1.1 Location of contemporary Dewas.
Source: Irina Glushkova.

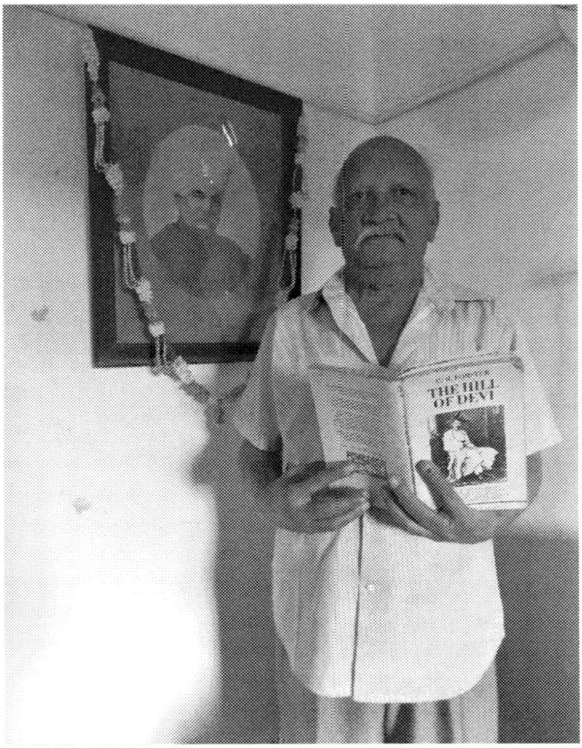

Figure 1.2 Mr. Vijay Pandit, a resident of present-day Dhar, next to a photo of his grandfather, a dewan of Dewas Senior during the times of Tukojirao III. In Pandit's hands is a copy of *The Hill of Devi* featuring an image of Forster.

Source: Photo by Irina Glushkova.

Dewas Junior, both worth fifteen-gun salute as per the British hierarchical table of military honours.

*

'Looking at any wall map or atlas, we see a world composed of states. The earth's surface is divided into distinct state territories. Each demarcated by a linear boundary, an edge dividing one sovereignty from the next. The division is accentuated when each territory is blocked out in a separate colour from neighboring states, implying that its interior is a homogeneous space, traversed evenly by state sovereignty. Our world is a jigsaw of territorial states, and we take this picture for granted'.[6] This quotation from Michael Biggs' insightful paper on cartography and state formation was on my mind when I tried to pin down on the few old maps within my reach a location of disjoined parts of the former Maratha principality known as the twin-states of Dewas (1728[7]–1948), in the historical region of Malwa.

The cartography of the Maratha Confederacy during its prime in the eighteenth century is usually shown as a coloured continuum slightly varying in size and configuration, which creates an impression of the Marathas' sway over a significant part of the Indian subcontinent. This ocular experience would have been unknown to actors of that turbulent period who had neither validated the very concept of the Maratha Confederacy[8] nor embraced fragments of the Maratha realm scattered here and there as an enclosed space or perceived them in terms of 'territory'. Besides their nucleus in Desh (i.e. *deś*, '[our own] country', a part of the west-central Deccan Plateau bounded by the Sahyadri range and its spurs, which eventually became a topographic designation of the geographical and historical region), the hold over vast areas beyond Maharashtra seems to have been never achieved simultaneously and evenly. The continuously yellow-coloured fragments of maps spreading and widening to the north off the seat of power in Pune also include the area of Malwa, and only roughly indicate their balancing claims to fiscal control neither certain nor secure at different points in time. These claims or rights 'always under sanction or pretended sanction of the Emperor' in Delhi were 'nothing but a prelude to the establishment of complete Maratha sovereignty', or *svarājya*, 'not to be defined as an abstract, territorially circumscribed, dominion complete in itself'.[9] This initial understanding of *svarājya* in the sense of non-*moṅglaī* is set by Andre Wink against *pararājya*, or *moṅglaī*, while both are 'intermingled ... to such an extent ... that the concept of territory becomes fallacious', and makes sense only as a reference to *mahārāṣṭra rājya*[10] located in Desh. These claims to the shared space were enforced by the distribution of *sarañjams*, such that the bonds with clans of leading commanders and their promotion to the rank of *sūbhedārs* in different parts of Malwa would pave the way to the 'slow conquest' of this buffer zone between Maharashtra and Hindustan[11] by the Southerners, as Marathas rooting outside Maharashtra had been recognized to the north of their nucleus. Therefore, the disparity of their 'conquered lands', including the specific case of Dewas with regard to either Maratha sovereignty or membership in the Maratha Confederacy, resists representation in terms of colours and border lines shown onto a cartographic space. These hallmarks were introduced by colonial historians for visual painting in red and pink the British expansion but later were put to use again through map renaming by students of Maratha history.[12]

Apart from the intermingling of *svarājya* and *moṅglaī*, some *pargannās* (an administrative unit of several villages) in various parts of Malwa as well as in Maharashtra were owned jointly by leading *sardārs*. This, while adding to the complexity of the 'territory' issue, also diminished a 'place' (*ṭhikāṇ*/*ṭhāṇ*[13]) value in the flexural space of the Maratha Confederacy.

This ambiguous, varied and dynamic kind of space[14] by no means resembled a homogeneous cartographic image of the Maratha Confederacy, which nowadays stands almost as its 'geobody' and 'logo-map' through its mass reproduction in school textbooks, historical literature and the internet.

The shift from the non-territorial concepts of *moṅglāī* and *svarājya* (in its initial meaning) had been manifested by the growth of the extraterritorial Maratha Empire, at a later date divided into quasi-states, known as principalities, princely states, *rājya*, *riyasāt*, *saṃsthān*, etc. As this process was regulated by the Europocentric mentality of the East India Company's administration, they were formed in accordance with the idea of a 'territory state' which had developed since the Peace Treaty of Westphalia (1648) and subsequent transformation of the European landscape. It seems problematic to trace Marathi analogues of 'territory' (derivative of Latin 'territorium', meaning 'the area of land surrounding and within the boundaries of a Roman city, municipium etc.') which is associated with 'place' and 'power' but is different from 'land' and 'terrain'. Marathi speakers substitute this notion of political geography for various lexemes related to spatial unity such as *deś*, *pradeś*, *bhūbhāg*, *prānt*, *mūlūkh*, *rāṣṭra*, etc., including Sanskrit *kṣetra*, by thus ignoring the historical context of each alternative. This substitution creates a sort of a 'territorial trap'[15] by juxtaposition of Indian glosses with outside concepts, especially with those which keep on being debated till now. Stuart Elden, tracing within Western political thought the emergence of the notion of 'territory' suggests that '[t]erritory clearly implies a range of political issues: it is controlled, fought over, distributed, divided, gifted, bought and sold. It is economically important, strategically crucial and legally significant'.[16] By the same token, the interplay of two words – 'place' and 'space' which form the title of this volume – are juxtaposed with and opposed to each other at the same time meaning different things to different scholars. Both are difficult to get planted into the Marathi language soil, and by trying it we may do injustice to indigenous concepts, which might indicate different approaches and modes to the creation of spatial and geographical meanings. The terminological gap within Marathi signifies the neglect of a diachronic semantic study of spatial lexemes and their usage similar to the one carried out by Wink in his seminal work (and by Elden's detailed treatment of English terms elsewhere), and forasmuch non-Marathi 'place' and 'space', not universal by themselves, are used throughout this chapter, implicitly maintaining their Western hues.

In the early periods of Maratha history, the family of Puars/Ponwars, now spelled as 'Pawars', appears to have been more distinguished than those of the Sindias, Holkars or Gaekwads. The Puars posed as Parmar Rajputs, the original rulers of Malwa, who had been forced to relocate to Maharashtra and had been since associated with Supa, a village they got hold of under the Nizamshahi rulers of Ahmadnagar. They ranked themselves as military commanders from the times of Chatrapati Shivaji and went on serving his grandson

Chatrapati Shahu of Satara rather than an incumbent peshwa of Pune. A fearless and wilful warrior from this clan, one Udaji Puar, is believed to have been among a Maratha vanguard squad which was the first ever to cross the Narmada river in 1698 to plunder parts of Malwa; he is also mentioned as having planted his own standard above the famous Mandu fort, then in Mughal possession.[17] Though this piece of information seems to have no historical support, the same Udaji Puar did accompany the peshwa Balaji Vishwanath during the Marathas' first expedition to Delhi in 1718–1719[18] and was the first general of promise and repute to have been granted half of the peshwa's revenues of several villages in Malwa (and Gujarat) at the earliest date of 1722;[19] in practical terms, this meant that he would own them if he managed to subjugate them. During the 1730s, at the time of strengthening of the Marathas' fiscal authority over Malwa, Bajirao I granted around forty *pargannās* to two branches of Puars of Supa who later became known as the Puars of Dhar (at the distance of about 100 km from Dewas, now another district headquarters in Madhya Pradesh), and the Puars of Dewas. Here starts the 'oddity', because the 1724 dues inclusive of Dhar (and Jhabua) had been singularly passed onto Udaji Puar,[20] while in 1734[21] an individual *sarañjām* of Dewas, Sarangpur, Bagod, Ingnod including a portion of the tributes from Banswada and Dungapur was granted jointly to Tukoji and Jivaji: it is this date that in 1936 Raghubir Singh names 'the beginning of the modern State of Dewas' and the reason for its later bifurcation.[22] On the way to modernity lay a number of stages, including the status of 'Joint Rajas of Dewas' at the time of the ratification of the 'Engagement' with the East India Company in 1818,[23] the choice of a single motto – 'Two branches grace one stem' – and regular surveys of cultivated lands continuing till the end of the nineteenth century.[24]

The succession of the Puars of Dhar held single ownership over their share of *pargannās* similar to the Sindias, Holkars and Peshwas, among whom other parts of Malwa were vivisected for direct tax collection through *chauth*, i.e. 'one-quarter of the revenue', and *sardeśmukhī*, or 'dues of the head'. Because Dewas and some other *pargannās* in Malwa were passed on to Tukoji and Jivaji brothers in co-ownership, every *sanad* would be simultaneously given to or withdrawn from both brothers, and they are popularly narrated to have held equal shares and lived amicably till some minor quarrel in 1739 over which they moved from a common dwelling to the eastern and western parts of Dewas, respectively. It may not be so as till much later, none of the leading generals of the Maratha Confederacy had been accustomed to stay in his headquarters in Malwa but had been in constant transit attending the peshwa in various campaigns in the south and in the north or following his own conspiracy. Later, the Gaekwads of Baroda adapted this maxim to their coat of arms – *jīn ghar jīn takht*, 'the saddle is my home and my throne'.

The Puars were not different, hence the petty settlement of Dewas along with Alot, Sarangam, Bagod, Khamkhera and other distant *pargannās* was given out on *ijārā*, i.e. on lease, by their nominated subordinates who routinely administered their masters' *sarañjāms*. Tukoji and Jivaji's immediate families, too, initially stayed behind in their individual estates near Supa – in Ganegav and Hingni, respectively. To cite Biggs again, 'Rulers certainly did not see the "medieval states" delineated so surely in our historical atlases. How, then, did they know the ground over which they claimed dominion? In the virtual absence of appropriate maps, the realm must have been known primarily as a succession of places'.[25] As was the practice of those days, the Puars used to control their domain through the repetition of clannish names (e.g. Tukojirao and Krishnajirao in Dewas S.) imposed on fiscal units; the passage from 'placelessness' to a realm of 'places' subdued in the process of tax collection may be indeed reconstructed by listing its component units from several historical studies including *Dewas State. Gazetteer. Text and Tables* by C.A. Luard (1869–1927), a Superintendent of the Gazetteers/Census for Central India (Luard, 1907), and *Saṃsthān Devās – Thorlī pātī. Pavār gharāṇyācā itihās* by M.V. Gujar, a historian from Dewas trained under G.S. Sardesai, a famous *riyasatkār*, a creator of the epic history of the Maratha Confederacy. It is Gujar's nationalist narrative that was imaginatively animated by Manohar Malgonkar's English rendering of *The Puars of Dewas Senior* with dedication to the incumbent Head of the Family[26] and the addition of the postcolonial events absent in the Gujar's narrative.[27] More *ṭhikāṇs*, i.e. component units, and their evasive belonging to or shuttling among various actors may also be traced from the published sources of the more famous Maratha families (the Sindias, Holkars and Gaekwads) among whom the Puars' dominion was squeezed, as well as from archival collections of Pune and Sitamau (to where Raghubir Singh shifted almost all bundles of documentation from Dewas J.) to the India Office of the British Library.[28] Most of these 'places' happened to be almost in constant transit from one master to another – initially as *sarañjāms* given and taken on the order of Pune, through takeovers following routine skirmishes, later as various forms of concessions to the colonizers and finally as modes of exchange to acquire a track of contiguous territory.

To this may be added that the Puars, being the ardent subordinates of Shivaji's descendants, thought of themselves not as 'rulers' but as *cākars*, 'servants', on *sarkār cākrī*, 'service to (one's) master'. They were referred to by military hereditary titles of *viśvāsrāv*, 'trustful', which was the title of the Puars staying in Supa, and *senāhaptasahsrī*, i.e. 'commander of seven thousand', which was bestowed upon Tukoji by Chatrapati Shahu. Contrary to other chiefs like Malharrao Holkar who was known as 'Subhedar Holkar' or Mahadji Shinde and whose appellative used to be 'Baba Patel', the Puars of Dewas had not been formally adorned with any title confirming their rights upon their quota in Malwa. The political instability along with the *sarañjāms*' movements and flux, as was reported by Michihiro Ogawa by the study of land grants and Shailendra Bhandare by the study of numismatic circulation, also added uncertainty to the status of the Puars.[29] With their *sarañjāms* to the north and south of Malwa occasionally withdrawn, or new *sarañjāms* not granted due to the peshwa's preferment of the Sindias and Holkars or for any other reason, the Puars' share in common revenue, too, would be less than that of the Sindias and Holkars. For some period, they were entitled to receive 23% of the tributes from Hindustan; later, from 1788 onwards, this became 12% of the levies of 'newly conquered country'. Sindia and Holkar also happened to be the direct cause of the ruin after 1797 of the Puars' estates in Malwa, irrespective of their acknowledgement of the Puars' superior rank. Even the reduced share as mentioned above was supposed to be divided between Tukoji and Jivaji and later between their successors. Be as it may, the petition signalling serious problems between the two brothers pended at the Pune court of the Peshwas beginning in 1781, while Luard clarified that '[u]ntil 1886 the two Branches exercised joint jurisdiction' after which the same year 'definite limits were assigned to each Branch, a new street being made to form the dividing line'.[30]

During the disturbances that followed the tragic death of Narayan Rao Peshwa in 1773,[31] which continued practically without intermission until 1818, the Puars of Dewas lost most of their possessions. John Malcolm, a Governor-General's nominee in negotiations with the Marathas leading to the Third Anglo-Maratha war and to a great extent an architect of Central India as we know it today, is also credited with creating the first genealogies of the leading Maratha dynasties of Malwa.[32] In his famous *A Memoir of Central India, including Malwa, and Adjoining Provinces*, he paid homage to the families of the Puar of Dhar and Dewas by placing the 'Puar' chapter (IV; Malcolm, 1823, pp. 97–115) ahead of much lengthier accounts of the Sindias (V) and Holkars (VI):

> Though their name always obtained them some respect from their more powerful Mahratta neighbours, the Puars of Dewas have suffered throughout the last thirty years the extreme of misery. They have been, in fact, the sport of every change. With territories situated in the most distracted part of Central India, and unable to maintain any force, they have alternately been plundered and oppressed, not only by the governments of Sindia and Holkar, but by … every freebooter of the day. A detail of their history during the last 25 years leaves an impression of wonder at their being in existence, or having an inhabited village in their country.[33]

Following the fall of the Maratha Confederacy in 1818 and masterful facilitation by Malcolm and his collaborates of subsidiary treaties the same year, the previously 'placeless space'[34] of Maratha rule in Malwa began to be mapped and delimited by the borders dividing one sovereignty from the next. As a result, multiple clusters of mostly hereditary *sarañjāms* attached to the families of the prominent generals of the Maratha Confederacy, especially to those who had fought the newcomers longer than others, were legalized and enhanced to the status of the princely states of Gwalior, Indore, Baroda, Dhar and Dewas. It aligns with Biggs' statement that 'By the early 19th century, the modern territorial state – with its cartographic techniques and mapped image – had been established in Europe. Since then, it has spread throughout the world. It was applied to lands conquered and colonized by Europeans, of course ...'.[35]

After rounds of diplomatic negotiations, the location of approved entities was pinned down to certain sites and their rulers were granted royal titles to compensate for their submission. By accepting limitations to their mobile, almost nomadic, style of life, including supervision of communication with their own compatriots of equal status, former grant lords and military commanders, i.e. new rajas and maharajas, became obliged to get down to particular social practices pertinent to the production of 'places', from constructing palaces, treasure-vaults, temples and stables (cavalry lines), laying out gardens for royal death memorials (*chatrī bāg*)[36] and inventing other symbols of interaction between a particular geographical spot and its masters.

Dewas, too, for better or worse, was brought under British protection, which curiously enough may be taken quite literally. Shrunk to the utmost by its ups and downs, its scattered land holdings became enclosed by carefully demarcated boundaries, and by this, Dewas stepped into a class of 'territorial states'. Starting from this date its kin duumvirate set about building their separate hereditary dynasties while still branding themselves as 'Two branches grac[ing] one stem'. The 'joint Rajas of Dewas' were recognized as equal in rank and authority. They were conditioned to share not only power but also (literally) a *gādī*, a throne, and made to accept that their administration be carried out through the same prime minister, as per the treaty's ruling. Completing a chapter on Tukoji Puar II, who sealed the treaty on behalf of Dewas S., Malgonkar remarks that, '[it] was perhaps a sign of the change-over from soldiering to administration that he was the first of his family to have died at Dewas [1827]; both his father and grandfather had died while they were away from their state, on active military service. A fine memorial in the Chhatri Bag marks the spot where he was cremated'.[37]

Parallel to Dewas-the-capital taking the path of successful transformation into a 'place', the territory of Dewas-the-principalilty turned into an arena of disintegration and administrative disputes accompanying an emergence of the twin-states. While both stayed indissolubly bound with each other, the mutual distrust led to each having its own prime minister from 1840. It was during this decade that as a result of the carve-up, their joint possessions became 'peppered in and out of each other'.[38] Each party received its own name in Hindi and Marathi – *Baḍī/Thorlī pātī* ('Older Share') and *Choṭī/Dhāktī pātī* (Younger Share) as well as in English – Dewas S(enior). and Dewas J(unior). While most of the territory was thus divided, the two major towns, Dewas and Sarangpur, were left in joint jurisdiction, although

Dewas J. made up his mind for a short time to shift his headquarters from Dewas to Sarangpur.

This emotional and formal separation was approved by the Political Department, and the names of the new states were augmented again by attachment of new additional markers – of Ganegavkar by the descendants of Tukoji from Dewas S., and of Hingnikar by the descendants of Jivaji from Dewas J. In order to move both parties away from their shared identity, these names connected them back with their indigenous places in Maharashtra and confirmed their individual loyalties to the land of their exodus. Still, the 'oddity' of Dewas may be ascribed not to its bifurcation which is known in examples of other Maratha States but to its mode of partitioning every bit of anything – a street, a road, a village and a sacred hill with its slopes, leading, eventually, to emergence of another *devī* – Tulja-Bhavani – besides the original Chamunda. Describing these peculiarities, Darling remarked:

> Here a flag was flying at half-mast, in whose honour, I wondered – to be told that it did no more than mark the division of the hill between Dewas Senior and Dewas Junior. For Dewas was the capital of two States, each with a fifteen-gun-salute Raja at its head, and each with its own territory and administration. Each too had its own temple on Devi. Mast and flag, on the other hand, were held in common; hence the curious position of the flag to mark the fact. School, hospital and Guest House were also joint; so much so that at the Guest House we were guarded by each State month by month in turn. In keeping with all this was a carriage which had been specially built for State occasions. That Government might have two Rajas with the minimum of discrimination it had been made wide enough for the two Rajas to sit facing the horses with the Agent to the Governor-General tucked in between them. Fortunately for all three parties Major Daly was of slender build.
>
> Each State had its own army, and never were armies less militant in their purposes. The Senior Branch had a muster-roll of 70 foot and 80 horse with a bodyguard of 14, plus 60 irregulars and 14 guns, two of them in actual use for firing the indispensable salutes. In the mornings the air is full of drums and tramplings for the Army drills. In the evenings the band plays. It numbers at least 10. It is therefore an important part of the State Forces![39]

He added that 'Senior Branch's territory measured only 442 square miles ... but providence has packed over 60,000 inhabitants into it'.[40] Junior Branch was almost of the same numbers in area and population. To this description, Forster added more details (Figures 1.3–1.5):

> At the time I knew them, their territories were inextricably mixed with each other and with the territories of surrounding states. The administrative confusion must have been even greater than normal, the

Figure 1.3 The goddess Chamunda, the famous devi of the hill.
Source: Photo by Irina Glushkova.

Figure 1.4 Sign for the two goddess temples divided between two families of Dhar S. and Dhar J.
Source: Photo by Irina Glushkova.

Figure 1.5 The goddess Tulja-Bhavani.
Source: Photo by Irina Glushkova.

> Government of India got periodically puzzled, and the two rulers made halfhearted attempts to escape each other's embraces. It was too difficult. They never succeeded. A map of their possessions lies before me. The Senior Branch (tinted green) owned 44 square miles, and had a population of 80,000, the Junior Branch (pink) was a little smaller. The district of Sarangpur (yellow) was administered jointly – I know not how, though on one occasion I took away a carful of rupees from it. The whole area was divided between the two states not by towns or sections, but by fields and streets. In Dewas City, S.B. would own one side of a street and J.B. the other. The arrangement must have been unique, and an authoritative English lady, who knew India inside out, once told me that it did not and could not exist, and left me with the feeling that I had never been there.[41]

Indeed, the inner complexity ran parallel to outside geographic and administrative confusion manifested by multiple enclaves and exclaves of neighbouring states peeping into each other. Even as late as the beginning of the twentieth century such an expert as Captain C.E. Luard, a Superintendent of the Gazetteer for Central India, introducing the position of Dewas state (as the title of the Gazetteer says) had to resort to a century-long measurement in geographic coordinates: 'The two States lie, except for the isolated *pargana* of Bagaud, entirely on the Malwa plateau. Their territories which are inextricably intermixed with the possessions of other Central India chiefs, especially with those of Sindhia [sic] and Holkar, lie roughly between latitude 22° and 24° N., longtitude 75°and 77° E'.[42] Thirty years later, this approach was still in demand,[43] as if no other markers could have been found, and Gujar referred to it by more careful detailing of the geographic location of the object of his narrative and demarcating it from Dewas J. only in name: 'The territory (*pradeś*) of the state of Dewas S. lies between latitude 22°16′ and 23°16′ N., longtitude 75°25′and 77° 46′ E ... This territory though is not continuous but breaks here and there by enclaves belonging to other states'.[44]

At the final stage of disaccord between the holders of the 'two branches grace one stem' motto, the colonial authority not only approved the split but also contributed to it by compiling a large map of the joint capital of both states, which I've come across in the British Library. Prepared by Major D.R. Wilmer in 1878–1879 and published in 1880, it is thickly loaded with Latin letters B (for Raja Kishan [Krishnaji] Rao [of D.S.]) and C (for Raja Narayan Rao [of D.J.]) written into geometrical figures of mostly polyhedrons constituting the map. The demarcation process helped to start the settlement of boundary disputes between the two branches, twenty-nine of which were disposed of in the same year.[45] It was accompanied by the inclusion of brief biographies of both incumbent rulers into the prestigious *Golden Book of India,* which again sharpened their identities by resorting to kin terms reminiscent of the patriarchs of both branches – the descendants of Tukoji Puar from Dewas S. were additionally distinguished as 'Baba [Father] Saheb' while those of Jivaji Puar from Dewas J. as 'Dada [Brother] Saheb'.[46] Both took efforts to differentiate their coats of arms and state flags, and Dewas S. substituted the 'two branch' motto for a new one in 1909.

All the same, it took much longer time to establish direct correspondence between a domain, i.e. territory, and its ruler invested with power, when the territorial 'oddity' was finally reshaped into some semblance of an orderly pattern. By 1939, still more than 400 border disputes were pending between the twin-states, when Vikramsinhrao Puar/Pawar,[47] the ruler of Dewas S., initiated an exchange of territories between two branches to connect bitty fragments into compact spatial entities and thus to simplify administration of both principalities. A passage from Malgonkar that describes Vikramsinh's all-India success in 'pig-sticking' sport and his frustration whenever a wild boar would cross over 'the invisible boundary into Dewas Junior'[48] is above all significant in this respect.[49]

The process happened to be logistically complex and emotionally charged, especially as relations between Dewas S. and Dewas J. had come to a dead end long ago; negotiations continued for over a year before an exchange procedure was settled and sent to the Political Department for approval. The east of the whole area went to the Senior Branch, and the west to the Junior Branch. The new arrangement came into force in September 1940 and resulted in over 90% of each state territory being released from the other branch's enclaves and encroachments, as illustrated in a cartographic comparison of Shobhana Jadhav's Ph.D. thesis on pre-independent Dewas.[50] Even the city of Dewas, which previously looked like a crazy quilt, was demarcated with sharp-cut boundaries, though the Samlat Road (Common Road) nowadays passing through the heart of the city's shopping hub is still remembered by its citizens as a border between two states. Thus, the process of 'territorization of rule' manifesting the symbolic fusion of political authority and geographic area eventually was achieved. In the case of the tiny twin-states under the tight grip of colonial politics of 'indirect rule', the 'symbolic fusion' could not really strengthen the rulers' standing but did facilitate the overall British surveillance of both principalities and their subjects, although for a very short period (Figures 1.6 and 1.7).

Figure 1.6 Clock tower at the Subhash Square (in former Dewas J.).
Source: Photo by Irina Glushkova.

Figure 1.7 A view of the desolated palace at Dewas S., now a residential building.
Source: Photo by Irina Glushkova.

A few other issues pertaining to disjoined lands still remained unresolved, such as the exchange of Bagod, an exclave enveloped into the territory of Indore at the distance of almost 75 miles from the capital city of Dewas, for any other village adjoining the domain of Dewas S. Though the ruler of Indore amicably agreed to transfer the villages of Nahar-Jhabua and Jarda, this trade was supposed to be done simultaneously with the exchange of the village of Padlya, adjoining Bagod. But its owner, Dewas J., failed to come to an understanding with the maharaja of Indore. The exchange was postponed, and in 1948, both states were integrated into independent India.[51] They merged with Madhya Bharat and Madhya Pradesh of independent India successively.

Fifteen years after the 1940 exchange deal, the newly reunited population of reintegrated postcolonial Dewas-the-capital and Dewas-the-district still kept in memory this event as a matter of pride to such an extent that K.G. Kavcale, a local historian, reproduced the congratulatory letter of Colonel G.T. Fisher, a resident, on the first page of his *Our Dewas* (*Āmce Devās*) historical sketch. That he also did not forget his own loyalty is evident by the letter's addressee – the maharaja of Dewas S.:

> I am very glad to inform Your Highness that His Excellency the Crown Representative has approved of the agreement for the transfer and redistribution of territories between the two Branches of Dewas, and I am to convey an expression of his Excellency's appreciation of the good will and hard work of your Highness which made possible the successful result of these delicate negotiations. I should like to add my own congratulations and to say that I believe that Your Highness and the Maharaja Sahib of Dewas Junior have set an example which I hope other rulers in Central India will be able to follow.[52]

Biggs' article also suggests, that '[i]t is easy to say "the state mapped its territory," implying that a preexisting entity increased the quantity of its knowledge. It is much harder to say that, through the process of mapping a new kind of territory and hence a new kind of state came into being. … Putting the state on the map meant knowing and imagining it as real – and, so, making it a reality'.[53] This is what I think happened to Dewas-the-capital which turned into a 'place'; it is also what happened to Dewas-the-principality: Dewas the principality found both a unique and anomalous configuration through subordination to the British and became an 'odd' place by bifurcation into two tiny kingdoms, or 'territorial states' without real statehood.

Notes

1 Malcolm Darling, *Apprentice to Power, India 1904–1908*, London: The Hogarth Press, 1966, p. 225.
2 E. M. Forster, *The Hill of Devi*, New York and London: Harcourt Brace Jovanovich, 1953, p. 194.
3 E. M. Forster, *A Passage to India*, London: Penguin Books, 1989 (1924).
4 E. M. Forster, *The Hill of Devi*, p. 8.
5 *Ibid.*, pp. 74 and 76.
6 Michael Biggs, 'Putting the State on the Map: Cartography, Territory, and European State Formation', *Comparative Studies in Society and History*, Vol. 41, no. 2, (1999), p. 374.
7 This date repeats the one given in Wikipedia though no event related to this particular year may be taken as a starting point of the beginning of a 'princely career' of Dewas.
8 Andre Wink mentions (though in passing) that '[t]he designation "confederacy" was often used by the British in the eighteenth and nineteenth centuries and was taken over by many modern Indian historians, first by M.G. Ranade' (Andre Wink. *Land and Sovereignty in India: Agrarian Society and Politics under the Eighteen-Century Maratha Swarājya*, Cambridge: Cambridge University Press, 1986, pp. 37–38, ft 93]. While a term of local origin, *peśvāī*, giving priority to a seat of power in Pune, also had been coined at some point, Stanley Wolpert suggested in one of his works a notion of 'pentarchy' which reflected, besides Pune, the might of the major Maratha dynasties (the Gaekwads, Holkars, Scindias and Bhosles) who finally also succeeded in carving out their own domains.

9 A. Wink. *Land and Sovereignty in India*, pp. 46–47.
10 *Ibid.*, p. 47.
11 See Gordon, 'The Slow Conquest: Administrative Integration of Malwa into the Maratha Empire, 1720–60'. In *Marathas, Marauders, and State Formation in Eighteenth-Century India*. Delhi: Oxford University Press, 1994.
12 Most known are the maps showing 'India in the times of Clive 1760 / Territory under Maratha control in 1760', 'Territories of the British India 1765', 'East India Company. India 1805', etc.
13 These are the words I have extracted from some letters of the eighteenth century corresponding to the meaning of 'place'. I cannot suggest any authentic gloss for the notion of 'space'.
14 The spatial fluidity of the Maratha Confederacy based on recitation of place names has been even acknowledged as a stage in *Empire: Total War* game by setting up concrete regions – 15 and 24 – to be captured and hold by 1750 and 1799, respectively [http://wili.totalwar.com/w/Maratha_Confederacy_(ETW_faction)]. A player (lusic29) asks at the *Empire* forum, 'How to stop the Maratha Empire? I hate the Maratha Empire. I like to play H/H and in every game the Maratha Empire grows very fast and begins invading America or Europe and this just ruin (sic) the game for me' [http://www.tvcenter.net/forums/showthread.php?648018-How-to-stop-the-Maratha-Empire] (both sites last accessed on 8 February 2018).
15 John Agnew, 'The Territorial Trap', *Review of International Political Economy*, Vol. 1, no. 1, (1994), pp. 53–80.
16 Stuart Elden, 'Chapter 17. Territory. Part 1', in *The Wiley–Blackwell Companion to Human Geography*, edited by Agnew John A. and James S. Duncan, Chichester: Blackwell Publishing, p. 261.
17 Raghubir Sinh, *Malwa in Transition or a Century of Anarchy. The First Phase. 1688–1765. With a Foreword by Jadunath Sarkar.* Bombay: D.B. Taporevala, Sons & Co, 1936, p. 85.

Many decades after discovery of a new manuscript in the archives of Jaipur, Raghubir Sinh, a historian and 'maharajkumar' of Sitamau, another princely state in Malwa ruled by the Rathore dynasty of Rajputs, brought more light on the process of penetration of 'invaders' into this region (Raghubir Sinh, "The Marathas in Malva [707–1719 A.D.]" in *Studies on Maratha and Rajput History*, Jodhpur: Research Publishers, 1989).
18 *Ibid.*, p. 130.
19 *Ibid.*, p. 144.
20 Hence Udaji Rao Pawar II of Dhar chose this date to celebrate a bicentenary anniversary of the state foundation in 1924, as I have found while going through archival materials kept in the British Library. Otherwise, Wikipedia mentions 1728 as the beginning of the State of Dhar [https://en.wikipedia.org/wiki/Dhar_State] (last accessed on 8 February 2018).
21 Here again other dates of the Dewas grant are found elsewhere: M.V. Gujar drawing from Peshwa Daftar names 1732 (1940, p. 63), while Malgonkar drawing from Gujar refers to 1731 when an idea of this was expressed in a letter of peshwas Bajirao to Holkar and Sindia (Malgonkar, 1963, p. 60).
22 *Ibid.*, p. 154, p. 279.
23 C. E. Luard, *Dewas State. Gazetteer. Text and Tables*, Bombay: Bombay Education Society, 1907, app. A, p. 80.
24 *Ibid.*, pp. 55–56.
25 Biggs, 'Putting the State on the Map', p. 378.
26 It seems that Dewas J. happened to be even more neglected as I have succeeded in retrieving only one publication (*Śrīmant mahārājā-sar-Malhārrāv Bābāsāheb*

mahārāj Pavār sarkār K.C.S.I. Rājya Dewās [Ju] yāñcā lekh-saṅgrah) of no significance to the theme of this paper. Still the information on Dewas J. used to be an inherent feature in any publication concerned Dewas S.

27 See M. V. Gujar, *Saṃsthān Devās– thorlī pātī. Pavār gharāṇyācā itihās.* [A State of Dewas Senior. History of the Pawar's Dynasty], Pune: M.V. Gujar, 1940 and Manohar Malgonkar, *The Puars of Dewas Senior*, Calcutta; London: Orient Longman Limited; Longmans, Green & Co. Ltd, 1963.

28 For example, I have come across a few files with correspondence dated 1944–1945 between various offices of colonial administrations in regard to exchange of territories between the Dewas J., Rajgarh and Narasingarh Darbars in the Oriental and India Office Collection in the British Library.

29 Michihiro Ogawa, 'Migration of Saranjamdars under the Marathas (1716–1818)' and Shailendra Bhandare, 'The "Slow Conquest": Maratha Settlement in Malva – a Numismatic Overview', papers presented at the 14th International Conference 'Maharashtra: Culture and Society', University of Mumbai, Mumbai, India, January 6–8, 2012.

30 Gujar, *Saṃsthān Devās*, pp. 265–270 and Luard, *Dewas State. Gazetteer. Text and Tables*, p. 64.

31 Narayan Rao was brutally killed in the Shanivarvada palace in Pune.

32 Jack Harrington, *Sir John Malcolm and the Creation of British India*, Palgrave Studies in Cultural and Intellectual History. New York: Palgrave Macmillan, 2010, pp. 99–128.

33 Malcolm, John. *A Memoir of Central India, including Malwa, and Adjoining Provinces.* Vol. I, London: Printed by S. and R. Bentley, 1823, p. 113. In reference to Sindia and Holkar, there are some folklore examples in this respect collected in Gujar, *Saṃsthān Devās*, pp. 307–311.

34 Few exceptions to this 'placelessness' may be named, the most striking would be Maheshvar on the Narmada river during the administration of Ahilyabai Holkar (1767–1795).

35 Biggs, 'Putting the State on the Map', p. 389.

36 Maratha death memorials/royal cenotaphs surrounded by thoroughly laid gardens in North India and Malwa as symbolic of princely power and statehood were a subject of my paper at the 14th International Conference "Maharashtra: Culture and Society": Irina Glushkova. *Between gardens and bazaars: Landscapes of Death and Their (Un)natural Beauty as Viewed in Former Maratha Principalities.* (Arizona State University, Tempe, USA), 23–26 April, 2014.

37 Malgonkar, *The Puars of Dewas Senior*, pp. 150–151.

38 Forster, *Hill of Devi*, p. 29.

39 Darling, *Apprentice to Power*, p. 142.

40 *Ibid.*

41 Forster, *Hill of Devi*, pp. 55–56.

42 Luard, *Dewas State. Gazetteer. Text and Tables*, p. 1.

43 The same latitude-longtitude approach, specifying the location of Ujjain/Gwalior, Indore/Maheshvar and Baroda is reproduced even today on the first page of all Ph.D. dissertations related to the Sindias, Holkars and Gaekwads I have come across in the respective universities.

44 Gujar, *Saṃsthān Devās*, app. A, p. 1.

45 *Report of the Political Administration of the Territories within the Central India Agency for 1878–79.* Calcutta: Office of the Superintendent of Government Printing, 1880, p. 82.

46 Roper Lethbridge, *The Golden Book of India*, London: Bennett, Coleman and Co, 1893, pp. 116–117.

47 After adoption to the throne of Kolhapur in 1947, Vikramsinhrao's name was changed to Shahaji II, and he became the last ruling maharaja of this princely state. For more details, cf. Jadhav (1985).
48 Malgonkar, *The Puars of Dewas Senior*, p. 285.
49 Exchange of territories for making the Holkar dominions (Indore) scattered far away outside Malwa more compact had begun as early as 1860s and lasted till 1930s (Singh, 1987, pp. 25–27) which might have made its impact as well on Vikramsinh's mind who was a close friend of the last maharaja of Indore.
50 Shobhana Jadhav, *Dewas under Vikramsinh Nanasaheb Pawar (1934–1947)*, Ph.D. thesis submitted to the Shivaji University, Kolhapur, for the Degree of Doctor of Philosophy in History, 1985. http://shodhganga.inflibnet.ac.in/bitstream/10603/140692/15/15_appendix%20b.pdf (last accessed on 8 February 2018).
51 Malgonkar, *The Puars of Dewas Senior*, p. 291.
52 K. G. Kavcale, *Āmce Devās*, Indur: S.K. Chaudhri, 1955.
53 Biggs, 'Putting the State on the Map', p. 399.

References

Agnew, John. 'The Territorial Trap'. *Review of International Political Economy* 1 (1): 53–80, 1994.

Bhandare, Shailendra. 'The "Slow Conquest": Maratha Settlement in Malva – A Numismatic Overview'. Paper presented at the 14th International Conference 'Maharashtra: Culture and Society' (University of Mumbai, Mumbai, India), January 6–8, 2012.

Biggs, Michael. 'Putting the State on the Map: Cartography, Territory, and European State Formation'. *Comparative Studies in Society and History* 41 (2): 374–405, 1999.

Darling, Malcolm. *Apprentice to Power, India 1904–1908*. London: The Hogarth Press, 1966.

Elden, Stuart. 'Chapter 17. Territory. Part 1'. in *The Wiley-Blackwell Companion to Human Geography*, edited by Agnew John A. and James S. Duncan. Chichester: Blackwell Publishing, 2011.

Forster, E.M. *The Hill of Devi*. New York and London: Harcourt Brace Jovanovich, 1953.

Forster, E.M. *A Passage to India*. London: Penguin Book, 1989 [1924].

Glushkova, Irina. 'Between Gardens and Bazaars: Landscapes of Death and Their (Un)natural Beauty as Viewed in Former Maratha Principalities'. Paper presented at the 14th International Conference 'Maharashtra: Culture and Society' (Arizona State University, Tempe), April 23–26, 2014.

Gordon, Stewart. *Marathas, Marauders, and State Formation in Eighteenth-Century India*. Delhi: Oxford University Press, 1994.

Gujar, M.V. *Saṃsthān Devās – thorlī pātī. Pavār gharāṇyācā itihās*. [A State of Dewas Senior. History of the Pawar's dynasty]. Pune: M.V. Gujar, 1940.

Harrington, Jack. *Sir John Malcolm and the Creation of British India*. Palgrave Studies in Cultural and Intellectual History. New York: Palgrave Macmillan, 2010.

Jadhav, Shobhana A. *Dewas under Vikramsinh Nanasaheb Pawar (1934–1947)*. Submitted to the Shivaji University, Kolhapur for the Degree of Doctor of Philosophy in History. [http://shodhganga.inflibnet.ac.in/bitstream/10603/140692/15/15_appendix%20b.pdf], 1985 (last accessed on 8th February, 2018).

Kavcale, K.G. *Āmce Devās*. Indur: S.K. Chaudhri, 1955.

Lethbridge, Roper. *The Golden Book of India*. London: Bennett, Coleman and Co, 1893.

Luard, C.E. *Dewas State. Gazetteer. Text and Tables*. Bombay: Bombay Education Society, 1907.

Malcolm, John. *A Memoir of Central India, including Malwa, and Adjoining Provinces*. Vol. I. London: Printed by S. and R. Bentley, 1823.

Malgonkar, Manohar. 1963. *The Puars of Dewas Senior*. Calcutta and London: Orient Longman Limited; Longmans, Green & Co. Ltd.

Ogawa, Michihiro. 'Migration of Saranjamdars under the Marathas (1716–1818)'. Paper presented at the 14th International Conference 'Maharashtra: Culture and Society' (University of Mumbai, Mumbai, India), January 6–8, 2012.

Report of the Political Administration of the Territories within the Central India Agency for 1878–79. Calcutta: Office of the Superintendent of Government Printing, 1880.

Sinh, Raghubir. *Malwa in Transition or a Century of Anarchy. The First Phase. 1688–1765. With a Forward by Jadunath Sarkar*. Bombay: D.B. Taporevala, Sons & Co, 1936.

Sinh, Raghubir. 'The Marathas in Malva (1707–1719 A.D.)'. in *Studies on Maratha and Rajput History*. Jodhpur: Research Publishers, 1989.

Singh, Ravindra Pratap. *Geography and Politics in Central India (A Case Study of Erstwhile Indore State)*. New Delhi: Concept Publishing Company, 1987.

Wink, Andre. *Land and Sovereignty in India. Agrarian Society and Politics under the Eighteen-Century Maratha Swarājya*. Cambridge: Cambridge University Press, 1986.

Chapter 2

The spatial analysis of the transition of the land revenue system in Western India (1761–1836), with special reference to Indapur Pargana

Michihiro Ogawa

Introduction

British colonial rule, which started in Western India in 1818, brought various changes in different places in the nineteenth century. The Ryotwari settlement, which was the land revenue system newly introduced by the British Government, is one of the main topics to study the British rule in Western India mainly for the following two reasons. First, the land revenue was the main financial source for the British government as well as Indian political powers in the eighteenth and nineteenth centuries. Second, this settlement reorganized agrarian society in Western India. Accordingly, many previous works focused on either the government revenue policy related to the Ryotwari settlement (e.g. Charlesworth [1985] 2002) or its impact on the local community, especially at the village level in Western India (e.g. Fukazawa [1983] 2008). These works tended to study changes in the colonial period only and did not have the long-term view of colonization in Western India. This chapter considers pre-colonial backgrounds to the introduction of the Ryotwari settlement, focusing on the political economy under Maratha rule, and clarifies the transition of the land revenue system from the pre-colonial to the colonial period. Under the Marathas, the land revenue was collected and remitted to the Peshwa Government with the sub-district called *pargana* as a unit. In the eighteenth century, the Peshwa Government assigned the land revenue from a village or parcel of land to commanders for military purposes. Many commanders were stationed in the assigned village or land and collected the assigned revenue instead of their salary. As discussed below, the assignment system was managed in the local administration at the sub-district level. This chapter will argue that the collapse of this assignment system at the sub-district level in the last phase of Maratha rule enabled the introduction of the Ryotwari settlement in Western India under the British rule. In other words, the most significant changes for the introduction of this new settlement occurred in the administration at the sub-district level, which was between the government and the local village community in the administrative hierarchy. Most previous works have overlooked the importance of the local administration at the sub-district level in the study of the land revenue system.[1] Therefore, this chapter defines 'place' as a local administrative territory of the sub-district called *pargana* and considers the transition of the land revenue system in the local administration at the sub-district level to show clearly how the Ryotwari settlement started in Western India.

The assignment system was first established in the Mughal Empire. Under the Mughals, the assignment as well as the assigned revenue came to be called *jagir* by the end of the sixteenth century.[2] The Mughal Empire gave a commander a military title and rank called *mansab*, according to which his military duty and income were determined. Irfan Habib argued that *jagirs* were constantly transferred after a short period so that a particular assignment was seldom held by the same person for more than three or four years (301). This prevented a commander stationed at one place for a long time from gaining too much power. In the eighteenth century, the Maratha Kingdom fought with the Mughal Empire and enlarged its territory northwards. In the process, the Maratha King or the prime minister called *peshwa*, who gradually replaced the Maratha King, promised that *jagir*[3] of the conquered territory would be given to commanders. Under the Marathas, *jagir* was not given for a specific period determined in advance. By the 1730s, in which its territory extended out of Deccan, a tendency developed towards longer tenure and hereditary confirmation. The development of the chief military commanders of the Marathas, such as Shinde, Holkar, Gaikwad and Bhonsle, was also based on *jagirs* in their conquered territories. These powers formed a confederacy nominally under the Maratha King and actually under the prime minister (*peshwa*) in the early eighteenth century. This unity was called the Maratha Confederacy, and Pune, wherein the *peshwa* established the government, was the central city of this confederacy.

The expansion policy of the Marathas was curtailed when they were defeated in the battle of Panipat in 1761. Madhavrao Ballal, who became *peshwa* just after this battle, changed the policy and initiated a period of internal reform in which many commanders were stationed in Indapur Pargana,[4] probably for the protection of Pune. As seen below, *jagirs* were given to commanders in Indapur Pargana. The Bhima and the Nira Rivers, which formed the boundaries of this *pargana*, made the soil on the banks fertile. Because Indapur Pargana was the nearest fertile area to Pune, this *pargana* occupied a strategic point both economically and politically. Indapur Pargana was given further significance under British rule, when the colonial government first introduced the Ryotwari settlement into this *pargana* in the Bombay Presidency in 1836. This chapter studies the *jagir* system and its historical influence on the British rule focusing on Indapur Pargana in the late eighteenth and the early nineteenth centuries.

Development of *jagir* system under the Marathas

Jagir systems in Indapur Pargana

Before discussing the *jagir* system in Indapur Pargana, this section briefly considers Indapur Pargana under the Marathas. In the eighteenth century, the territory of the Marathas was divided into thirteen provinces, called *subha*, which in turn were subdivided into several *parganas*. A *pargana* was composed of many villages. Among these three segmental units, a *subha* was administered by a governor who was sent by the government, while a village was administered a hereditary village headman called *patil*. Between *subha* and village, a *pargana* was managed by both an officer sent from the government and by a hereditary local officer. The former was called the *kamavisdar*, who represented the central government, and the latter was the *desai* or *deshmukh*, who represented the local community. Under the Marathas, a *pargana* was a very significant 'place' for government control over local areas. In the eighteenth and the early nineteenth centuries, Indapur Pargana consisted of eighty-six villages.

Under the land revenue system, this sub-district could be divided into three types of villages, viz., *inam* villages, *jagir* villages and government villages. In all types of villages, however, the village headman (*patil)* was responsible for collecting land revenue. In government villages, the village headman paid the land revenue to the government local officer called *kamavisdar*, who remitted money to the government in Pune. In *inam* villages, the village headman gave the land revenue to the holder of *inam*, which were privileges given for various reasons. To the government, these villages appeared to be tax-free villages. In *jagir* villages, the collection of land revenue was assigned to commanders for military purposes. In Indapur Pargana, *jagir* was generally given with the village as a unit.[5] Figure 2.1 shows the arrangement of villages in Indapur Pargana under the Marathas. The bottom part represents Inam villages, the middle part stands for jagir villages, and the top part is for government villages.

While the number of *inam* villages was invariably five during this period, the number of *jagir* villages began to increase significantly in the 1770s, and continued to increase gradually in the 1780s and 1790s, reaching sixty-two in 1802. Figure 2.2 shows that the number of *jagir* villages drastically decreased at the beginning of the nineteenth century. This point will be considered below.

Between 1768 and 1818, Indapur Pargana saw a total of 138 assignees. In the deed in which the assignment of the collection of the revenue from a village was ordered, the terms of an assignment were not mentioned. In many cases at Indapur Pargana, *jagir* was given to *paga* (regular cavalry) and to *silahdars*, or the irregular soldiers who equipped themselves with arms and horses and then participated in military activities. In Indapur Pargana, *jagir* was given to commanders under the Shinde and the Holkar

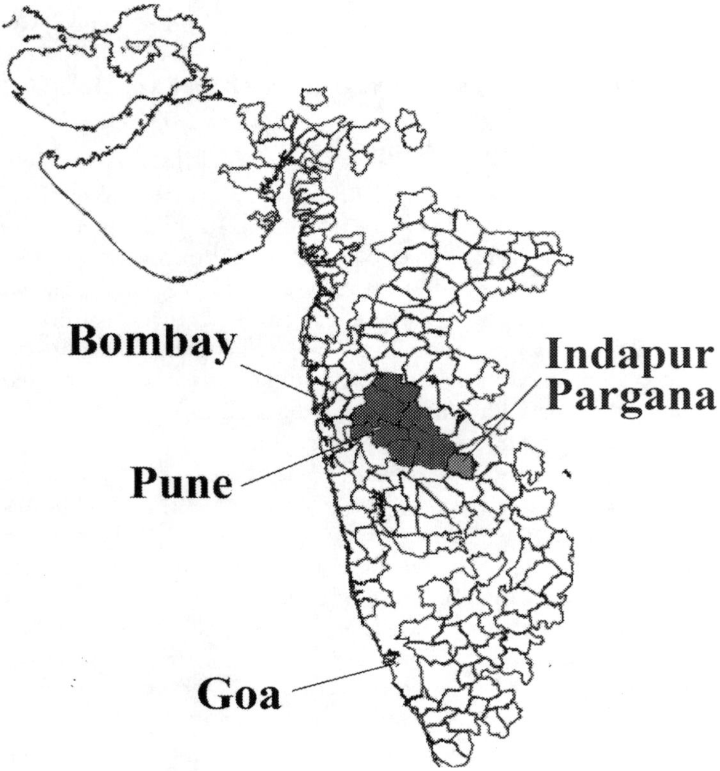

Figure 2.1 The location of Pune District and Indapur Pargana in Bombay Presidency.
Source: Created by Michihiro Ogawa.

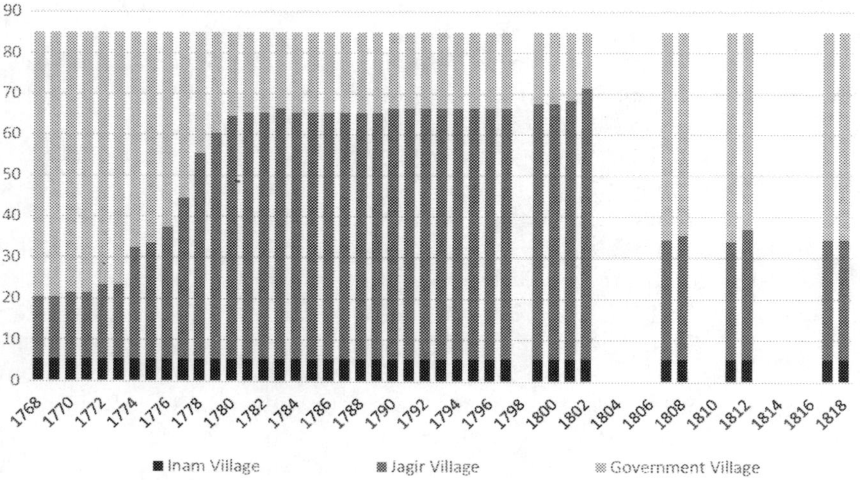

Figure 2.2 The arrangement of villages in Indapur Pargana in the period of 1768–1822.
Source: Taleband Pargana Indapur, Prant Ajmas, Pune, Rumal nos. 56–63, Maharashtra State Archives, Pune.

families.[6] As *jagir*, one village was assigned to the Patwardhan family, powerful commanders under the *peshwa*. In short, various classes of commanders under the Marathas were given *jagirs* in Indapur Pargana. In this situation, some commanders were actually stationed in their *jagir* villages and others were not. The next section considers how commanders managed their villages under the *jagir* system.

Management of jagir villages

Whether a holder of *jagir* stayed in the assigned villages or not, the village headman of a *jagir* village paid the revenue to the holder. After the government decided to assign a village to a commander, *kamavisdar* produced the deed, called '*tainat jabta*', or the muster roll for pay. His assigned revenue was written down both in the accounts of Indapur Pargana and in '*tainat jabta*', which showed how the assignment was settled between a holder of *jagir* and the government. In the case of the village of Wadepuri, where the revenue was assigned to Jiwaji Raghunath in 1780,[7] the assigned revenue consisted of (i) *ain jama* (the land revenue), (ii) miscellaneous items such as the tax for alms (*dharmaday patti*) and tax on a servant (*shagirthpesha*) and (iii) the *anthatsa* or the payment to the prime minister (*peshwa*). While (ii) miscellaneous items were re-distributed in a village[8] and (iii) the amount of the *antasthan* was remitted to the prime minister in Pune as in the government village, the holder of *jagir* received (i) *ain jama* as his income. Another commander, Fakirji Fadtare, to whom the revenue of Babhulgaon in Indapur Pargana was assigned in 1778, held the revenue of two villages in Satara Subha, a quarter of the revenue of a village in Karnataka Subha, the assigned land for various services called *shet-sanadi* in Junnar Prant as *jagir*.[9] This case shows that the rights of *jagir* of a commander spread over different provinces (*subhas*) under the Marathas.

Unfortunately, the expenditure list in assigned villages was not found in the Pune Archives. Therefore, it is difficult to precisely ascertain how a holder of *jagir* used the revenue from his assigned village which was located in Indapur Pargana. This point is considered separately according to whether a holder of *jagir* was stationed in his assigned village in Indapur Pargana or not. The above case of Fakirji Fadtare is a good example to consider the management by the holder who did not stay in his assigned village. Fakirji Fadtare was not in Babhulgaon in Indapur Pargana. He sent his staff to the village, who remitted money to him.[10] This case indicates that the locations of his *jagir* villages did not matter to Fakirji Fadtare himself. For him, in other words, these *jagir* villages were places treated in financial accounts only. Actually, his staff sent money to Fakirji Fadtare, who was distant from Indapur Pargana, quite often by use of *warat* or the bill of exchanges issued by the government. In this situation, the system of remittance developed.

The following deed concretely shows the purpose for giving a *jagir* village in which a commander would stay:

> 18 Jamadilakhar (the sixth Islamic month) or Ashwin (the seventh Hindu month) Kanhoji Khalate, who had regular cavalry, had no villages in which to post his cavalry. Therefore, Kumbhargaon in Indapur Pargana and its meadow, which had belonged to Shamrav Narayan, were given [to Kanhoji Khalate] for his cavalry. Meadow even in the village should be registered as the meadow in his charge for the expenditure in his cavalry. This is the deed given to *kamavisdar.*
>
> Present [a copy of] this deed (*sanad*) to the above person [*viz*. Kanhoji Khalate] and let him start managing the village.
>
> Two documents [at the total].[11]

This deed, which was originally issued to the *kamavisdar*, clearly mentioned that the reason for giving a commander a *jagir* village was he did not hold any fields in which to raise his horses. A commander was stationed in the assigned village to raise horses. It is noteworthy in this case that he could not freely use natural resources, viz., meadows in his assigned village. In this sense, the place for his *jagir* was clearly separate from natural spaces in a village. Many deeds in which *jagir* was given for a commander to procure the field in which to raise horses are found in Maharashtra State Archives, Pune. Under the *jagir* system, the main duty of its holder was generally the maintenance of his equipment in the village and his military service to the government. The above quotation indicates that many commanders were stationed in Indapur Pargana to raise horses, which were the most important equipment for *silahdars* (the irregular soldiers) and *paga* (regular cavalry). According to the lists of feed and allowances, horses were fed with vetch, sorghum and other cereal crops, as well as fodder. Rice, wheat flour, salt, butter, ghee, jaggery, pepper and mixed spices were sometimes also given as nutritious foods to not only ill horses but to pregnant horses. In short, military horses under the Marathas were not only imported from other regions but were bred in Indapur Pargana. The banks of the Bhima and the Nira rivers were famous for breeding and raising domestic horses. However, they were considered to be for commercial uses.[12] The above documents clarified the government arranged *jagirs* in Indapur Pargana, which was the nearest fertile areas from Pune, for military horse breeding in order to protect this city in the internal reforms after 1761.

The details on keeping horses can be found from some particular cases. In the case of Sakhoji Kate to whom the village of Kalasi was assigned at Rs. 588-8, it was fortunately found that it cost Rs. 40 per year in 1787 to feed his horses with vetch, cereal crops, salt and sugar.[13] However, this is an exceptional case. The data about the price of the crops that were given to horses could not be generally collected in the list of feed and allowances or other documents. It is inferred that these crops were not procured from the market but brought to the holder of *jagir* directly from the fields. However, he had to purchase at least rice and salt, which were produced mainly in the coastal area. The fodder given to the horses of a commander was cut in meadows of his assigned village. The forced labourers were brought from its neighbouring government villages, who worked to cut and pile fodder when an assignee was ordered to set out for military service.[14] Bonded labourers were also used for the collection of fodder, the payment to whom was fixed at Rs. 1–8 per 1,000 bundles.[15]

According to the list of feed and allowances, mainly female domestic slaves called *kumbin*, *Mahars*, and boys worked for a commander. Their allowance was paid in kind only. Besides these, a commander employed some staff. Although the members of the staff varied according to the village, they mainly consisted of one or two clerks (*karkuns*), a water-carrier (*palkhi*), a meadow guard (*kurnya*) and bodyguards who were made up of *Marathas* (farmers and soldiers), *Mahars* and *Mangs*.[16] Sometimes a goatherd (*shelkya*) and a cowherd (*gaykya*) were added to the list of allowances. The allowances for these staff members were paid in money. Carpenters (*Sutars*), potters (*Kumbhars*), *Mahars* and *Mangs* in a *jagir* village were also obligated to work for a commander at forced labour annually. For example, carpenters in Daij in Indapur Pargana, where the cavalry of Khandoji Jagthap were stationed at least in 1768, cut fifty acacias in meadows of this village and then made a one-story house for him.[17] Although these artisans basically worked according to the roles in the local community, the work a commander demanded was the extra labour that was not to be arranged in the local community. In this sense, the *jagir* system thus affected the local labouring system in the village community.

To maintain equipment such as horses, holders of *jagir* not only spent money but also used grain and fodder directly from the field and paid in kind. While his formal rights were converted into money in *Tainat Jabta*, his actual service in his village was not completely monetized at least in the late eighteenth century. Therefore, the assignment of a village by which not only money but also provisions for his duties were easily available was favourable to holders of *jagir* as payment for his military service. Furthermore, the space for raising horses seemed to be the most important of the benefits they enjoyed under the *jagir* system. However, the assignment of the whole village as *jagir* did not mean a holder of *jagir* could freely control natural and human resources in his *jagir* village. The resources he could use were to be registered for the expenditure in keeping his horses, etc.

In consideration of previous studies of the local administration, the present analysis of *jagir* system indicates the diversity of the administrative 'place' under the Marathas. The previous works clarified the distribution system of grain and labour in the local community, which was headed by the hereditary headman called *patil* in a village and *deshmukh* in a *pargana*. The rights and duties of peasants, artisans, local officers, etc., which were called *watan*, were inheritable, transferable and salable.[18] The *jagir* system

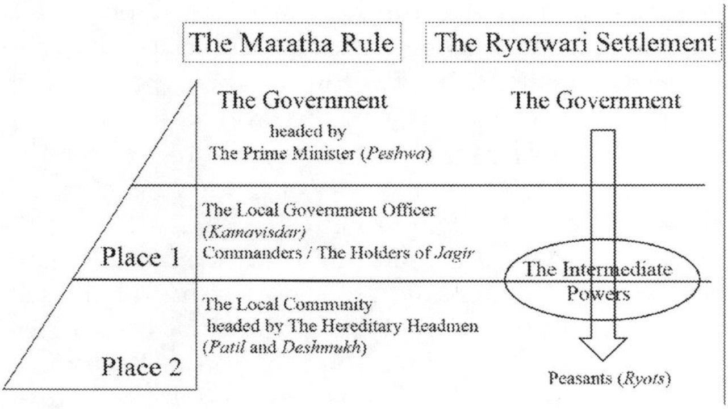

Figure 2.3 The structure of administrative place under the Maratha rule.
Source: Created by Michihiro Ogawa.

was not related to this distribution system except through the payment by the village headman and was different from the distribution system in that the *jagir* system was based on the government order. It can be said in this sense that these systems operated on different layers. Furthermore, Figure 2.2 shows that government villages under *kamavisdar* and *jagir* villages under commanders were complementary. *Kamavisdar* worked on the same layer as commanders under the *jagir* system. In short, as Figure 2.3 shows, the administrative place could be divided into three layers. The government headed by the prime minister (*peshwa*) was on the top layer of the administrative place. The local distribution system operated on the bottom (Place 2 on Figure 2.3). Between the government and the local community, *kamavisdar* and commanders worked on the middle layer (Place 1). The middle layer (Place 1) was created by the government for its local administration, while the bottom layer (Place 2) emerged chiefly in the local customs. This structure could be seen not only in Indapur Pargana but in the whole territory of the Marathas.

To raise horses successfully, some commanders in Indapur Pargana utilized natural resources and the distribution system more vigorously in certain restrictions. In short, Place 1 gave more influence on Place 2 in Indapur Pargana than other *parganas*. This made this *pargana* special under the Maratha rule. As seen later, Figure 2.3 shows that this point is related to the introduction of the Ryotwari Settlement into Indapur Pargana.

Arrangement of *jagir* villages under the Marathas

According to the government order, *jagir* or the assignment of collecting the land revenue from a village in Indapur Pargana, was transferred in various contexts, although this transfer was not regulated unlike in the Mughal Empire. This section studies how *jagir* was transferred and a *jagir* village was arranged in order to consider the concept of 'place' under Maratha rule.

Transfer of jagir

Jagir was removed, seized, and exchanged for various reasons under the Marathas. It is considered from an institutional perspective how *jagir* villages were arranged by seeing the main reasons of their transfer.

Political reasons: Assignment of *jagir* was based on the settlement between the government and a commander. A strong reason was required for removing *jagir* and thus violating the settlement. For example, Man Singh Mane to whom Sugaon had been assigned was deprived of his *jagir* because he rose in rebellion in 1777. After this deprivation, this village was assigned to Raghnath Baji Diwan.[19] The *jagir* in Padasthal in Indapur Pargana, which belonged to Krishna Singh Bais, was seized in 1767 because he did not carry out his military duties.[20] In this case, the settlement was violated because the holder of *jagir* did not perform military services. It seemed the government strictly checked his military performance even in time of peace. The *jagir*'s seizure was released as soon as his military performance was confirmed.[21]

Some cases of removal were related to huge political disputes. In 1776, Manaji Shinde, to whom the revenue of Bhabulgaon and Shelgaon in Indapur Pargana had been assigned, joined the plot to eliminate Nana Phadnis from the government and bring Raghunatrao, who helped Manaji to become the head of the Shinde family in 1764, to Pune as *peshwa*.[22] In 1777 Manaji defected to Hyder Ali's camp, betraying the Marathas at the battle against Mysore.[23] His *jagir* in two villages was seized immediately because of his malfeasance. In 1778, the revenue of Babhulgaon was assigned to Fakirji Fadtare as mentioned above. *Jagir* in villages of Kharochi and Ajoti, which had belonged to Darkoji Nimbalkar, was seized in 1779 because he supported Raghunatrao. Madhavrao Narayan and Nana Phadnis were at war with Raghunatrao over the Peshwaship in 1774–1782. After this dispute, the winners (Madhavrao Narayan and Nana Fadnis) gave *jagirs* in Indapur Pargana to a new commander, who probably supported them. The political issues at the central government influenced the arrangement of *jagirs* in Indapur Pargana.

Military reasons: It was a very important military service especially in Indapur Pargana to keep horses. *Jagir* villages were arranged so that commanders there could raise horses in better circumstances. For example, the revenue of Kumbhargaon was assigned to Manshing Khalate in 1780 because he did not hold any fields in which to raise horses.[24] As seen above, however, this village had been given to Kanhoji Khalate as *jagir* for the same reason. Therefore, *jagir* of Sirsodi was given to Kanhoji Khalate in

1780 so that he could continue to keep military horses. With the transfer of *jagir*, Kanhoji Khalate himself shifted to Sirsodi in order to deploy his horses and then be stationed there.[25] The government tried to provide the fields in which to raise horses to as many commanders as possible. For more effective arrangement, the government sometimes changed the commander who was stationed in Indapur Pargana from one village to another. This change was accompanied by his actual migration. In 1778, the *jagir* of Kalambradi in Barshi Pargana was removed from Pandurang Naik, and then the *jagir* of Pimpli in Indapur Pargana was given to him instead.[26] As seen in Figure 2.4, Pandurang Naik and his father Bapuji Naik carried out the large scale management of military horses in Indapur Pargana. The government intended to move his *jagir* in order to enlarge their management of horses there.[27]

Financial reasons: In many cases, the transfer of *jagir* occurred subsequent to another transfer of *jagir* for the above reasons. In the above case of Mansing Khalate and Kanhoji Khalate, for example, the *jagir* of Kanhoji Khalate was transferred not for his own reason but as a result of the assignment to Mansing Khalate. The government gave *jagir* of Sirsodi to Kanhoji Khalate to guarantee his income and fields for his horses. In this sense, this assignment was not only military but also concerned financial matters. In the above case of Pandurang Naik, the revenue of Pimple had been assigned to Mahimaji Pudhe. By the order dated on the same day as this village was given to Pandurang Naik,[28] the revenue of Kalambradi in Barshi Pargana was given to Mahimaji Pudhe. In short, the assigned revenue was exchanged between Pandurang Naik and Mahimaji Pudhe. The government carried out this exchange to guarantee the income of Mahimaji Pudhe. In the above case of Fakirji Fadtare, the land called *shet-sanadi* in Kurali, Chakan Tarf was removed by the order dated on the same day as the revenue of Babhulgaon in Indapur Pargana was assigned to him. The revenue from the former amounted to Rs. 50 only, while the latter amounted to Rs. 2,700. By the removal of the former, the government controlled his financial promotion of *jagir*. Because he was stationed neither in Kurali nor in Babhulgaon, this change was chiefly a financial matter. Once *jagir* for political and military reasons was transferred, the government controlled and rearranged *jagir* villages, lands, etc. in order not to worsen the financial situation of all the *jagir* holders related to the transfer. Here these subsequent transfers or exchanges are categorized as 'financial reasons'.

The analysis of transfer of *jagir* has clarified that it moved in different provinces under the Marathas. This indicates that the middle layer on Figure 2.3 seemed to spread over the whole territory of the Marathas while the bottom layer was chiefly limited to a *pargana*. However, the promotion of horse breeding in Indapur Pargana seemed to make the movement and activities of commanders different from others. The next part focuses on the *jagir* system in Indapur Pargana.

Arrangement of jagir villages in Indapur Pargana

This part spatially analyses the arrangement of *jagir* villages. Figure 2.4 shows the locations of *jagir* villages in Indapur Pargana in the late eighteenth century. Each area of the maps stands for a village territory. On the maps, different commanders are recognized according to a difference in shades.

In 1768, five different villages were assigned to five different assignees. As seen above, the number of *jagir* villages greatly increased between 1769 and 1774. In this period, villages on the banks of rivers, which were covered with fertile soils by the rivers, were assigned to the commanders who were stationed in Indapur Pargana to raise horses. Dotted areas, which belonged to Bapuji Naik and Pandurang Naik, extended in this period. From 1774 to 1786, the number of *jagir* villages still increased politically because *jagir* villages were given to new commanders after the dispute over the peshwaship in the late 1770s. While dotted areas extend slightly on the map of

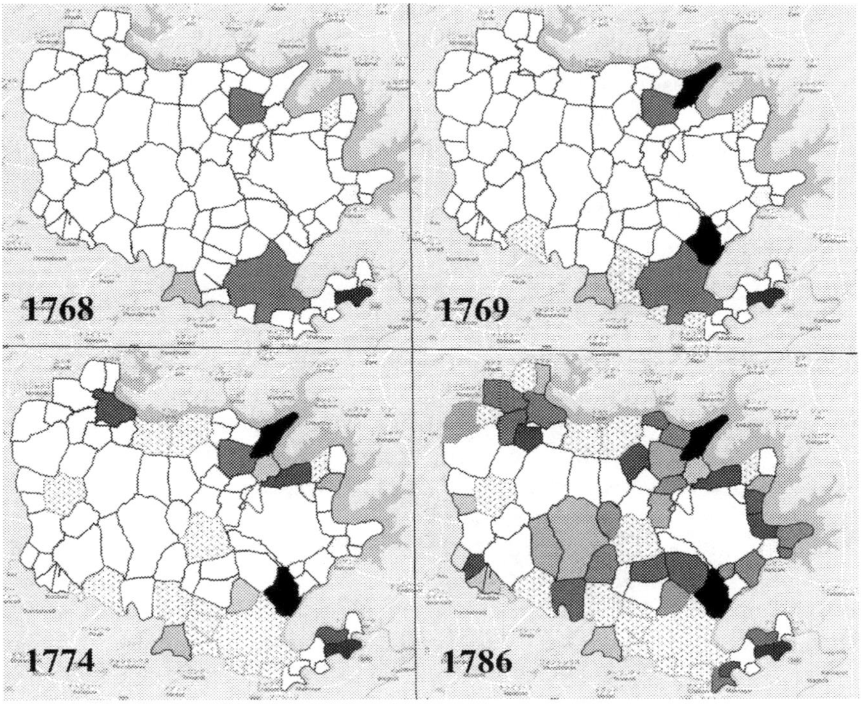

Figure 2.4 Location of *jagir* villages in Indapur Pargana in the late eighteenth century.
Source: Created by Michihiro Ogawa.

1784, different shades of territories can be seen, which represents the diversification of commanders in Indapur Pargana. In this phase, fertile land to raise horses effectively began to run short. Less fertile lands in inland villages were thus also used. Although villages in Indapur Pargana were rearranged to use more villages for keeping horses, political situations also influenced this rearrangement.

In 1802, the army of the Holkar family attacked Pune, the central city, and its surrounding areas, including Indapur Pargana in the civil war over the peshwaship of Bajirao II, and in 1803, drought hit the areas around Indapur Pargana. These two disasters devastated Indapur Pargana. The annual accounts do not contain enough data to show the arrangement of villages in which the land revenue could not be collected. Therefore, the data between 1803 and 1806 in Figure 2.2 is blank. After these two disasters, many commanders in *jagir* villages left Indapur Pargana. When the settlement of the land revenue restarted in 1807, the number of *jagir* villages was substantially reduced to only twenty-nine. This change is understood more clearly when considering the military system of the Marathas. In the civil war in 1802, Bajirao II concluded a treaty with the English East India Company to gain its military support. According to this treaty, the artillery and the army of the English East India Company were stationed in Pune to protect Bajirao II. In other words, horses and cavalry became less useful under the military system of the Marathas in this phase. This institutional change also influenced the great decrease in the number of *jagir* villages in Indapur Pargana.

After 1807, the number of government villages in which *kamavisdar* collected the land revenue and remitted it to the government increased greatly. The power of this officer, or more precisely, his supporter, Sadashiv Mankershwar,[29] had risen highly in the administration of Indapur Pargana between 1807 and 1818. *Kamavisdar* began to survey dry land, pasture and fallow land in order to find as much cultivatable land as possible. In the new styles of accounts, dry land and pasture were separately entered, from which it is found that the area of dry land in government villages increased every year. In the 1810s, the concept of land use changed at least in government villages. However, the map of 1807 (Figure 2.5) shows many of the *jagir* villages that survived the two disasters were still located on the banks. Manohar Gir, or the powerful commander who served under the *peshwa,* directly held villages on the bank of the Nira River, whose territory is surrounded with a cross line (++++) in Figure 2.5, as *jagir* partly replacing *jagir* villages of Pandurang Naik. This arrangement indicates that the government still supported the military activities of commanders with cavalry under the Marathas, though this system itself was to be abandoned under the above treaty. In short, this was the period of transition in which old and new styles of administration coexisted.

The *Peshwa* directly fought against the East India Company in 1817 and was defeated in 1818, when British rule began in Western India. Many

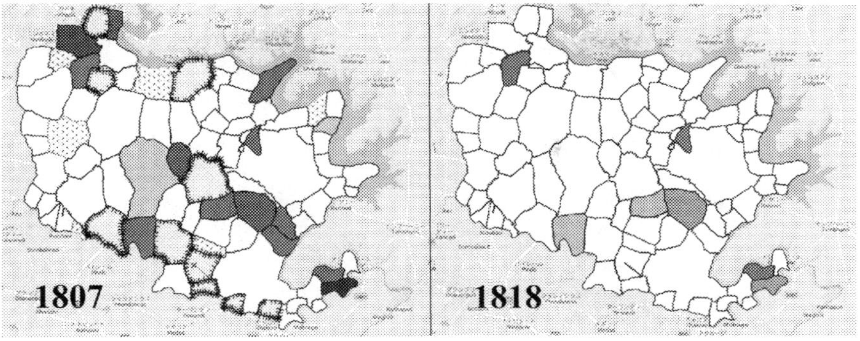

Figure 2.5 Location of *jagir* villages in Indapur Pargana in the early nineteenth century.
Source: Created by Michihiro Ogawa.

commanders including Manohar Gir joined this battle. Under British rule, most of the *jagir* villages which survived the two disasters were converted into government villages. The number of *jagir* villages was reduced to seven, and most of the commanders left Indapur Pargana by 1818. The map of 1818 (Figure 2.5) shows that the location of seven villages was not always suitable for raising horses. The holders of *jagirs* in these seven villages came from the Patwardhan family and the Holkar family, which were the princely states in British India. The Assistant Collector, who was in the lowest position for a British officer in India, was appointed to administer a *pargana,* which was generally renamed *taluka*. The Assistant Collector of Indapur Pargana, who replaced the position of *kamavisdar*, and Sadashiv Mankeshwar carried out the introduction of the Ryotwari settlement in 1836. In this context, the collapse of the *jagir* system in the last phase of the Maratha period made the introduction of the Ryotwari settlement in the British period possible.

It can be clearly understood by use of the above model (Figure 2.3) why the Ryotwari settlement was introduced into Indapur Pargana first. This colonial policy aimed at the settlement of the land revenue between the government on the top layer and peasants on the bottom layer (Place 2) excluding intermediate powers, who worked on Places 1 and 2.[30] The policy itself developed in the colonial administration and already started in the Madras Presidency in 1790s. The disruption around Pune in the last phase of Maratha rule would influence both Places 1 and 2. However, the peculiarity of Indapur Pargana can be found in changes on Place 1, in which most commanders holding intermediate powers in the late eighteenth century had left Indapur Pargana and the powers promptly concentrated into one person, viz., Sadashiv Mankeshwar. The replacement of his position easily enabled the exclusion of powers on Place 1, unlike in other *parganas*.

At this point, Indapur Pargana was selected as the first place for the Ryotwari settlement in the Bombay Presidency. However, peasants were on the bottom layer (Place 2). This chapter does not cover changes on Place 2; the local powers and their changes on Place 2 will be studied in the near future.

Conclusion

This chapter considered the introduction of the Ryotwari Settlement in Western India from a long-term viewpoint, focusing on the administrative territory of the sub-district called *pargana,* which was defined as 'place'. The analysis of the *jagir* system clarified its structure with three layers, and especially the layer on which the government officers and commanders operated. As *jagir* was transferred in a very wide area, this layer seemed to spread over the whole territory of the Marathas while the layer for the local community was limited to a *pargana*. In this sense, these two layers were different. In this situation, however, commanders in Indapur Pargana got involved in matters on the layer for the local community for horse breeding more deeply than in other areas. The collapse of the *jagir* system in Indapur Pargana in the last phase of Maratha rule caused a temporary gap in the intermediate powers and then its excessive concentration. This change made the introduction of the Ryotwari settlement in Indapur Pargana easier, at least in the layer for commanders and government officers. In other words, very significant changes for the introduction of the Ryotwari Settlement occurred in the layer between the government and the local community just before British rule started in 1818. However, this does not mean the local community in Indapur Pargana easily accepted this settlement. The Ryotwari Settlement introduced sub-district viz., *pargana* to sub-district in the nineteenth century. Previous works clarifying this settlement saw various forms of resistance in the Bombay Presidency, but they did not recognize the difference in the layers on which the resistance occurred.[31] The structure of the administrative place this chapter clarified will work for better understanding of colonization, too.

Notes

1 Ravinder Kumar considered the process of establishing the Ryotwari settlement at the sub-district level in the nineteenth-century Western India (Kumar [1968] 2014, pp. 88–127). The present study develops this from the long-term perspective by studying the economic and political backgrounds to the new settlement.
2 Irfan Habib, *The Agrarian System of Mughal India 1556–1707*. 2nd edition. Reprint, New Delhi: Oxford University Press, [1999] 2010, pp. 299–301.
3 Under the Marathas, the word '*saranjam*', meaning materials, provisions or supply, was used for the revenue assignment most common in the eighteenth century. However, the term '*jagir*' was also used under the Marathas, and these two terms were often used interchangeably within a single letter. This chapter unifies the synonyms to the word '*jagir*' (Wink [1986] 2008, pp. 319–320).

4 A. R. Kulkarni, *Medieval Maratha Country*. Reprint, Pune: Diamond Publications, [1996] 2008, p. 202.
5 Previous studies on revenue assignment in pre-colonial India were inclined to deal with the assignments whose territory covered the whole *pargana*, or sometimes even the whole *subha*, which was the upper territorial unit of *pargana*. For example, the work of H. Fukazawa focused on the assignment to the Patwardhan family, whose assignment area extended over many *parganas* under the Marathas. In this study, the assignee worked like a government in collecting the land revenue (Fukazawa 1991, pp. 77–90). However, Andre Wink has pointed out most of the assignments under the Peshwa Government were much tinier than these large assignments (Wink [1986] 2008, p. 325). In this context, this study clarifies the actual management of *jagirs* in pre-colonial India.
6 Two villages in Indapur Pargana were directly under Manaji Shinde, who had been the head of Shinde family, as his *jagir* from 1764 to 1768.
7 Michihiro Ogawa, 'Mapping the Transition of the Land Revenue System in Western India from the Pre-Colonial to the Early Colonial India: Evidence from to Indapur Pargana (1761–1836)', *Journal of Asian Network for GIS-based Historical Studies* 3, 2015, pp. 14–15.
8 For example, the holder of *jagir*, more precisely the village headman, paid the whole amount of the tax for alms (*dharmaday patti*) to local religious establishments such as a Hindu temple as the alms called *dharaday*.
9 27 Jamadilawal Shuhur 1164, bundle (Fadke) Fakirji Fadtare, Ghadni Rumal no. 454, 26 Safar Shuhur 1178, Fadke no. 3, Ghadni Rumal no. 395, and 3 Ramajan Shuhu 1176, Fadke no. 3, Ghadni Rumal no. 395, Maharashtra State Archives, Pune (hereafter MSAP).
10 26 Safar Shuhur 1178, Prant Ajmas, Pune, Rumal no. 547, MSAP.
11 18 Jamadilakhar, Prant Ajmas, Pune, Rumal no. 503, MSAP.
12 James M. Campbell, *Poona District,* Vol. 18–1 of *Gazetteer of the Bombay Presidency*. Bombay: The Government Central Press, 1885, p. 61.
13 23 Jilhej Shuhur San 1187, Prant Ajmas, Pune, Rumal no. 503, MSAP.
14 3 Jilhej Shuhur 1175, Fadke Khanderao Jiwaji Siledar, Ghadni Rumal no. 404, MSAP.
15 29 Moharam Shuhur 1186, Prant Ajmas, Pune, Rumal no. 547, MSAP.
16 *Mahars* and *Mangs* were entitled to carry all the dead bodies of animals, cows and buffaloes in their villages. They worked in various services for the local community.
17 7 Sawal Shuhu 1168, Prant Ajmas Pune, Rumal no. 547, MSAP.
18 Hiroshi Fukazawa, 'Agrarian Relations and Land Revenue – The Medieval Deccan and Maharashtra', in Vol. 1 of *The Cambridge Economic History of India*, edited by Tapan Raychaudhuri and Irfan Habib, Reprint, New Delhi: Cambridge University Press, [1982] 2007, pp. 252–256.
19 16 Jilhej Shuhur 1178, Prant Ajmas, Pune, Rumal no. 503, MSAP.
20 No date Safar Shuhur 1168, Prant Ajmas, Pune, Rumal no. 503, MSAP.
21 26 Safar Shuhur 1178, Prant Ajmas, Pune, Rumal no. 547, MSAP.
22 N. G. Rathod, *Great Maratha Mahadaji Scindia*, New Delhi: Sarup & Sons, 1994, pp. 4, 13, 14.
23 Charles Augustus Kincaid and Dattatraya Baḷavanta Prasnis, *From the Death of Shahu to the End of the Chitpavan Epic*. Vol. 3 of *Comprehensive History of the Maratha Empire*. Reprint, Delhi: Anmol Publications, [1925] 1986, p. 120.
24 30 Rabilawal Shuhur 1181, Prant Ajmas, Pune, Rumal no. 547, MSAP.
25 21 Rajab Shuhur 1180, Prant Ajmas, Pune, Rumal no. 547, MSAP.

26 25 Falgun Shuhur 1178, Fadke Mahimaji Mudhe, Ghadni Rumal no. 454, MSAP.
27 Ogawa, 'Mapping the Transition of the Land Revenue System in Western India from the Pre-Colonial to the Early Colonial India', 2015, pp. 17–18.
28 25 Falgun Shuhur 1178, Fadke Mahimaji Mudhe, Ghadni Rumal no. 454, MSAP.
29 Sadashiv Mankeshwar was one of the chief officers under Bajirao II. He replaced *kamavisdar* of Indapur Pargana by supporting him financially.
30 *Deshmukh* on Place 2 as well as commanders and *kamavisdar* on Place 1 held the intermediary powers under the Marathas.
31 While *khots* or the hereditary revenue farmer in Ratnagiri of Konkan were on the layer for the local community, *talukdars* in Gujarat were on the other layer. For the details, see Charlesworth ([1985] 2002, pp. 47–56).

References

Campbell, James M. *Poona District,* Vol. 18-1 of *Gazetteer of the Bombay Presidency.* James M. Campbell. Bombay: The Government Central Press, 1885.

Charlesworth, Neil. *Peasant and Imperial Rule, Agricultural and Agrarian Society in the Bombay Presidency, 1850–1935.* Reprint, Cambridge: Cambridge University Press, (1985) 2002.

Fukazawa, Hiroshi. 'Agrarian Relations and Land Revenue: The Medieval Deccan and Maharashtra'. In Vol. 1 of *The Cambridge Economic History of India*, edited by Tapan Raychaudhuri and Irfan Habib, Reprint, New Delhi: Cambridge University Press, (1982) 2007, pp. 248–260.

Fukazawa, Hiroshi. 'Agrarian Relations: Western India'. In Vol. 2 of *The Cambridge Economic History of India*, edited by Dharma Kumar, Reprint, New Delhi: Cambridge University Press, (1983) 2008, pp. 177–206.

Fukazawa, Hiroshi. *The Medieval Deccan, Peasants, Social Systems and States, Sixteenth to Eighteenth Centuries.* Delhi: Oxford University Press, 1991.

Habib, Irfan. *The Agrarian System of Mughal India 1556–1707.* 2nd edition. Reprint, New Delhi: Oxford University Press, (1999) 2010.

Kincaid, Charles Augustus and Dattatraya Baḷavanta Prasnis. *From the Death of Shahu to the End of the Chitpavan Epic.* Vol. 3 of *Comprehensive History of the Maratha Empire.* Reprint, Delhi: Anmol Publications, (1925) 1986.

Kulkarni, A.R. *Medieval Maratha Country.* Reprint, Pune: Diamond Publications, (1996) 2008.

Kumar, Ravinder. *Western India in the Nineteenth Century*, Reprint, London: Routledge, (1968) 2014.

Ogawa, Michihiro. 'Mapping the Transition of the Land Revenue System in Western India from the Pre-Colonial to the Early Colonial India: Evidence from to Indapur Pargana (1761–1836)', *Journal of Asian Network for GIS-based Historical Studies* 3, 2015: 12–20.

Rathod, N.G. *The Great Maratha Mahadaji Scindia*, New Delhi: Sarup & Sons, 1994.

Wink, Andre. *Land and Sovereignty in India Agrarian Society and Politics under the Eighteenth-century Maratha Svarajya.* Reprint, Cambridge: Cambridge University Press, (1986) 2008.

Chapter 3

Creating spaces for indigeneity from Nizam's Hyderabad state to Maharashtra

Bina Sengar

Idea of an indigenous space

> Not being in control of the land, or not being able to protect it or have access to the natural foods and medicines that grow on it, gives us a really shaky future.
>
> Ramona Peters,[1] a Mashpee Wampanoag and indigenous rights activist.

Land as space is not limited to property rights. Land shapes the culture and identities of communities. In this way, space can be seen as connected to the cultural and political practices of land governance and social connectivity which help to create community identities. The notion of identity, which is often considered individualistic, is inherently an outcome of humans' association with the land and the concept of space associated with it (Stump, 2008). Indigenous peoples' relationship with their traditional lands and territories is said to form a core part of their identity and spirituality, which is deeply rooted in their culture and history. In respect to the sovereignty of indigenous peoples globally, in 2007 the UN declared 46 Articles which aimed to recognize the land rights and contributions made by indigenous people.[2]

However, at a time when global connectivity and policies are changing tremendously, the issue of the rights of ethnic minorities and indigenous peoples has reached an extremely sensitive position in comparative constitutional law as well as in international law. Notwithstanding its importance, there are serious disagreements regarding the definition of 'peoples', 'minorities' and 'indigenous peoples'. The primary reason for this controversy is that although 'people' and 'indigenous peoples' have a right to self-determination, under contemporary international law 'minorities' do not enjoy the same rights. As the International Labour Organisation Convention 169 (entitled the Convention Concerning Indigenous and Tribal Peoples in Independent Countries [1989)]) and the Draft United Nations Declaration on the Rights of Indigenous People confirm, indigenous peoples are increasingly being recognized as having the right to self-determination. This right, if accorded widespread recognition, could make a difference between the rights to independent statehood as opposed to mere entitlement to cultural, linguistic or religious existence within established international boundaries.[3]

The introductory ideas of identity, land rights and indigenous people's entitlement to spaces of their own form the backdrop of the present study. This chapter will explore how space and indigeneity are understood for the largest indigenous or tribal group[4] of India, i.e. the Gonds. The Gonds as an indigenous community or conglomerate of several clans or sub-clans are considered to be one of the oldest human societies of South Asia. Over the last two millennia, the social and political status of the Gonds has undergone several changes. However, the predominant change that occurred in their indigenous space began with the evolution of empire states in Western India after the beginning of the seventeenth century. This chapter will delve into the spatial changes that became evident in Gond societies when new land rights were introduced. Shifts in governance led to alternative concepts of cultural spaces which consequently changed the Gond people's world view. Consequently, their fate as an indigenous group changed radically over time, as empire states and rulers, specifically the Mughals, Marathas (Bhonsle of Nagpur state), later the Nizams (Asafjahi rulers of Hyderabad state) and Britishers, grappled with the Gonds' territorial land and cultural sovereignty. In the following narrative, historical transitions within Gond spaces are discussed in congruence to the Gondi spaces in Maharashtra and Western India. The present chapter focuses especially on the cultural and space sovereignty binaries which evolved historically because of conceptual scaffolding. In the process of the linguistic-based state formation in independent India, those parts of the Gondwana region which are now part of Maharashtra and Telangana (formerly Andhra Pradesh) states underwent the process of scaffolding; this significantly differs from the process of acculturation. Change which occurred within the Gond culture over time and led to formation of different strata within their own spaces is discussed through this research.

As we further delve into this question, it is useful to note that the problematic of land ownership and the right to sovereignty not only determines cultural integrity; it also determines how people govern themselves and whether they are considered rulers or the *ruled*. According to Benedict Anderson, the 'classical concept' of a nation is an imagined political community, a metaphorical kinship of people who will most likely never know each other.[5] Despite its imaginative nature, national identity encourages people to be willing to sacrifice themselves in order to defend the nation. The whole idea of collective identity as a nation comes with the development of print media and the development of capitalism. The structuring of land-associated identities with metaphorical cultures thus leads to the formation of binary identities, which are constructed or construed to be part of national identity.[6] In the context of South Asia, the inclusion of indigenous communities and regional cultures in national identities raises questions pertaining to their spaces of cultural identity and sovereignty. Stella Tamang, an indigenous leader from Nepal, summarizes the relationship between indigenous people and the land this way:

> [I]ndigenous peoples ... have an intimate connection to the land; the rationale for talking about who they are is tied to the land. They have clear symbols in their language that connect them to places on their land ... [I]n Nepal, we have groups that only can achieve their spiritual place on the planet by going to a certain location.[7]

As we further explore the ideas of nation states and regional and localized/indigenous spaces in South Asia and India in specific, we come across several variations which led to the formation of multiple binaries and regional spatial dichotomies in the context of indigenous spaces. The theories of political philosophers have helped us to understand societies; however, in localized native communities or in the field, when we try to apply these theories, then the facts don't readily conform.[8] As in the words of Evans-Pritchard (1940, RP-2015): 'Political philosophy has chiefly concerned itself with how men *ought* to live and what form of government they "ought to have", rather than with what are their political habits and institutions'.[9] When we study the so-called primitive political states, it becomes evident that mere differences in modes of livelihood do not determine differences in political structures (Evans-Pritchard, 2015). The mode of livelihood may neither lessen their concept of state and hegemony nor will it minimize their notions of sanctity and the superiority of space in their own ecological conditions (Bhukya, 2017). The sacrilege or sanctity of space and political institutions are interwoven with beliefs, practices and their connectedness with the land and the norms of land ownership. As in the studies about '*Dang Rajas*' (Skaria, 2000) and on Zulu society (Gluckman, 2012), the ownership of land and the idea of ruling classes were not alien concepts to tribal communities; in a conception similar to that of the nation state, Zululand, for example, constituted a large number of varying sizes of tribes. In Zulu theory, the chiefs (or their ancestors) of all these tribes were 'raised up' by one or another of the kings.[10] By the mid-1970s, such observations had become common in the Latin American homeland of the folk-urban continuum as well as in ethnographies by Gluckman's colleagues and others throughout sub-Saharan Africa. As the gestalt shifted from the antithesis of the rural-urban to the synthesis of the 'translocal' cultural order, study after study groped for a suitable terminology. Scholars spoke variously of 'a bi-local society', 'a single social and resource system', 'a non-territorial community network', a 'common social field' uniting countryside and city, a 'single community spanning a variety of sites on both sides of the border', 'a single social field in which there is a substantial circulation of members' or some new species of the like.[11]

Over the years, scholars have developed the idea that complex narratives are underpinned by a 'concrete and stable system of symbols'. 'Conceptual scaffolding' is erected to construct new ideologies or to modify existing ones;[12] a 'primary framework' helps to transform '[w]hat would otherwise be a meaningless aspect of [a] scene into something that is meaningful' by offering a point of comparison, or a conceptual structure, through which people can digest information.[13] When the pre-colonial and colonial authorities imposed Gond societies with a set of rules in their indigenous cultural space, the outcome was conceptual scaffolding. The aspects of scaffolding which are reflected in the Gond society are studied in the presented essay. In the main cultural, scaffolding in Gond society could be analysed as the set of rules that enabled binary opposition within their cultural myths, symbols and values. The fundamental cultural oppositions, introduced in Gond societies, such as those of changed gender equations, induced political and cultural hierarchy of rules to structure within the Gond's social and cultural patterns. The aspects of the evolution of scaffolding – which is other than acculturation – that happened in the Gond society of Maharashtra will be discussed further in the second part of this chapter.[14]

Similarly, the law of nations and the principles of territorial sovereignty have shaped concepts of governance,[15] where abstract or multiple binaries serve to organize and produce a social hierarchy that people use in the struggle to claim cultural and physical spaces.[16] Moreover, dualism in administrative and legal procedures further constrains the division between existing cultural and identity binaries.[17] The binary of rulers and ruled has shaped the conception of indigenous people across time and space (especially in the context of India). Whether the political community was an empire, a princely state, a colony, a republic, chiefdom or kingdom, all have been conceived as part of a centre or a periphery, as ruler and ruled or as either us and them.[18] Within a 'state-centric' approach to 'peripheral cultures', tribal community cultures are often defined as 'forest dwellers'. The ecological contexts of 'space' in tribal societies thus become the entire idea of being tribal. With such an approach, the tribal/native/indigenous societies are seen through narrow perceptions of being primitive or as representing archaic forms of human institutions. In such studies, the idea of space and spatial structures of communities are largely ignored (Suykens, 2009), unlike the complexities of state and organized political systems of these communities which is explained in the studies by Pritchard (1940, 1987), Skaria (2000), Gluckman (2012) and Bhukya (2017).[19]

Comparative study of the various ethnological data from different native communities in the spaces of the world encouraged scholars to seek connectivity in the narratives. Moreover, these studies suggested interconnectedness in most of the known historic traditions of culture.[20] Thus, the 'naive attempt to hold peoples hostage to their own histories', as one anthropologist has said, thereby deprived them of history.[21] These indigenous communities underwent historical transition in their own cultural spaces and evidence change and continuity. The change in the culture and core power structures of indigenous political spaces significantly determined their relationships with the power owners in the empire and people of the peripheries.[22]

Space and spatial identity of Gonds

The idea of indigenous or tribal spaces is associated with the terms 'rural/peripheral states' or 'forest dwellers'. Whenever we emphasize or comprehend the rural/forest space and people in them and their relations with land, then we overwhelmingly delve into the rural/forest land systems and their administration and seek the answers for the overall destruction/reconstruction of space in rural or indigenous regions with the human intervention in forest tracts and land areas. These ideas are often substantiated through various empirical studies, and our overall impressions very often lead to the colonial or capitalist practices which encouraged destruction of the space and the heritage of the ecological spheres of the indigenous societies.[23] Considering the above discussion in this chapter, this researcher will engage into the space destruction of the forest or rural communities of Gond by the over powering agencies of pre-colonial Mughals, Marathas and Nizam of Hyderabad and colonial British rule. These authoritative agencies brought significant changes in the land rights and administration of the Gonds, the different aspects of which will be stated in the following discussions.

However, when we consider the way Gondwana as a state emerged and evolved, then the appropriateness of the thoughts of Pritchard and Suykens become viable for consideration. The notion that the idea of state is associated with people of disconnected identities (Anderson, 2006) is not always applicable to societies whose histories have proven to have a close association with land and space, as posited by Suykens and Pritchard and further substantiated by the works of Haimendorf, Skaria and Bhukya. The horizontal division of Indian societies into hierarchically ranked castes, subcastes and communities has been the subject of a considerable literature.[24] In the narrative below, this chapter seeks to understand how the formation of these hierarchies within the social and political structure in India affected Gondwana and Gond spaces.

With the coming of the colonial era, new forest laws, trade administration and land ownership changed and so did the idea of native states *vs.* princely states. In the post-colonial era, we have carried forward many of the policies of colonial times. Although partial territorial rights were given to the tribal states, territorial hegemony and power remain a question among the indigenous populations in India. In these circumstances, this chapter critically investigates the regional political questions of the Gond as indigenous:

1 How do we define territorial and sovereignty rights and cultural spaces of Gond/indigenous community in native and colonial states?
2 What binaries of identity of the Gonds were used in Hyderabad state's Marathi/Maharashtrian and Telugu/Telangana regions?
3 How can we discuss cultural exclusivity and the sovereignty of political space for indigenous communities in the nexus of the regional and national frameworks in colonial times?

Gond and Gondi descent: present and past

Before we can understand the past and the complexities of the Gond as a universally unique identity which experienced ruptures in its own structures of cultural spaces and places, it becomes essential to look into how the Gond as an identity is understood in the twenty-first century. The 2011 census says that the total population of the Gond tribe in the country is 11,344,629. The census also lists the total Gondi-speaking population as 2,713,790. But according to Gond community leaders and observers, the actual numbers could be much higher, given the fact that huge concentrations of Gondi-speaking people are located in the Naxalite-affected areas of Madhya Pradesh, Maharashtra, Chhattisgarh and Andhra Pradesh; in most of these areas, there has been no census. The actual number of Gondi speakers, say community members, is many times the number reflected in the census. Gondwana Ganatantra Party (GPP) President, Hira Singh Markam,[25] says that based on surveys carried out by the party, the total number of people with Gondi as their first language is an estimated 20 million. 'Quite a few of the Scheduled languages in India cannot boast of this big a number of speakers', says Markam. 'Yet government has not included this language in the schedule'.[26] Even the official figure of 2.7 million is higher than the number of speakers of languages like Dogri, Bodo and Manipuri, all of which have been included in the Scheduled list of languages of India.[27] Gondi has also not been included under the Technology Development for Indian Languages (TDIL) programme of the Department of Electronics and Information Technology, which is developing a unicode – a programme for computers, which allows the user to type in any of the twenty-two Scheduled Indian languages.[28] The complexity presented highlights the linguistic questions of the Gonds in contemporary society; these can be further explored by delving into the historicity of the spatial and cultural identities of theirs which are constructs of the past.

The Gondwana region, which lay between the Narmada and the Godavari rivers and which later constituted parts of the British Central Provinces and now parts of the states of Madhya Pradesh, Maharashtra and Telangana, was marked as the country of the Gonds during the Mughal period. Although the region geographically occupied the centre of the Mughal Empire, it remained politically at the periphery of the empire due to its geographical setting as well as to the contested histories of its people. Gondwana was ruled by four powerful Gond dynasties for almost 300 years from the middle of the fifteenth century to the middle of the eighteenth century. The four independent Gond kingdoms arose more or less simultaneously in Garha in the north (present Mandla and Jabalpur districts), in Deogarh and Kherla (present Chhindwara and Betul districts) in the centre and Chanda (present Chandrapur district) in the south.[29] The Gonds of Chanda divided themselves into four endogamous tribes: the Raj Gonds, the Maria or Madia Gonds, the Dhurve Gonds and the Khatulwar Gonds. There were also other minor sub-tribes, such as the Koyas, the Gaitas, the Pardhans and the Kolams, who would not class themselves with any of the above tribes and were few in number. These sub-tribes all spoke dialects of the Gondi language (Figure 3.1).[30]

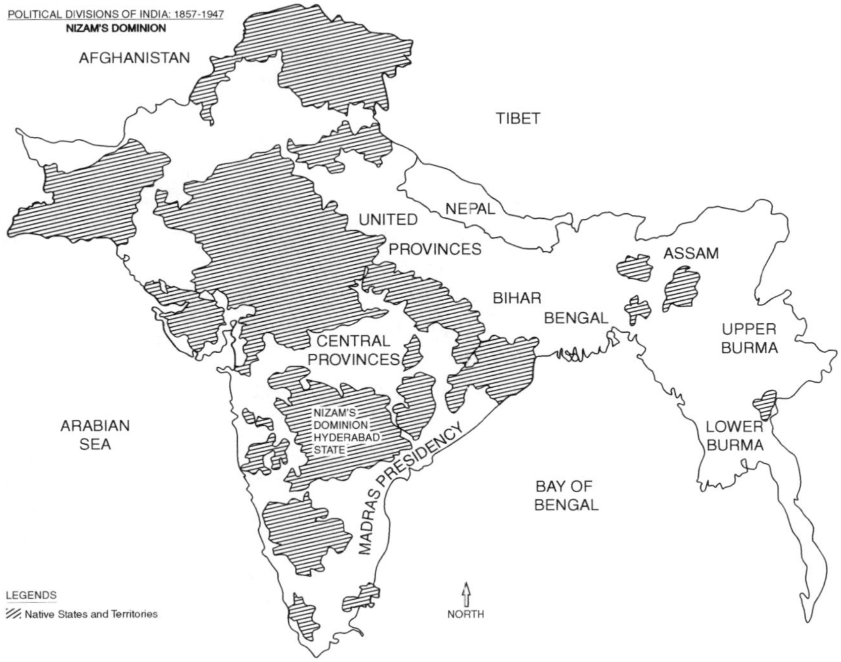

Figure 3.1 The Gond region in the Central Provinces of British India.
Source: Bina Sengar.

Historically, prior to the Mughal intervention, Gondwana remained in the geographical understanding of the Indian scriptures and mythologies. In the *Puranic* literature, Gondwana was understood as 'Lanka'; Gonds, who are also known as *Kittur* in their folklore, refer to Ravana as a Gond king, and in their oral narratives, they have a king similar to Ravana.[31] To substantiate the theories that the Gond have pre-historic existence in the South Asian Deccan plateau, in the nineteenth century when geologists were working on the idea of a continental drift, they were impressed by the finding that in the Gondi language of the Gond people of Central India, they referred to their land as '*Gond-wana*', where '*Wana*' means 'Land'; they also found that the jigsaw of the Gondwana land of the Paleozoic era matched with the fossils of the Gondwana land.[32] The early history of the Gond rajas of all the forementioned states of Gondwana is not clear. Moreover, the oral legends and stories of the Gond community speak abundantly of their rule in the region. Haimendorf arrived at the conclusion that the Gonds and Khonds are the survivors of tribes of different origins, and he thus prefers to class them as 'Gondi-Speaking populations'.[33]

According to oral legends, the Gonds descended from the legendary Gond brothers, who were thrown into a cave by Lord Mahadev and rescued by the Gond hero, Pari Kupar Lingo, who settled them, found brides for them and otherwise laid the foundations of social and political life among the Gonds.[34] From these two ancestors, the Gonds now claim to have more than 750 *akharas* or clans.[35] The Gonds living in erstwhile Hyderabad state (now spread over Chhattisgarh, Madhya Pradesh, Maharashtra and Telangana) claim to have been pushed from the river valley region of Pen-Ganga in the north and Godavari in the south.[36]

The Gond Rajas claimed to have ruled an extensive region, based first in Sirpur, then Ballarshah and finally Chanda. The northern boundary of their rule, it was said, reached the Wardha basin and the southern boundary to the northern bank of the Godavari river.[37] The region enjoyed considerable prosperity under the rule of the Gond rajas. Gond rajas, as per the legends, claimed their rule not just over Gond tribes but also over the migrants and settlers whom they encouraged to settle in Gondwana's territorial sovereign spaces. They rewarded their Gond *tarvels* (warriors) with a large amount of forest land, making them subordinate rajas, or *zamindar*s, of those tracts. They encouraged both *adivasi* and non-*adivasi* cultivators to settle on the land and bring it under cultivation. The *zamindar*s subtitled the land to the actual cultivators on a lease system and at nominal rents.[38] In this way, large areas were brought under cultivation, bringing into existence the notion of a state under Gond rajas, where the homogeneity of the community identity of Gond acculturated with other communities. The concept of state within the Gonds' history, where Bhim Ballal Singh established an indigenous state, thus contests the notions of homogeneity and peripheral identities, which are often associated with tribal spaces.[39]

As we further proceed to the late sixteenth- and seventeenth-century histories of Gond states and how they interacted with the imperial states of those times, we come across a characteristic transition and shift in the balance of power. The gradual deconstruction and fragmentation in the spaces of Gondwana as sovereign space is evident from the shift in the core of the Gond state by the beginning of the sixteenth century. The dominant power in the areas of Central India in the late Mughal era was the Gond kingdom, which was centred on and around Nagpur. The extended Gond family had already suffered from feuds, and one member of the ruling power converted to Islam in 1686 under the title 'Bakht Buland' in order to secure the Mughal emperor Aurangzeb's support in his quarrel against competing heirs.[40] He founded the city of Nagpur, which his successor made his capital. The Deogarh kingdom, at its widest extent, embraced the modern districts of Betul, Chhindwara and Nagpur, with parts of Seoni, Bhandara and Balaghat. In the south of the province, Chanda was the seat of another Gond dynasty, which first came into prominence in the sixteenth century. The three Gond principalities of Garha-Mandla, Deogarh and Chanda were nominally subject to the Mughal emperors. In addition to the acquisitions made in the north at the expense of Garha-Mandla, the Mughals, after the annexation of Berar, established governors at Paunar in Wardha and Kherla in Betul. Having thus hemmed in the Gond states, however, they made no effort to assert any effective sovereignty over them; the Gond rajas for their part were content with practical independence within their own dominions. Under their peaceful rule, their territories flourished, until the weakening of the Mughal Empire and the rise of the invasive policies of the Bundela and Maratha powers, which through their feudal levies of *Chauth* and *Sardeshmukhi* brought misfortune upon them.[41]

When Bakth Buland founded Nagpur city, it was a new beginning in the Gond kingdom; through the new city of Nagpur and evolving Gond states in the Vidarbha and Marathwada region, he could initiate the process of cultural schisms within Gond society and scaffolding with the neighbouring states of Mughals, Marathas as well as with the local cultural practices of Vidarbha and Marathwada; this consequentially led to the formation of 'multiple binaries' within the Gond identity as will be discussed below. It could be highlighted here that Nagpur was never the founding seat of power of the Gond dynasty. There is no historical record of Nagpur prior to the beginning of the eighteenth century, when it formed part of the Gond Kingdom of Deogarh, in Chhindwara district. Bakht Buland, the ruler of Deogarh, visited Delhi and afterwards was determined to encourage the development of his own kingdom. This Gond king is said to have embraced Islam to save his royal power and continued as a king under the pressure of the Mughals. During his rule, he invited Hindu and Muslim artisans and cultivators to settle in the plain country and help found the city of Nagpur. His successor, Chand Sultan, continued the development of his country and moved their capital to Nagpur.[42] The Gond continued to rule from their capital

Deogarh (Devgad), located in Chhindwara district till the late nineteenth century.[43] The Kingdom of Nagpur came under the rule of the Marathas of the Bhonsle dynasty in the mid-eighteenth century. The kingdom clashed with the expanding British in the early nineteenth century, becoming a princely state of the empire in 1818, and was annexed to British India in 1853.[44] The Chanda kingdom (Chandrapur in Maharashtra), a contemporary of the Kherla and Deogadh kingdoms, produced several remarkable rulers who developed excellent irrigation systems and the first well-defined revenue system among the Gond kingdoms.[45]

'Gond': the indigenous spaces under pre-colonial and colonial era

The process of land and power acquisition and deprivation within the cultural spaces of Gond has been documented in historical sources, where the people of the Gond region were identified as Andhra and Abhira; the ancient legacy continued to remain a major focus of a political balance of power in the medieval era when Mughals retained control and a relationship of alliance with the Gond (as discussed above).[46] The extraction of land as resource and political-cultural space continued to occur in the post-Mughal era as well. From the late eighteenth to twentieth centuries with the decline of the Mughals, land alienation expanded in the region of the Gonds with both the rise of Maratha confederacy and later Britishers in the Central Provinces and the Mughal *Mansabdar* as Nizams in the parts of Deccan *suba* and later as Hyderabad state.[47]

As with the coming of the Mughals, the influence of the direct infiltration of the non-Gondi population in the Gond areas began. The Mughals' use of gunpowder efficiently defeated the tribal Gonds in their own areas.[48] It was also to be noted here that Utnur, a region of Adilabad or Chanda state, passed to the Mughals as part of Berar and was the seat of a Sarkar, or a sub-district, during the Mughal period. It was then known as Nabinagar. It has been generally assumed that the non-Gondi or non-tribal population thereafter began to infiltrate into the tribal areas.[49] According to Prasad, the kind of land grant records available under the Mughals determined that pre-colonial, caste-based, natural resource management regimes were well defined and had authority over land ownership, which in terms of stability and coherence, were more powerful than that of the colonial regime over the indigenous Gond spaces.[50] When we compare the land acquisitions and methods of space utilization of the Gondwana by the British colonialists in comparison to the Mughals, Marathas and Post-Mughal Asafjahi Nizams of Hyderabad, we come across changes to governance which were more dominating and disallowed the notion of political space among the Gond community and its leadership. This could be understood through the history of the Gondwana, where the social and political marginalization of the Gonds was a result of the changing nature of zamindari power and the creation of private property rights in early colonial India.[51] In the name of the Mughal Emperor, the Peshwa (as his grantee) demanded 'restitution' of all lands Bhopal had 'usurped'. John Malcolm,[52] a nineteenth-century administrator and historian, described the outcome as follows; his words are further corroborated by the writings of Gordon and Dahiwale:

> Resistance appeared unavailing, and the minister, Byjeeram, negotiated a treaty by which the Bhopal government made a sacrifice of half its territories to save the remainder. By this engagement, it lost the whole of its possession in Malwa, except a few towns; what remained, which was chiefly in Gondwana, was confirmed to the family by treaty with the Peshwa. After this settlement Bhopal, as such, disappeared from the Peshwa's revenue records and new directly-administered *parganas* appeared – Ashta, Devipura, Duraha, Bhilsa, Shujalpur, and Sehore.[53]

The Bhonsle state of Nagpur was established in 1743, usurping the throne of the Gond Raja of Deogarh. But the Brahmins were in the administrative services of the Gonds and the Bhonsles. David Baker states that the Bhonsles laid the foundations of Brahmin dominance by establishing them on land and appointing them in their administrative services. In Yavatmal district, for instance, of the 1,397 *watandars*, there were 301 Brahmin *watandars*[54] and 830 *maratha-kunbi watandars*.[55] Moreover, commerce and financing were under the control of the immigrant *marwari-gujaratis* of the north.

As stated in the land records of certain villages in the Central Provinces that were in erstwhile Gondwana region, they had been founded by or greatly improved by the ancestors of the old *patels*,[56] which came in the territories in the late sixteenth and seventeenth centuries. But these administrators were ousted during the period of Maratha rule from 1830 to 1853 to make way for officials or other influential land holding communities and personnel. In these villages, the *Patels* received the proprietary right if they continued to cultivate in the village. Where the *malguzars* (Revenue Collector of a subdivision of '*Mahal*') were absentee landlords (which was common), the proprietorship was conferred on some of the leading resident peasants if they were willing to take it (and along with it the responsibility to pay the land revenue); otherwise, the proprietary right was conferred on the existing lessees, frequently Brahmins.[57] According to the statistical records presented in the study of land records and settlement reports by R.H. Craddock[58] and further detailed in the study by Harnetty[59]:

> Of the 1,281 villages in this district, proprietary right was vested in the existing *malguzars* in 982 villages (77 per cent). As a result, Brahmins became the landlords in one-third of all the villages of Chanda. In Bhandara, the Settlement Officer came down heavily on the side of

> those who were presently holding village leases which, because of the proximity of the district to the former Bhonsla capital of Nagpur, often meant Maratha Brahmins. Out of a total of 1,448 villages in Bhandara, 314 were thus conferred on Brahmins.[60]

Another prominent group among the new landlords were tribals, particularly Gonds, who predominated in hilly and jungle areas and were strongly represented in Hoshangabad, Mandla, Chhindwara, Nimar and Chanda. It was on the credulity of Gond people that persons from the money-lending castes, such as the Marwari Seth Gokuldas, were to build their fortunes. Many *malguzars* came from the cultivating castes: Lodhis and Kurmis were conspicuous in the northern wheat districts; Kunbis and Marathas in southern districts, especially Wardha, Nagpur and Chanda.[61]

The Settlement Reports of the other districts reveal a similar story that all over the Central Provinces in the late nineteenth century, banking and trading castes, Marwaris, Banias and Kalars, were gaining at the expense of the aboriginal landlords – Gonds, Raj Gonds and Korkus – while the agricultural or cultivating castes remained about where they were. This is brought out most strongly by one of the ablest Settlement Officers of his generation, R.H. Craddock, who was the Settlement Officer of Nagpur. In his report of 1899, he attacked the widespread assumption that the original proprietary body were all agriculturalists by caste and profession and argued that every transfer represented a loss by agriculturists and a gain by non-resident, grasping and unsympathetic money-lenders.[62]

The status and economic prosperity of the tribal community began to decline with the fall of the Raj-Gond states from the sixteenth century under the Mughals. All non-tribal rulers in central India furthered this decline.[63] When the British came to power, they tended to emphasize the homogeneity of the indigenous forest dwellers among the Gond and in Gondwana. As discussed above, in the indigenous spaces of Gond there were incursion and infiltration of the non-tribal population, which further evolved the cultural binaries in the context of occupancy rights and cultural praxis.[64] Even then the British administration of the Central Provinces identified the Gonds as homogeneous autochthons and forced them out of the forests and into more settled agriculture in an effort to 'improve' them and create a market economy.[65]

The indigenous communities of India are commonly known as Scheduled Tribes;[66] since colonial times, there were several administrative changes conferred upon their spaces. These administrative changes led to redefining their forest-community relationships, land rights and ideas of their cultural spaces. An administrative approach towards an exclusive cultural space often differed within the native *vs.* colonialist binary. A valuable function of the metaphor of space is that it solidifies cultural memories of place in representational form and in material textures, which together form what we might call a 'culture of landscape'[67] or a politico-cultural identity which is closely associated with their space.[68] The experience, memory or culture of a place can be re-presented through a culture of space. Memory is central to an understanding of the value of a space. Memory, along with the shifting contexts and sites of home, is a significant factor in shaping the nature of geographies of belonging, being and desire.[69]

During the nineteenth and early twentieth centuries, the colonial state radically transformed various land and labour relationships throughout the subcontinent. These changes in the state-indigenous land relationships were evident in the Moplah, Santhal, Bhil and Gond regions in specific. The state responded with atrocious force, and as a result, we come across in history the rebellions by the space owners in the indigenous territories when the land transition policies were adopted by the colonialists; these rebellions by the indigenous space owners resulted in bloody and brutal confrontations from both sides.[70] In contrast, the native states or princely states more or less adopted the political-cultural spaces of indigenous or indigenized communities; although the cultural destruction and loss is evident in these regions, the nature of its displacement is different from those and the colonial territories.[71]

Nizam and political space of Gond: 1720–1956

When Nizams as the commanders in chief of the Mughals gained control over territories adjoining Gondwana in the Mughal and post-Mughal era, the Gond were the ruling indigenous population of Central India, and their lands included vast tracts from the Deccan plateau to the undulating hill ranges of Vindhanyanchal and Satpuda; their influence was also not unknown in Bundelkhand, Baghelkhand and Rajputana. The Gonds were the royal protégés of the Mughals and had a position of aura and prestige among the rulers both of Delhi and the Deccan. With their ever-encompassing valour and hegemony over land territory, the Gonds maintained their culture, power and sovereignty.[72] The Gond territories of erstwhile Hyderabad state (1720–1956) were in those times spread across the British Colonial territory of Central Provinces (as discussed above). Before the States Reorganization in 1956, the Gond territories of Hyderabad state of Nizam were spread over parts of Adilabad district which included certain territories of the state of Maharashtra, including Yavatmal district, Chandrapur district, Gadhchiroli district and subdivisions (taluka places) of Mahur, Kinwat, Himayatnagar of the Nanded district and Hingoli and Kalamnuri subdivisions (taluka places) of Hingoli district.[73] Several regions of present Nanded district were previously part of Adilabad and Asifabad districts (presently known as Kumarram Bheem district) of present Telangana state. In 1956, Nanded district consisted of six talukas of Nanded, Kandhar, Hadgaon, Deglur, Biloli and Mudhol together with the two *mahals*[74] (district subdivision) of Mukhed and Bhokar. After the reorganization, the Bichukonda and Jukkal circles of the Deglur taluka and the Mudhol taluka (except the Dharmabad circle) were transferred from the district of Nanded to the district of

Nizamabad, and the Kinwat and Rajura talukas and the Islampur circle of the Boath taluka from the Adilabad district were added to it. The Islampur circle was attached to the Kinwat taluka and the Dharmabad circle to Biloli. Since the Rajura (present Chandrapur) taluka was far removed from the district, it was subsequently transferred to Chanda district to which it remained contiguous.[75] The reorganization of the administration and cultural space of Gond territories began in the beginning of the twentieth century when the Hyderabad state underwent land reforms because the territories of Berar were taken over by the Britishers.[76] With the loss of territories and changed administrative systems in the neighbouring territories of Gond in the areas governed by the Britishers, it became necessary for the Nizam to reframe policies for the Gonds. As stated above, in the British-dominated territories of the Gond, the purpose was to develop the concept of land as private ownership of Gond, hence, to appropriate the capitalist benefits from the land as a resource. Unlike the British territories in Central Provinces, in the Hyderabad state, land was a domain of autonomy for the Gond communities who were governing it (Figure 3.2).[77]

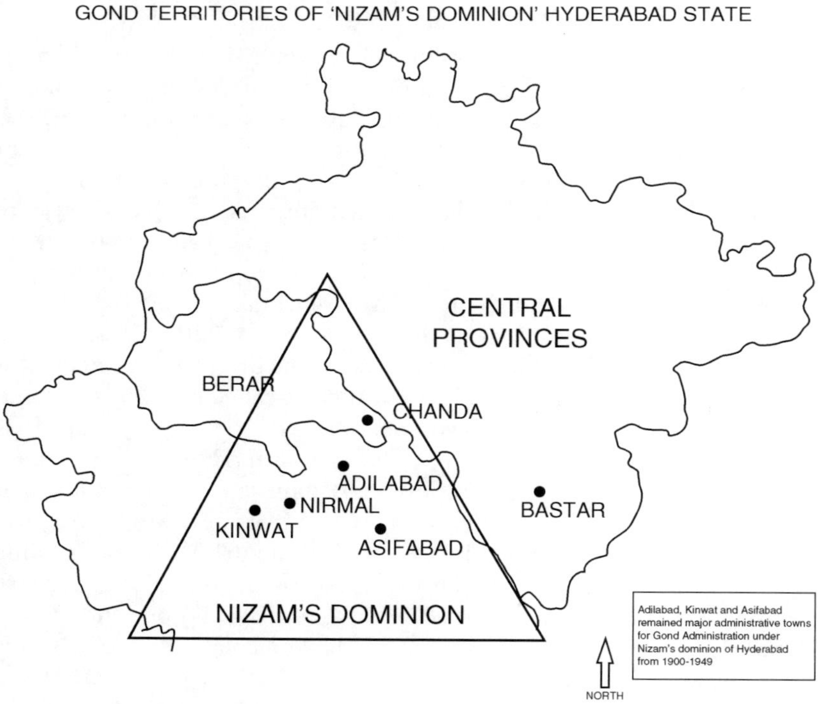

Figure 3.2 Gond territories of Hyderabad state.
Source: Bina Sengar.

The territories held under the Marathas were shared by Nizam's Hyderabad state and Britishers after the fall of the Marathas in 1818, and the British took charge of Nagpur state as protectorate in the 1860s. The regions of Rajura, Kinwat, Mahur and Adilabad started experiencing incursions from the British territories in Hyderabad state.[78] However, the kind of administration which was arranged by the Marathas continued to exercise its powers till the last decades of the nineteenth century. *Mokashi* (a land grant under Maratha land revenue system) rights were merely jurisdictional rights conferred to Gond chiefs, whereas rights of revenue collection remained under Patels and Deshmukh *watandars*.[79] The kind of arrangement developed by the Marathas made *watandars* the superiors of hundreds of villages inhabited by Gonds, and consequently, many of the Gonds were left in penury. In the changed circumstances, the Nizams of Hyderabad state tried to curtail the powers of these *watandari* without leading them into conflicts with the state.[80]

Administrative changes: Land reform of the Gond-dominated areas of Hyderabad state began when the Nizam of Hyderabad explored the forest and mining potential of the region. In these parts, raw materials were abundantly available. Hence, the Adilabad-Chanda-Kinwat Gond areas underwent a qualitative structural change in 1874 with the construction of a railway line from Hyderabad to Paloncha for mining operations.[81] The Nizam now provided the land free of cost to a railway private company to build the railway line, which opened in 1874 in Hyderabad state,[82] and by late 1909, it entered the areas of Adilabad-Kinwat as Indian Peninsular Railways connecting regions across Godavari and its tributaries.[83] In due course, the Nizam's state offered large tracts of tribal areas to others on lease in the second half of the nineteenth century.[84] By the beginning of the twentieth century, the Nizam reorganized the Gond and the administrative systems of other tribal regions. In Hyderabad state, the district of Adilabad according to the Census of 1901 had a population of 477,848. Adilabad district was comprised of eight *talukas*: (i) Adilabad (or Edlabad), (ii) Sirpur, (iii) Rajura, (iv) Nirmal, (v) Kinwat, (vi) Chinnur, (vii) Lakhsetipet and (viii) Jangaon. The towns were Adilabad, the district head-quarters, Nirmal and Chinnur. About 80% of the population was constituted by Hindus; Adilabad had a Hindu temple, where an annual fair was held.[85] It also had a busy grain market. More than 10% of the population was Gonds, and the remaining population constituted by non-Gondi communities. The revenue demand was about 6.5 lakhs. The district was divided into three subdivisions for administrative purposes: One consisting of the Adilabad (or Edlabad), Sirpur and Rajara/Rajura *talukas*, placed under a second *taluqdar*,[86] while the second comprising Lakhsetipet, Chinnur and Jangaon and the third consisting of Nirmal and Kinwat, were each under a third *taluqdar*.

The first *taluqdar* was the Chief Magistrate as well as the Civil Judge of the district, having a judicial assistant, called the *adalat-madadgar*, who was also a Joint Magistrate, who exercised powers during the absence of the first *taluqdar* from head-quarters. The second and third *taluqdars* and the *tahsildars* exercised second- and third-class magisterial powers. The second and third *taluqdars* had no civil jurisdiction, but the *tahsildars* presided over the *tehsil* civil courts. Local boards were established in the district. Adilabad taluk (or Edlabad) in Adilabad district, Hyderabad state, had an area of 2,220 square miles. The population in 1900, including *jagirs*, was 112,314 compared with 99,332 in 1891.[87]

In 1905, part of the *taluqa* was transferred to the new taluk of Kinwat. Adilabad was very sparsely populated, containing extensive uncultivated wastes. Besides the offices of the first *taluqdar*, the police superintendent, the customs inspector, the forest *daroga* (police inspector), a dispensary, a post office and a school were situated there.[88] By these new arrangements, the Nizam attempted to gain more land revenue and began leasing out some areas to British colonial trade interests – especially in the forest regions of erstwhile Adilabad district, which had regions of present Maharashtra and Telangana in it. The opening up of the Chandrapur-Balharshah railway line in 1929 helped to connect the Adilabad forest areas with the outside world.[89] As a result of continuous troubles and exploitation caused by the outsider absentee landlords, conflicts began in the Gond area by the late nineteenth century. In 1862, a government treasury was robbed in Chanda, which was followed by what is known as the Rompa Rebellion from 1879 to 1880. Moreover, in the districts of Adilabad, Asifabad and Kinwat, the indigenous Gond reached a desperate state of mind.[90] The Nizam state had started grazing taxes on the cattle of the Gonds.[91] In 1940s, unrest became evident in the tribal regions of Adilabad, Asifabad and Kinwat, against which the well-known Kumaram Bhimu or Kumra Bhimu initiated one such movement against Hyderabad state in 1940s from Asifabad region.[92] To understand and resolve the tribal and state conflicts, the Nizam appointed Christoph von Fürer-Haimendorf as the Advisor for Tribes and Backward Classes to the Nizam's government. Haimendorf spent several years among the Raj Gonds in this district from 1941 onwards. The anthropologist came to India in 1936 on a fellowship to carry out his studies on aboriginal tribes. It was his work among the primitive Raj Gonds in Adilabad district that stood out. Haimendorf was assisted in his studies by his wife Elizabeth and came to the area to study the problems besetting the tribes in the northern region of Hyderabad state following the famous uprising led by legendary Gond martyr Komram Bheem at Jodeghat. The couple camped at Marlavai village in a hut built by the local chieftain Lachu Patel.[93] He also accepted a teaching appointment at Osmania University which he later relinquished, after ten years in India, to accept a lectureship at the School for Oriental and African Studies in 1949.[94] In the course of Haimendorf's work, he set up various educational and other schemes for tribal peoples, all with the aim of preserving and safeguarding indigenous cultures and languages. Later, it was decided to start cooperative activities in the tribal area. In 1943, Marlavai near Utnoor's Jainoor-mandal became the centre of educational and other cultural activities among the tribal population of Gonds. A teacher training centre was started, which provided Gond teachers for the Gond village school and other subordinate posts near the villages. Haimendorf also started tribal cooperatives, and apparently by the end of 1945, thirty cooperative activities were started in Marlavai.[95] Based on their success, the programme was extended and a Rural Bank at Mankapur in the northern part of Utnoor was started in 1946.[96] Practices of agricultural improvement were also started in Marlwai, which encouraged education and updated skills of economic and educational empowerment.[97] In 1953, Haimendorf returned to work among the Gonds of Andhra Pradesh, and further elaborated on his expertise on tribal affairs in Hyderabad.[98] During his short stay of another two years, he expanded his concept of primary teaching of Gond students in Gondi language. Marlavai village of Jainoor subdivision, thus, became a centre for tribal students' learning.[99]

By 1956, Kinwat (which was now part of Nanded district)[100] became part of Marathwada division and got separated from Adilabad-Andhra Pradesh to become part of the state of Maharashtra by 1960.[101] With the beginning of a new era, in the two different parts of the same cultural space Adilabad-Kinwat-Chanda (Chandrapur) divisions developed three separate cultural spaces of Marathi-Gondi of Marathwada, Marathi-Gondi of Vidarbha and Telugu-Gondi of Telangana. The policies adopted in later phases were unlike the earlier policy of non-interference; the traditions inculcated in the later phase of Hyderabad state were to empower tribals through education, cooperatives and by being part of the administration. This was all part of a policy to assimilate Gonds in mainstream society. After the territories of Chandrapur and Kinwat were incorporated into Maharashtra as part of the national policies for tribals, the assimilative policies[102] continued and the autonomy of the tribal states was minimized by their wider inclusion in the nation-state system. Many Gond men and women received education in the universities of Hyderabad, Aurangabad and Nagpur as per their locations in the Vidarbha, Marathwada and Telangana regions of Andhra Pradesh (now Telangana state) after 1956 and 1960, which contributed to the further assimilation of their spaces with the spaces of the Maharashtra and erstwhile Andhra Pradesh provinces of the Indian Union.

When we evaluate the changes in the Gond spaces which were promulgated by the Hyderabad state from the end of the nineteenth to the mid-twentieth centuries, then we can notice several fractions within the Gond's cultural sovereignty. The multiple binaries which were created in their spaces were based on administrative, linguistic and socio-economic structures. The scaffolding within the Gond spaces of political and cultural sovereign was not the outcome of the colonial phenomena; it was a process which evolved from the seventeenth century and continued to evolve and solidify as multiple schisms formulated because of administrative structures and the scaffolding cultural concepts of states and national phenomena. That multiple binaries within the Gond states of Gondwana would continue to form became apparent during the colonial era when the colonial structures were further created as part of a capitalist regimen of railways and market networks in the Gond regions of Hyderabad state and the Berar region of the Central Provinces. The further emergence of the linguistic states of Andhra Pradesh and Maharashtra brought a linguistic binary within the so-called homogenized notion of Gondi language when the Gondi spaces of Maharashtra and Telangana (erstwhile Andhra Pradesh) evolved the Gondi-Telugu and Gondi-Marathi dialects. The creation of the new states of Maharashtra and Andhra Pradesh by the 1960s contributed to the creation of multiple spaces within the larger Gond space of Gondwana.

Notes

1 *Indigenous People Indigenous Voices*, www.un.org/esa/socdev/unpfii/documents/6_session_factsheet1.pdf (last accessed on 7 February 2018, 10:00 p.m.).
2 'United Nations Declaration on the Rights of Indigenous People', *Resolution Adopted by the General Assembly, 61/295, 2007.* www.un.org/esa/socdev/unpfii/documents/DRIPS_en.pdf (accessed on 26 December 2017).
3 Asaf Hussain, 'Ethnicity, National Identity and Praetorianism: The Case of Pakistan', *Asian Survey*, 1976, 16 (10), pp. 918–930. Also see: Shaheen Sardar Ali and Javaid Rehman, *Indigenous Peoples and Ethnic Minorities of Pakistan: Constitutional and Legal Perspectives*, London: Routledge, 2013. Shaheen Sardar Ali and Anne Griffiths, *From Transnational Relations to Transnational Laws: Northern European Laws at the Crossroads*, London: Routledge, 2016.
4 In India, the predominant term used for indigenous communities is 'Scheduled Tribe' or Tribal; there are also corroborative terms used such as *adivasi* (indigenous) *vanvasi* (forest dwellers), etc. *as* there are academic and constitutional debates in India as who are the indigenous. The present chapter will not delve into the debate, although in some of its discussions this problematic will appear.
5 Karina V. Korostelina, *Constructing the Narratives of Identity and Power: Self-Imagination in a Young Ukrainian Nation*, New York: Lexington Books, 2013, p. 23.
6 Bina Sengar, 'Defining and Redefining Political Status of Gond Tribe of Maharashtra', *Marathwada Itihaas Parishad*, Hingoli, 25–26 November 2016 (working research paper).
7 Ibid., p. 1.
8 M. Fortes and E. E. Evans-Pritchard, *African Political Systems*, London: Routledge Revival, 2015.
9 Ibid.
10 Max Gluckman, *Politics, Law and Ritual in Tribal Society*, London: Aldine Transactions, 2012.
11 Marshall Sahlins, 'On the Anthropology of Modernity or, Some Triumphs of Culture over Despondency Theory', In Antony Hooper (ed.), *Culture and Sustainable Development in the Pacific* (Open Access Book, pp. 44–61), Canberra: ANU Press, 2005.

12 Linnda R. Caporael, James R. Griesemer, and William C. Wimsatt, *Developing Scaffolds in Evolution, Culture, and Cognition*, Cambridge: MIT Press, 2013, p. 73.
13 Hank Johnston, *Culture, Social Movements, and Protest*, Burlington: Ashgate Publishing Ltd., 2009, p. 140.
14 Ibid., p. 173.
15 Jon M. van Dyke, Sherry P. Broder, Seokwoo Lee, and Jin-Hyun Paik, *Governing Ocean Resources: New Challenges and Emerging Regimes: A Tribute to Judge Choon-Ho Park*, Leiden: Martinus Nijhoff Publishers, 2013, p. 428.
16 Margery Fee, *Literary Land Claims: The 'Indian Land Question' from Pontiac's War to Attawapiskat*, Waterloo: Wilfrid Laurier University Press, 2015.
17 Ben Chigara, *Re-conceiving Property Rights in the New Millennium: Towards a New Sustainable Land Relations Policy*, Routledge, 2013, pp. 10–11.
18 Joya Chatterjee and David Washbrook, *Routledge India Handbook of the South Asian Diaspora*, New Delhi: Routledge, 2014.
19 Fortes and Evans-Pritchard, *African Political Systems*. Also see: John Sorenson, 'History and Identity in the Horn of Africa', *Dialectical Anthropology*, 1992, 17 (3), pp. 227–252.
20 Alan Lomax, Conrad M. Arensberg, Riva Berleant-Schiller, Gertrude E. Dole, Arthur E. Hippler, Knud-Erik Jensen, Abraham Makofsky, Andrew Sherratt, John L. Sorenson, and B. Turyahikayo-Rugyema, 'A Worldwide Evolutionary Classification of Cultures by Subsistence Systems', Discussion, *Current Anthropology*, 1977, 18 (4), pp. 659–708.
21 Sahlins, Marshall, *Op. cit*, p. 48.
22 Bhangya Bhukya, *The Roots of the Periphery: A History of the Gonds of Deccan India*, New Delhi: Oxford University Press, 2017.
23 Sengar Bina, *Colonial Landscape in a Princely State: British Land Policies in Rural Spaces of Ajanta*, Conference Souvenir Old and New Worlds: The Global Challenges of Rural History, International Conference, Lisbon 27–30 January 2016: https://lisbon2016rh.files.wordpress.com/2015/12/onw-0118.pdf (last accessed on 7 February, 2018, 10:00 p.m.). Also see: Y. Whelan, 'The Construction and Destruction of a Colonial Landscape: Monuments to British Monarchs in Dublin before and after independence', *Journal of Historical Geography*, 2002, 28 (4), pp. 508–533.
24 CVF Haimendorf, 'The Descent Group System of the Raj Gonds', *Bulletin of the School of Oriental and African Studies*, 1956, 18 (3), pp. 499–511.
25 http://asifabad.telangana.gov.in/district-profile/ (last accessed on 7 February, 2018, 10:00 p.m.).
26 Ibid.
27 Ibid.
28 www.downtoearth.org.in/news/gondi-language-victim-of-government-neglect-46707.
29 Bhangya Bhukya, 'Enclosing Land, Enclosing *Adivasis*: Colonial Agriculture and *Adivasis* in Central India, 1853–1948', *Indian Historical Review*, 2013, 40 (1), pp. 93–116.
30 Ibid.
31 U. P. Shah, 'The Sālaka Shah, e and Land ', *Journal of the American Oriental Society*, January–March 1976, 96 (1), pp. 109–113.
32 Ron Redfern, *Origins: The Evolution of Continents, Oceans, and Life*, Norman: University of Oklahoma Press, 2001, p. 20.
33 CVF Haimendorf, *The Raj Gonds of Adilabad*, MacMillan and Co., 1948, quoted by R. E. Enthoven', *Journal of the Royal Asiatic Society*, 1950, 82 (3–4), p. 199.

34 Setu Madhavrao Pagdi, *Op.cit.*, p. 3. [According to Setu Madhavrao Pagdi, 'There Is a Difference of Versions Whether the Gonds Rescued Were Four in Number of Twenty Two'.]
35 Ibid., p. 10.
36 Ibid., p. 13.
37 Mehta, Behram H., *Gonds of the Central Indian Highlands*, Vol-I, New Delhi: Concept Publishing, 1984, pp. 260–306.
38 Ibid., pp. 260–306.
39 Bhukya, 'Enclosing Land, Enclosing *Adivasis*.
40 Mehta, *Op. cit.*, pp. 260–306.
41 Ibid., p. 284.
42 Gundeboina Naresh Mudiraja, *Great History of Mudiraja Caste*. http://mudiraja.weebly.com/gond-kingdoms-of-central-india.html (last accessed on 7 February, 2018, 10:00 p.m.).
43 Shashishekhar Gopal Deogaonkar, *The Gonds of Vidarbha*, Delhi: Concept Publishing Company, 2007, pp. 35–36.
44 Mehta, *Loc. cit*, pp. 279–282.
45 Deogaonkar, *The Gonds of Vidarbha*, pp. 38–40.
46 Mehta, *Op. cit.*, pp. 236–237.
47 Setu Madhavrao Pagdi, *Op. cit.*, pp. 17–20.
48 J. J. L. Gommans, *Mughal Warfare: Indian Frontiers and Highroads to Empire 1500–1700*, London: Routledge, 2003.
49 Setu Madhavrao Pagdi, *Op. cit.*, pp. 20–21.
50 Prasad, Archana, 'Military Conflict and Forests in Central Provinces, India: Gonds and the Gondwana Region in Pre-colonial History', *Environment and History*, 1999, 5 (3), pp. 361–375.
51 Ibid.
52 John Malcolm, *A Memoir of Central India and Adjoining Provinces with History and Copious Illustrations of Past and Present of That Country-Vol. 1*, London: Kingbury, Parbury and Allen, 1823, p. 360.
53 Stewart N. Gordon, 'The Slow Conquest: Administrative Integration of Malwa into the Maratha Empire, 1720–1760', *Modern Asian Studies*, 1977, 11 (1), pp. 1–40.
54 Land grant given to the army personal under Maratha land revenue system.
55 S. M. Dahiwale, 'Consolidation of Maratha Dominance in Maharashtra', *Economic and Political Weekly*, February 11, 1995, 30 (6), pp. 336–342.
56 A village headman who was responsible for the village and land management and revenue collection responsibility in the village.
57 Peter Harnetty, 'The Landlords and the Raj: The Malguzars of the Central Provinces, 1861–1921', *Studies in History*, 1987, 3 (2), p. 189.
58 R. H. Craddock, 'Notes on the Status of Zamindars of the Central Provinces, 1889', In J. F. Dyer (ed.), *Introduction to Revenue and Settlement System in Central Provinces*, Nagpur: Govt. Press, 1956.
59 Harnetty, 'The Landlords and the Raj', p. 189.
60 Ibid., p. 187.
61 Ibid., p. 187.
62 Ibid., p. 199.
63 David Baker, 'State Policy, the Market Economy, and Tribal Decline: The Central Provinces, 1861–1920', *IESHR*, 1991, 28 (4), pp. 341–370, K. S. Singh, 'Ecology, Identity and Culture: The Human Landscape', *India International Centre Quarterly*, 2000 and 2001, 27/28 (4/1), pp. 201–214.
64 Ezra Rashkow, 'Making Subaltern *shikaris*: Histories of the Hunted in Colonial Central India', *South Asian History and Culture*, 2014, 5 (3), pp. 292–296.

65 David Baker, *Op. cit.*, pp. 371–372.
66 Govind Sadashiv Ghurye, *The Scheduled Tribes of India*, Delhi: Transaction Publishers, 1980, p. 1.
67 Bina Sengar, 'Colonial Landscape in a Princely State: British Land Policies in Rural Spaces of Ajanta', https://lisbon2016rh.files.wordpress.com/2015/12/onw-0118.pdf (last accessed on 7 February, 2018, 10:30 p.m.). Also see: Divya P Tolia-Kelly, 'Mobility/Stability: British Asian Cultures of `Landscape and Englishness', *Environment and Planning*, 2006, 38, pp. 341–358.
68 Bina Sengar, *Op. cit.*, pp. 2–3.
69 Gerald Roche, '"Flows and Frontiers": Landscape and Cultural Dynamics on the Northeast Tibetan Plateau', *The Asia Pacific Journal of Anthropology*, 2014, 15 (1), pp. 1–25.
70 Manu Bhagavan, 'Princely States and the Hindu Imaginary: Exploring the Cartography of Hindu Nationalism in Colonial India', *The Journal of Asian Studies*, 2008, 67 (3), pp. 881–915.
71 Setu Madhav Pagdi, *Among the Gonds of Adilabad*, Bombay: Popular Book Depot, II Edition, 1952, p. 1.
72 Mehta, *Op. cit.*, pp. 56–59.
73 Deogaonkar, *The Gonds of Vidarbha*, pp. 14–17.
74 *Mahal*: Mughal terminology of administrative sub-division similar to '*rani*' means forest, '*abaadi*' is population and '*mahal*' is district sub-division in Urdu language.
75 District Gazetteer-Nanded.
76 Ibid.
77 Interview of Madhavrao Maraskolla was taken at village Jawarla, taluka: Kinwat, district: Nanded, Maharashtra. 17 February 2017.
78 Bhangya Bhukya, *Op.cit.*, p. 52.
79 Setu Madhavrao Pagdi, *Op. cit.*, pp. 32–35.
80 Ibid., pp. 35–36.
81 B. Ramdas, 'A Separate Telangana: Promises and Prospects for Tribal Peoples', *Economic and Political Weekly*, 2013, XLVIII (29), pp. 118–122.
82 Latika Chaudhary and Jared Rubin, 'Religious Identity and the Provision of Public Goods: Evidence from the Indian Princely States' (Working paper, 2015). Also see: M. A. Nayeem, *The Splendour of Hyderabad: The Last Phase of an Oriental Culture, 1591–1948 A.D*, Bombay: Jaico Pub. House, 1987.
83 Ramdas, *Op. cit.*, pp. 118–122.
84 Ibid.
85 Sanjay B. Salunke, 'Case Study of Keslapur Nagoba Jatra or Fair: A Socio-Anthropological approach', *International Journal of Advanced Research*, 2014, 2 (4), pp. 1046–1051.
86 *Taluqa* implies for administrative sub-division and *Taluqdar* implies for administrative sub-divisional officer.
87 Wilson William Hunter, *Imperial Gazetteer of India*, Vol. V (5), London: Claredon Press, 1909, pp. 23–24.
88 Ibid., p. 24.
89 Ramdas, *Op. cit.*, p. 119.
90 Mehta, *Op. cit.*, p. 292, Also see: Subhas Ranjan Chakraborty, 'Colonialism, Resource Crisis and (Forced) Migration', http://mcrg.ac.in/PP42.pdf (last accessed on 7 February 2018, 10:30 p.m.).
91 Interview of Madhavrao Maraskolla of village Jawarla, Tal Kinwat on 17 February 2017 and also details in Christoph von Fürer-Haimendorf, *Tribal Hyderabad*, Hyderabad: The Revenue department, Govt. of HH The Nizam, 1945, p. 107.

92 Ibid., pp. 122–123 and also see Bhangya Bhukya, *Op. cit.*, pp. 132–137.
93 S. Harpal Singh, Haimendorf's Ashes for Marlavai Village, *The Hindu*, Adilabad Edition, 23 February 2012.
94 Alan Macfarlane and Mark Turin, 'Professor Christoph von Fürer-Haimendorf 1909–1995', Bulletin of the School of Oriental and African Studies, University of London, vol. LIX, pt.3, (1996) 2000, www.alanmacfarlane.com/TEXTS/cfhsoasobit.pdf (last accessed on 7 February 2018, 10:30 p.m.).
95 Setu Madhavrao Pagdi, *Op. cit.*, pp. 120–122.
96 Ibid., p. 122.
97 Alan Macfarlane and Mark Turin, *Op. cit.*, 'In each area he (C.V. Heimendorf) studied the languages and culture of between three and six societies. He published ten ethnographic monographs based on his field-work, including *The Chenchus* (1943), *The Reddis of the Bison Hills* (1945), *The Raj Gonds of Adilibad* (1948)'. Later as his last wish to be buried in Marlavai in 2012, his ashes were brought to the region and tribals of the village have constructed a memorial in his honour. www.alanmacfarlane.com/TEXTS/cfhsoasobit.pdf (last accessed on 7 February 2018, 10:30 p.m.).
98 Ibid.
99 S. Harpal Singh, *Op. cit.* www.thehindu.com/todays-paper/tp-national/haimendorfs-ashes-for-marlavai-village/article2921816.ece (last accessed on 7 February 2018, 10:30 p.m.).
100 P. V. Kate, *Marathwada under the Nizams, 1724–1948*, New Delhi: Mittal Publications, 1987, p. 119.
101 Asha Sarangi, 'Ambedkar and the Linguistic States: A Case for Maharashtra', *Economic and Political Weekly*, 14–20 January 2006, 41 (2), pp. 151–157.
102 Bina Sengar, 'Gandhian Approach to Tribals', *Proceedings of Indian History Congress*, 62nd Session, Kolkata, 2001, pp. 327–336.

References

Anderson, Benedict. *Imagined Communities: Reflections on the Origin and Spread of Nationalism*. London: Verso, 2006.

Arondekar, Anjali. *For the Record: On Sexuality and the Colonial Archive in India*. Durham: Duke University Press, 2009.

Baker, David. 'State Policy, the Market Economy, and Tribal Decline: The Central Provinces, 1861–1920'. *IESHR*, 1991, 28 (4): 341–370.

Bhagavan, Manu. 'Princely States and the Hindu Imaginary: Exploring the Cartography of Hindu Nationalism in Colonial India'. *The Journal of Asian Studies*, August 2008, 67 (3): 881–915.

Bhattacharyya, Pranab Kumar. *Historical Geography of Madhya Pradesh from Early Records*. Delhi: Motilal Banarsidass Publisher, 1977.

Bhukya, Bhangya. 'Enclosing Land, Enclosing *Adivasis*: Colonial Agriculture and *Adivasis* in Central India, 1853–1948'. *Indian Historical Review*, 2013, 40 (1): 93–116.

Bhukya, Bhangya. *The Roots of the Periphery: A History of the Gonds of Deccan India*. New Delhi: Oxford University Press2017.

Caporael, Linnda R., James R. Griesemer, and William C. Wimsatt. *Developing Scaffolds in Evolution, Culture, and Cognition*. Cambridge: MIT Press, 2013.

Chakraborty, Subhas Ranjan. 'Colonialism, Resource Crisis and (Forced) Migration', http://mcrg.ac.in/PP42.pdf (last accessed on 7 February, 2018, 10:30 p.m.)

Chatterjee, Joya and David Washbrook. *Routledge India Handbook of the South Asian Diaspora*. New Delhi: Routledge, 2014.
Chaudhary, Latika and Jared Rubin. 'Religious Identity and the Provision of Public Goods: Evidence from the Indian Princely States' (Working paper, 2015).
Chigara, Ben. *Re-conceiving Property Rights in the New Millennium: Towards a New Sustainable Land Relations Policy*. London: Routledge, 2013.
Craddock, Reginald H. 'Notes on the status of Zamindars of the Central Provinces, 1889'. In J. F. Dyer (ed.), *Introduction to Revenue and Settlement System in Central Provinces*. J. F. Dyer, Ed. Nagpur: Govt. Press, 1956, p. 61.
Dahiwale, S. M. 'Consolidation of Maratha Dominance in Maharashtra'. *Economic and Political Weekly*, 11 February 1995, 30(6): 336–342.
Deogaonkar, Shashishekhar Gopal. *The Gonds of Vidarbha*. Delhi: Concept Publishing Company, 2007.
Enthoven, R.E. '[Review of] The Raj Gondo [sic] of Adilabad." *Journal of the Royal Asiatic Society*, July 150, 82 (3–4): 100.
Fee, Margery. *Literary Land Claims: The 'Indian Land Question' from Pontiac's War to Attawapiskat, Waterloo*. Waterloo: Wilfrid Laurier University Press, 2015.
Fortes, Meyer and Edward Evan Evans-Pritchard. *African Political Systems*. London: Routledge Revival, 2015.
Fürer-Haimendorf, Christoph von. *Tribal Hyderabad*. Hyderabad: The Revenue Department, Govt. of HH The Nizam, 1945.
Fürer-Haimendorf, Christoph von. *The Raj Gonds of Adilabad*, MacMillan and Co., 1948.
Fürer-Haimendorf, Christoph von. 'The Descent Group System of the Raj Gonds'. *Bulletin of the School of Oriental and African Studies*, 1956, 18 (3): 499–511.
Ghurye, Govind Sadashiv. *The Scheduled Tribes of India*. Delhi: Transaction Publishers, 1980.
Gluckman, Max. *Politics, Law and Ritual in Tribal Society*. London: Aldine Transactions, 2012.
Gommans, Jos J. L. *Mughal Warfare: Indian Frontiers and Highroads to Empire 1500–1700*. London: Routledge, 2003.
Gordon, Stewart N. 'The Slow Conquest: Administrative Integration of Malwa into the Maratha Empire, 1720–1760'. *Modern Asian Studies*, 1977, 11 (1): 1–40.
Harnetty, Peter. 'The Landlords and the Raj: The Malguzars of the Central Provinces, 1861–1921'. *Studies in History*, 1987, 3 (2): 187–209.
Hussain, Asaf. 'Ethnicity, National Identity and Praetorianism: The Case of Pakistan'. *Asian Survey*, 1976, 16 (10): 918–930.
Hunter, William Wilson. *Imperial Gazetteer of India Vol. V: 'Abazai to Arcot'*. Oxford: Claredon Press, 1908.
Johnston, Hank. *Culture, Social Movements, and Protest*. Burlington: Ashgate Publishing Ltd., 2009.
Kate, P. V. *Marathwada under the Nizams, 1724–1948*. New Delhi: Mittal Publications, 1987.
Koreti, Shamrao. 'Socio-Cultural History of the Gond Tribes of Middle India'. *International Journal of Social Science and Humanity*, 2016, 6 (4): 288.

Korostelina, Karina V. *Constructing the Narratives of Identity and Power: Self-Imagination in a Young Ukrainian Nation*. New York: Lexington Books, 2013.

Lobo, Brian. *A Status of Adivasis/Indigenous Peoples Land Series – 3: MAHARASHTRA*. Delhi: Aakar Books, 2011.

Lomax, Alan, Conrad M. Arensberg, Riva Berleant-Schiller, Gertrude E. Dole, Arthur E. Hippler, Knud-Erik Jensen, Abraham Makofsky, Andrew Sherratt, John L. Sorenson, and B. Turyahikayo-Rugyema. 'A Worldwide Evolutionary Classification of Cultures by Subsistence Systems'. *Current Anthropology*, 1977, 18 (4): 659–708.

Macfarlane, Alan and Mark Turin. 'Professor Christoph von Fürer-Haimendorf 1909–1995'. *Bulletin of the School of Oriental and African Studies*, University of London, 1996, LIX (3) http://www.alanmacfarlane.com/TEXTS/cfhsoasobit.pdf (last accessed on 7 February, 2018, 10:30 p.m.)

Madsen, Stig Toft. *State, Society and the Environment in South Asia*. London: Routledge, 2013.

Malcolm, John. *A Memoir of Central India and Adjoining Provinces with History and Copious Illustrations of Past and Present of That Country-Vol. 1*. London: Kingbury, Parbury and Allen, 1823.

Mehta, Behram H. *Gonds of Central Indian Highlands*. Vol. 1, New Delhi: Concept Publishing, 1984.

Pagdi, Setu Madhav. *Among the Gonds of Adilabad*. Second Edition. Bombay: Popular Book Depot, 1952.

Pallavi, Aparna. 'Gondi Language: Victim of Government Neglect'. *Down to Earth*, 1 October, 2014.

Prasad, Archana. 'Military Conflict and Forests in Central Provinces. India: Gonds and the Gondwana Region in Pre-colonial History'. *Environment and History*, 1999, 5 (3): 361–375.

Ramdas, B. 'A Separate Telangana: Promises and Prospects for Tribal Peoples'. *Economic and Political Weekly*, 2013, XLVIII (29): 118–122.

Rashkow, Ezra. 'Making Subaltern *shikaris*: Histories of the Hunted in Colonial Central India'. *South Asian History and Culture*, 2014, 5 (3): 292–296.

Redfern, Ron. *Origins: The Evolution of Continents, Oceans, and Life*. Norman: University of Oklahoma Press, 2001.

Roche, Gerald. '"Flows and Frontiers": Landscape and Cultural Dynamics on the Northeast Tibetan Plateau'. *The Asia Pacific Journal of Anthropology*, 2014, 15 (1): 1–25.

Sahlins, Marshall. 'On the Anthropology of Modernity or, Some Triumphs of Culture over Despondency Theory'. In *Culture and Sustainable Development in the Pacific*. Anthony Hooper, Ed. (Open Access Book, pp. 44–61). Canberra: ANU Press, 2005.

Salunke, Sanjay B. 'Case Study of Keslapur Nagoba Jatra or Fair: A Socio-Anthropological Approach'. *International Journal of Advanced Research*, 2014, 2 (4): 1046–1051.

Sarangi, Asha. 'Ambedkar and the Linguistic States: A Case for Maharashtra'. *Economic and Political Weekly*, 14–20 January, 2006, 41(2): 151–157.

Sardar Ali, Shaheen & Javaid Rehman. *Indigenous Peoples and Ethnic Minorities of Pakistan: Constitutional and Legal Perspectives*. London: Routledge, 2013.

Sardar Ali, Shaheen & Anne Griffiths. *From Transnational Relations to Transnational Laws: Northern European Laws at the Crossroads*. London: Routledge, 2016.

Sengar, Bina. 'Gandhian Approach to Tribals'. *Proceedings of Indian History Congress*, 62nd Session, Kolkata, 2001: 327–336.

Sengar, Bina. 'Defining and Redefining Political Status of Gond Tribe of Maharashtra'. *Marathwada Itihaas Parishad*, Hingoli, 25–26 November, 2016 (Working Research Paper).

Sengar, Bina. 'Colonial Landscape in a Princely State: British Land Policies in Rural Spaces of Ajanta'. https://lisbon2016rh.files.wordpress.com/2015/12/onw-0118.pdf (last accessed on 7 February, 2018, 10:00 p.m.)

Sengar, Bina. *Colonial Landscape in a Princely State: British Land Policies in Rural Spaces of Ajanta*. Conference Souvenir Old and New Worlds: The Global Challenges of Rural History, International Conference, Lisbon, 27–30 January 2016: https://lisbon2016rh.files.wordpress.com/2015/12/onw-0118.pdf (last accessed on 7 February, 2018, 10:30 p.m.)

Shah, U. P. 'The Sālakaṭaṅkaṭas and Laṅkā'. *Journal of the American Oriental Society*, January–March, 1976, 96 (1): 109–113.

Singh, K. Suresh. 'Ecology, Identity and Culture'. *India International Centre Quarterly The Human Landscape*, 2000 and 2001, 27–28 (4 and1): 201–214.

Singh, S. Harpal. 'Haimendorf's Ashes for Marlavai Village'. *The Hindu*, Adilabad Edition, February 23, 2012.

Sorenson, John. 'History and Identity in the Horn of Africa'. *Dialectical Anthropology*, September 1992, 17 (3): 227–252.

Spencer, Dorothy M. 'Folk Tales of Mahakoshala, Verrier Elwin-.IX. Book Review: London, Oxford University Press, 1944', *American Anthropologist*, 1946, 48: 641–642.

Stump, Roger W. *The Geography of Religion: Faith, Place, and Space*. Lanham, MD: Rowman & Littlefield Publishers, 2008.

Tolia-Kelly, Divya P. 'Mobility/stability: British Asian Cultures of "'Landscape and Englishness"'. *Environment and Planning*, 2006, 38: 341–358.

Van Dyke, Jon M., Sherry P. Broder, Seokwoo Lee, and Jin-Hyun Paik. *Governing Ocean Resources: New Challenges and Emerging Regimes: A Tribute to Judge Choon-Ho Park*. Leiden: Martinus Nijhoff Publishers, 2013.

Whelan, Yvonne. 'The Construction and Destruction of a Colonial Landscape: Monuments to British Monarchs in Dublin before and after Independence'. *Journal of Historical Geography*, 2002, 28 (4): 508–533.

Weblinks

http://www.un.org/esa/socdev/unpfii/documents/6_session_factsheet1.pdf (last accessed on 7 February 2018, 10:00 p.m.)

http://asifabad.telangana.gov.in/district-profile/ (last accessed on 7 February 2018, 10:30 p.m.)

http://mudiraja.weebly.com/gond-kingdoms-of-central-india.html (last accessed on 7 February 2018, 10:00 p.m.)

http://www.doccentre.org/docsweb/RWH-dw/land.htm (last accessed on 7 February, 2018, 10:30 p.m.)

http://www.downtoearth.org.in/news/gondi-language-victim-of-government-neglect-46707

http://www.thehindu.com/news/national/telangana/Asifabad-to-become-a-district-again-after-75-years/article15476025.ece (last accessed on 7 February 2018, 10:30 p.m.)

http://www.un.org/esa/socdev/unpfii/documents/DRIPS_en.pdf (last accessed on 7 February 2018, 10:30 p.m.)

https://joshuaproject.net/assets/media/profiles/maps/m16855.pdf (last accessed on 7 February 2018, 10:30 p.m.)

http://www.downtoearth.org.in/news/gondi-language-victim-of-government-neglect-46707 (last accessed on 7 February 2018, 10:30 p.m.)

Chapter 4

Internet as an emancipatory space

Case study of Dalits in Maharashtra

Shraddha Kumbhojkar

Voltaire, writing in 1764, remarked on the constructed and contested nature of historical narratives. 'All ancient histories, as one of our wits has observed, are only fables that men have agreed to admit as true. With regard to modern history, it is a mere chaos, a confusion which it is impossible to make anything of'.[1] Voltaire's remark is as much about the conspiracy of consent regarding the constructed nature of ancient history, as it is about the uncontrollable and contested nature of modern historical narratives. If one applies his words to the case of Maharashtrian Dalit[2] narratives of history, it becomes evident that historical narratives about a distant past are, indeed, traditionally monopolized by the powers that be. However, in the case of the recent past, more and more voices are being heard, though some may be deemed as 'mere chaos'.

History and traditions have been harnessed for legitimizing the *Dalits*' lowly status, and consequently, it has been very important for the Dalit public to search for a counter-historiographical tradition. Major revolts against caste oppression and other inequalities in Indian history seem to have used a two-pronged strategy: first, claiming the authority to write independent historical narratives from one's own point of view and, second, discrediting the grand narratives constructed by those in power. Thinkers starting from Buddha made efforts to effectively communicate the ideals of equality and social justice both to the oppressors and the oppressed. Charvaka's (before 500 C.E.) criticism[3] of the creators of Vedic literature or Tukarama's (seventeenth century) claim[4] that 'we are the only ones who truly understand the meaning of the Vedas' – these were manifestations of the thinkers' efforts to discredit the grand narratives and claim the authority to ascribe meaning to the scriptures. The modern period of history also saw efforts such as the Satya Shodhak Samaj (Society of Truth Seekers established in 1873), which attempted to offer an alternative cultural narrative that exonerated the lower castes from the responsibility of their plight.[5] All these efforts can be seen as attempts to claim the agency to historicize one's own past. In the nineteenth and the twentieth centuries, thinkers such as Phule and Ambedkar used print media for sharing their emancipatory counter-historiographies with the Dalit public. Twenty-first-century Maharashtra has seen the communication revolution and a concomitant democratization of knowledge. It is argued here that Dalits in twenty-first-century Maharashtra are creatively using the internet as an emancipatory space. They may not be able to fully utilize the potential of the internet, nor are they working in an organized and unidirectional manner. However, a review of their activities in cyberspace attests to the fact that just like Gutenberg's revolution, the internet is acting as a catalyst in a number of interconnected phenomena that are useful for Dalit emancipation.

A technocrat at a world summit of the G-8 nations in 2011 thus described the potential of the internet for disadvantaged people:

> The critical change produced by the digital network environment is the radical decentralization of the capacity to speak, to create, to innovate, to see together, to socialize, the radical distribution of the poor means of production, computations, communications [...] that which gets us together inside the experience, being there on the ground.[6]

This ability to share things as they happen is a remarkable thing for any society. For the people who have been historically deprived of the agency to tell their own stories, the importance of the internet and the opportunities it offers for networking with fellow human beings cannot be overemphasized. Maharashtrian Dalit youth have definitely taken to the internet in the last few years. That the figures of internet penetration among the Indian population have been growing at a breathtaking speed is no secret.[7] However, specific caste-wise data of network usage or connectivity are not available. In such a scenario, case studies become an important tool of understanding how the internet is used by the Dalits, who have been deprived of opportunities to create and share knowledge.

What is worth the attention of researchers of Maharashtrian place and space perhaps is the fact that Dalit youth in Maharashtra are increasingly making use of the internet as a space that offers emancipatory opportunities. The present chapter argues that Dalits in Maharashtra have learnt to make use of the internet in support of their emancipatory politics. More than any public space that is physically identifiable, the Dalits in Maharashtra are comfortably making use of the internet to voice their concerns about inequality, document instances of unfair treatment, rally together for a common cause and share their successes and failures in their fight for equality. This is not to say that by virtue of the huge potential of the internet that Dalits have successfully achieved what they want. Far from it. However, the fight for equality would have been much less visible and much less effective had the Maharashtrian Dalits not been able to use the internet as effectively as they do. What a Zimbabwean journalist has said of her local context can be relevant in this case, too. Delta Milaya Ndou says that 'the mere presence of women in online spaces does not constitute emancipation unless they can exercise agency and use those spaces to assert themselves'.[8] Similarly, Dalits in Maharashtra, it is argued here, have been able to exercise their agency in their use of the internet and have effectively used it to assert their ideas and voices. A large chunk of the Dalit population even today is definitely on the wrong side of the digital divide. However, a review of the various creative ways in which Dalits have used the internet helps us paint a picture of resistance, a picture of hope and also of melancholy.

Beyond a few web pages that have largely gone un-archived, source materials relevant for Dalit emancipation began to appear online in the year 2000. This was also the year when the International Dalit Solidarity Network was established. From 2001 onwards, Dr. Ambedkar's speeches reported in *The Hindu*, a daily newspaper, back in 1951 found their way into the online edition of the newspaper, which was indexed and archived by Francis Pritchet in his pages on the website of Columbia University.[9] Though these were not direct contributions by Maharashtrian Dalit people, they have proved to be important for the emancipation movement as widely used source materials to date. A Maharashtrian Dalit engineer had begun the work of Dalit emancipation and solidarity from a different location a few years before this. The first ever Dalit International Conference was organized through the Dalit International Organization (DIO), Malaysia, in October 1998 in Kuala Lumpur by Mr. Rajkumar Kamble and his colleagues.[10] While the internet may not have been used for organizing the conference, its documentation has been preserved with the help of the internet. After twenty-odd years, the pamphlets and photographs of the conference are preserved on the website of the organization that bloomed from the conference, Dr. Ambedkar International Mission (AIM). The AIM has not only organized a number of follow-up conventions of Dalits in Paris and the U.S., it has also been instrumental in organizing a Conference at Columbia University, USA, in 2013 to commemorate Dr. Ambedkar's arrival there a hundred years before.

Around 2008, the internet came to be effectively used as a medium to achieve what the Truth and Reconciliation Commissions were able to achieve in the Western world. In September 2006, members of a Dalit family were abducted, raped and killed in eastern Maharashtra, with no witnesses ready to testify. Mainstream media did not report the news for weeks together. A Dalit government officer used the potential of the internet by publicly uploading the report of the Fact Finding Commission that documented the findings about the crime.[11] This was quickly taken down from the website, but by then it had been widely shared and reported in the mainstream media. Whether the action helped secure justice for the sole surviving member of the family is a different issue, but the internet was usefully harnessed to at least give voice to an otherwise voiceless victim.

The arrival of YouTube and Facebook in India are two phenomena that gave a further boost to the idea of using the internet specifically for purposes relevant to the Dalit people. Dalit music had always been very popular in Maharashtra. In fact, a Marathi saying, though perpetuating caste-based labels, acknowledges that Brahmin households have writing and Mahar households have music.[12] The YouTube videos of Ambedkarite songs are some of the most viewed videos in the world of Marathi music. Non-Bollywood Ambedkarite songs by the famous family – Anand, Milind and Adarsh Shinde – have easily garnered more than a million views each.[13] Dalit Camera is a popular YouTube channel operating since 2007 that has more than 6 million views for its videos, films and documentations relevant to Dalit lives.[14] A number of films pertaining to the issues that the Dalits are interested in are easily available and widely shared on YouTube. There are films featuring Dr. Ambedkar's speeches, his funeral procession, clips of Dalit leaders' speeches, episodes of television series such as *Samvidhan* which dealt with the making of the Indian Constitution and even videos of untoward incidents such as the riots in early 2018 at Bheema Koregaon filmed and shared by the members of the public. Facebook also is a very popular medium for bringing about Dalit solidarity.

Facebook became popular in India over the second decade of the twenty-first century as the number of smartphone users went up. In 2013, the number of active mobile phone Facebook users in India was 57.5 million and is expected to reach 167.7 million users in 2018.[15] WhatsApp, a popular internet-based messaging application for smartphone users, has also been bought by Facebook. Both Facebook and WhatsApp have opened unimagined new vistas for Dalits who wish to come together or share any ideas while enjoying the anonymity of the social network. There are dozens of Facebook pages related to the Ambedkarite movement and managed by Maharashtrian Dalit youth. Vaibhav Chhaya[16] is a Dalit activist and media professional who has been organizing a festival to commemorate the Dalit poet Namdeo Dhasal. The festival, entitled *Sarva Kahi Samashtisathi*, has been popularized with the help of his Facebook page. The schedule of the festival, changes to and details of the programme are shared on the Facebook page.

In times of crisis, too, internet technology and the power of Facebook has shown that it can be harnessed for larger good. On 6 December 2017, when hundreds of thousands of Ambedkarites began to gather in Chaitya Bhoomi in Mumbai to pay annual homage to Dr. Ambedkar, Vaibhav Chhaya and dozens of Dalit activists realized that there was a cyclone warning sent out for Mumbai. With the help of Facebook and WhatsApp, they organized tonnes of food to be cooked by friends and families and distributed throughout designated places in Mumbai where thousands of Ambedkarites had to take shelter for a couple of days.

Besides the social network part, where one can easily organize like-minded people without too much of fear of caste labelling, the internet has proven useful for fearlessly presenting Dalit viewpoints about almost anything. In 2014, a new edition of Dr. Ambedkar's *Annihilation of Caste* with an introduction by Arundhati Roy was published. Many Dalit activists found that Roy's introduction did not convey what Dr. Ambedkar wanted, and they felt that in fact her introduction was unfairly taking the readers' attention away from Dr. Ambedkar's essential argument. A number of Dalit scholars and thinkers as a part of the Ambedkar Age Collective wrote their rejoinders around the theme and even published a book called *Hatred in the Belly* as an 'answer back' to Roy's arguments. Gaurav Somvamshi is a part of this collective, which is associated with the website called roundtableindia.co.in. He is one of the authors who have, while pursuing their independent careers, taken up issues of caste inequality and its justification. He wrote a seven-part article on roundtableindia, which dealt with the various questions that he faced as a Dalit in the present day.[17] The articles garnered a lot of views and discussion through the website as well as through his personal Facebook page. This is a case that goes to show that social media and websites can go hand in hand or complement the content that each of them offers.

WhatsApp is an application that lets users share digital media in a closed group setting. Umesh Hattikat is a research student who has recently submitted his M.Phil. dissertation that studies the history of the Vhalar subcaste. This is a subcaste that is found scattered in South Maharashtra and which has a very low literacy rate. When Hattikat set out to study the caste group, he was not sure how he could get information regarding the recent history of the Vhalar people. However, to his surprise, he found that the Vhalar youth had organized themselves in a caste group via WhatsApp and were all approachable through that messaging service. His survey work became very easy after this discovery, and he hopes the dissertation will have some policy implications for eventually bettering the lives of the Vhalar community members.[18]

The examples dealt with so far have primarily shown how the internet has helped Maharashtrian Dalits in exploring ways to emancipate themselves. The story obviously has a grim side, too. A Dalit smartphone user was murdered in Shirdi over an altercation regarding his use of an Ambedkarite song as his ringtone in 2015.[19] This is by no means a solitary instance. The Bheema Koregaon riots in the New Year week of 2018 also had a strong relationship with the content spread through social media. Competing and contradictory narratives of history were floated by the Dalits as well as non-Dalits in the build-up to the event that commemorated the battle of Bheema Koregaon, which had taken place 200 years earlier. Videos were virally circulated with the aim of fanning communal hatred, and they resulted in loss of at least one life and property worth millions of rupees. Present-day contestations for social acceptance are almost always played out in the field of historical narratives. The Bheema Koregaon riots were no exception.

To conclude, the internet has been used by the Dalits in Maharashtra as an emancipatory space. With the help of the internet, they are getting access to authentic sources of information and an audience with a genuine interest in their stories. The internet helps them document their own history through their own gaze by bringing people together, protected by the comparative anonymity of cyberspace. These processes, of course, come with a concomitant set of challenges. By connecting virtually, are Dalits able to retain the connection with the grass roots, the masses? After all, the Dalit movement was always known for its rootedness. Is it that the new media are creating a cultural hegemony of the digitally advantaged Dalits over the disadvantaged ones? Online catharsis might lead to a certain degree of distancing of Dalits from their own lived experiences, and this may lead to an eventual apathy about real-life events. And finally, while the internet can be a highly supervised and supervisable medium, there is a possibility that it may be used for socially engineering the opinions and activities of Dalits. While the future holds the answers to many of these questions, from the point of historiography, one can see Voltaire's argument coming true. There is a slow but steady transition from a universe of Grand Narratives of Dalit history to a multiverse of competing memories and histories taking shape.

Notes

1 Voltaire (François-Marie Arouet), *Jeannotet Colin*, Cramer, Geneva P. 101. Accessed on 10 January 2018. https://books.google.co.in/books?id=mxFAAAAAcAAJ&q=%22fables+convenues%22&redir_esc=y#v=snippet&q=%22fables%20convenues%22&f=false.

2 The word *Dalit* in Sanskrit literally means crushed or trampled upon. This is a word used for the people of the formerly untouchable castes in South Asia. Many other words have been used to describe the same group of people, e.g. Untouchables, *Shudras*, *Pariahs*, Depressed Classes, *Harijans*, etc. These nomenclatures are rejected for various reasons by the Dalits themselves. Even the word *Dalit* is not unchallenged as some prefer the name Ambedkarite. I have stuck to Dalit here, primarily because of its widespread usage and acceptance.

3 'The Creators of the three Vedas are the Cunning, the Clever and the Night-wanderers'. Charvaka, quoted in Sayana Madhava's *Savadarshanasamgraha*, p. 14. Accessed on 10 January 2018. https://archive.org/details/Sarva-darsana-sangrahaOfMadhavacharya (translation mine). Charvaka was one of the ancient Indian philosophers who negated the authority of the Vedas as repositories of knowledge.

4 Tukaram, *Gatha*, 2256. Accessed on 12 January 2018. https://mr.wikisource.org/wiki/%E0%A4%A4%E0%A5%81%E0%A4%95%E0%A4%BE%E0%A4%B0%E0%A4%BE%E0%A4%AE_%E0%A4%97%E0%A4%BE%E0%A4%A5%E0%A4%BE/%E0%A4%97%E0%A4%BE%E0%A4%A5%E0%

A4%BE_%E0%A5%A8%E0%A5%A7%E0%A5%A6%E0%A5%A7_%E0%A4%A4%E0%A5%87_%E0%A5%A8%E0%A5%AA%E0%A5%A6%E0%A5%A6 (Translation mine.) Tukaram was a seventeenth-century poet renowned for his humanistic ideas and progressive views.

5 For a detailed discussion about the Satya Shodhak Samaj's efforts at creation of an alternative history and culture, see Shraddha Kumbhojkar, 'Denial of Centrality to Vedic Texts', in Willy Pfändtner & David Thurfjell (eds.), *Post-colonial Challenges to the Study of Religion*, Interreligiösarelationer, Uppsala: Swedish Science Press, 2008.

6 Yochai Benkler, co-director of the Berkman Center for Internet and Society, *Interview* at the e-G8 Summit, Paris, 30-05-2011. Accessed from www.cbsnews.com/news/g8-hails-power-of-the-internet-as-an-instrument-for-emancipation/ on 10 December 2017.

7 In 2014, India had shown a 240% growth in the number of internet users in the previous five years. In 2015, the number of internet users in India was 259.88 million. In 2017, it grew to 331.77 million people. Source: Statista.com accessed from www.statista.com/statistics/292488/fastest-growing-internet-populations/ and www.statista.com/statistics/255146/number-of-internet-users-in-india/ on 28 January 2018.

8 Delta Milayo Ndou, 'Being online will not guarantee emancipation', in *The Herald*, 27-10, 2016. Accessed from www.herald.co.zw/being-online-will-not-guarantee-emancipation/ on 11 December 2001.

9 https://web.archive.org/web/20050206045328/http://www.columbia.edu:80/itc/mealac/pritchett/00ambedkar/timeline/1950s.html accessed on 24 January 2018.

10 http://ambedkarmission.org/about-aim.html accessed on 24 January 2018.

11 www.pucl.org/major_reports/Report%20on%20Khairlanji%20Massacre,%202007-2.pdf accessed on 10 November 2017.

12 The original Marathi saying goes - *Baamnaghareelivne, Mharaghareegaane.*

13 www.youtube.com/watch?v=t0wVhY5XYVM accessed on 28 January 2018.

14 www.youtube.com/user/kadhirnilavan/about accessed on 20 January 2018.

15 www.statista.com/statistics/380559/number-of-mobile-facebook-users-in-india/ accessed on 14 January 2018.

16 www.facebook.com/vaibhav.chaya accessed on 1 February 2018.

17 http://roundtableindia.co.in/~roundta3/index.php?option=com_content&view=article&id=9190:seven-questions&catid=119:feature&Itemid=132 accessed on 1 February 2018.

18 Interview with Umesh Hattikat, December 2016.

19 www.thehindu.com/news/national/other-states/dalit-youth-killed-for-ambedkar-song-ringtone/article7232259.ece accessed on 1 February 2018.

Part II

Constructing space and place

Material culture and public spaces

Chapter 5

Place, space and money in Maharashtra, c. 1750–1850

Some insights

Shailendra Bhandare

Prologue

The monetary history of pre-modern Maharashtra is a subject that has received little attention in the wider discourse about histories of Maharashtra in general. Traditionally, an emphasis on 'positivist' style of history-writing in Maharashtra has shifted the focus too much towards reconstructing of political events, their veracity and establishing of an overarching 'narrative' that threads various political processes in a seamless stream. Conceivably, economic undercurrents and practicalities underpinned many political activities of the eighteenth and the nineteenth centuries in Maharashtra, and money played a massive role in their orchestration. A cursory glance at the amounts of money exchanged as tributes, levies, ransoms and other such transactions that were politically motivated and transpired between Maratha and other polities would be sufficient to see that vital role. In spite of its importance, monetary history has been largely overlooked, and this chapter is an attempt to highlight some important aspects of it, with the rhetorical devices of 'place' and 'space' deployed to present the story.

The mapping of places and spaces leads us to conceive a 'geography' of money. This can emerge as a 'conceptual' as well as a 'physical' subject category. Money is usually defined as anything that is accepted in payments; coins are only one of the forms of money. An essential characteristic of money is that it circulates as a medium of exchange. These two aspects are crucial in creating the 'geography' of money – as a medium of exchange and/or mode of payment, monetary objects like coins can travel the world and create their own characteristic 'spaces'. A familiar international example of this can be the circulation and acceptability of the US dollar across the globe. Another example of how money works out its own geography would be the creation of a 'monetary union' like the Eurozone, where several countries willingly gave up the use of their national currencies and accepted a mutually agreed upon single currency. Needless to say, the mechanics of how money performs these roles are complicated, but one can safely surmise that working out a notion of 'geography' for money is crucial to understand them.

In this chapter, I propose to use the concept of 'geography of money' and some of its constituent elements to highlight how 'places' and 'spaces' can be deployed to throw light on the monetary history of eighteenth- and nineteenth-century Maharashtra, particularly with respect to coins, their issue, circulation and consumption. To this effect, I will employ some concepts outlined by Benjamin Cohen in his book *The Geography of Money*.[1] Cohen's study is not aimed at Maharashtra, or for that matter, India; instead, it focuses on the wider world, and he paints a canvas far more wide than I do. However, I found some initial concepts that he has outlined quite useful to understand coinage in pre-modern Maharashtra, particularly in the context of 'space' and 'place'. I will, therefore, extend these concepts into some new areas, which will help us explain how money circulated in Western Maharashtra in an interesting light. At the outset, I must clarify that the 'Maharashtra' I focus on here is by and large the 'Maharashtra' we know today – that is, the state inhabited by Marathi-speaking people that came into existence on 1 May 1961. In pre-modern times, the notion of 'Maharashtra' was obviously different. I have opted for the modern definition of Maharashtra mainly to restrict the scope of this chapter to a particular and smaller area, in order not to lose its focus. I will also confine the discussion to higher value currency regimes, mainly silver rupees. This is not because what I intend to analyse and argue for is applicable only to high value coins but because the inherently complex nature of copper currency in eighteenth- to nineteenth-century Maharashtra would require a much longer paper.

The conceptual framework for investigation

To populate the concept of 'geography of money', Cohen takes into account and defines some salient theoretical terms. His aim is to investigate money in terms of 'spatial organizations', and how 'monetary domains are configured and governed' (3, 8). In his approach, he sees a need for 'monetary geography to be reconceptualised in functional terms' (5). A crucial concept he deploys in his investigative reconceptualization is that of 'networks'. At their basis, monetary networks are essentially 'transactional'; the transactions money performs are all linked up and as such create a web of their own. Cohen explains what a 'network' is in detail (12), adding that transactional networks underpin 'the functional domains of individual currencies: the range of their effective use for various monetary purposes'. Cohen also contends that monetary geography is 'fundamentally grounded in key social structures' (13).

To go beyond physical geography, or to 'de-territorialize' the study of monetary geography, Cohen advocates a separation of 'physical and functional notions of space'. A notion of 'functional space' is difficult to articulate and visualize, because it is not rooted in reality and cannot always be drawn on a map. Such spaces are often created by human contact and are, therefore, 'social' spaces. With particular reference to money, such a space might be called a 'monetary space' or a 'monetary sphere', which can be visualized as consisting of a network of payments (22). Arjun Appadurai has used the word 'finanscapes (or financescapes)' to describe such monetary spaces in context of globalization.[2] According to Appadurai, financescapes are one of the five 'flows' that constitute a 'deterrorialized' notion of the modern 'global world'. He describes them to be imaginary landscapes generated by the movement of vast amounts of capital.

Monetary spaces can often be described as 'currency domains'. It would be worthwhile to reproduce Cohen's ideas of these domains, almost verbatim, because much of what I will argue later in this chapter to highlight the role of 'place and space' in the monetary history of eighteenth- to nineteenth-century Maharashtra will have a bearing on these conceptual terms. The domains Cohen refers to are three (23):

1 Territorial domain – the traditional domain in which money operates, which is its 'space-of-place'. It is defined by the jurisdiction of a government who issues the money and it corresponds to the conventional/physical imagery of political geography.
2 Transactional domain – this corresponds to the functional imagery consisting of transactional networks and creates a 'finanscape'. Unlike territorial domain, the transactional domain cannot always be represented by conventional imagery like a map. It is a 'space-of-flows', as Cohen calls it, which is defined by how currencies respond to the demand of being used in monetary purposes, either in their own country or elsewhere.
3 Authoritative domain – Cohen calls this a 'new concept', that 'brings together both functional and physical dimensions of money in a single amalgam, of use and authority'. He thus concedes that currency domains are not purely a function of transactions alone but also of authority. Elements of dominance and dependence clearly enter the picture too, as a result of either market forces or political decision (24). The 'authoritative domain' thus captures and spans, according to him, '... [the] hierarchical links between currencies as well their individual networks of use'. This hierarchical relationship is typically described as a monetary 'bloc' or 'zone' (48).

As can be evident, much of how Cohen proposes to see the geography of money is based on 'spaces', be it a defined physical space in which money operates or spaces in which it 'flows', both in social and transactional senses. This kind of conceptual visualizing also makes us think about how these 'spaces' might have reacted with each – what the internal dynamics of money circulating within a space it creates (intra-spatial dynamics) were, and how these spaces interact between each other (inter-spatial dynamics). Cohen does not include numismatics in the scope of his discussion, so it will also be interesting to see how the numismatic characteristics that money carries, such as type, legends, denomination, etc., fit into these dynamics of spaces and places. This will involve populating Cohen's concepts with material data and exploring how the two respond to each other. This is what I propose to do with coinage in late eighteenth-century to early nineteenth-century Maharashtra.

There are a couple of points one needs to understand and appreciate before we go any further. In the pre-modern period, currency all over India was 'real', i.e. the constituent coinages were worth what they were in real metal terms. A 'rupee' was designated to be 1 *tola* (approx. 11.6 gm) of pure silver. Any variance in weight or purity would affect the value of a 'rupee' coin – it would be discounted from its full worth. When Mughal rule was at its zenith in the seventeenth century, its currency apparatus was solid – mints were rigorously controlled, and their output was standard in terms of weight and purity. This helped the rupee to be established as a pan-imperial currency and create its 'territorial domain'. With the gradual fragmentation of the Mughal Empire in the eighteenth century, the right to coin was farmed out, as revenue sources were rapidly alienated from the central power. Various emerging political entities secured these rights, either through official arrangement with the deputies (Nawabs) of the Empire or without any such sanction. Many of the deputies, like the Nawab-Wazir of Awadh or the Nizam of Hyderabad, assumed these rights and began operating mints of their own. Such centrifugal activities made the reliability and standard of the rupee a thing of the past – instead of a single Mughal rupee, there came to exist several rupees, and it became far more likely for the currency regime to be constituted of coins of varying weights and purity. These various 'rupees' nominally still had the name of the Mughal emperor impressed upon them, but in reality had little to do with Mughal sovereign authority. As such, they were 'quasi-Mughal' in their form and substance. The emergent polities exercised their own monetary authority through such coins, so the 'authoritative domain' of money in the eighteenth century consisted of many overlapping 'spaces' created by the issue and circulation of these coins. In a very basic sense, there was a 'sovereign space', which was essentially Mughal, all in but name, but there were several 'subordinate spaces' which were populated by various issuing authorities.

The second significant aspect about currency in pre-modern Maharashtra was that coins were a 'commodity' like any other, and their issue was regulated by demand and supply. Minting access was 'free', meaning anyone could go to the mint and convert bullion into coins as per their requirements. However, minting was not 'free' – the mint operators levied a charge for striking the coins, and the loss of metal suffered during processes such as refining and bringing it to the requisite purity standard. An example is found in papers of the Sawantwadi state; a charge of 10 Annas per 100 rupees struck is mentioned as the levy and the total income of the mint from this charge being one hundred rupees per year.[3] More productive mints, such as those located in larger cities like Pune, might have accrued greater income and might even have lowered the levy. The mint administrator (or the licensee, in case of mints where rights to coin were farmed out) would pay the government's dues, and pay for his staff and raw materials from this income.

The monetary environment of Maharashtra in late eighteenth–early nineteenth centuries

The geographic landmass of today's Maharashtra was divided into three broad political regions or 'zones' in the eighteenth century. Western Maharashtra was largely the political domain of the Peshwa and his acolytes, although the rulers of Satara and Kolhapur, scions of Chhatrapti Shivaji, the original founder of the Maratha 'Swaraj', held weak control of their fiefs. Central Maharashtra or 'Marathwada' was largely under the rule of the Nizam, while Eastern Maharashtra or Vidarbha was under the sway of the Bhonsla Rajas of Nagpur. On the coast, there were other entities – the European presence was dominated by the British after the Portuguese were ousted by the Marathas from their strongholds of Vasai and Chaul by the mid-eighteenth century, and the Dutch trading post at Vengurla steadily declined. Among coastal powers, the maritime warlord Angrey family, and the Sidis of Janjira exercised considerable might, till the Angre navy was scuttled in the mid-eighteenth century by family feuds and the Peshwa's intervention. In a numismatic sense, each of these political authorities occupied a certain space, which was defined largely by places – mint towns – which struck coins of particular types. The typology of these coins helps us to define the circulatory spaces they inhabited; we will see this in more detail further in this chapter.

The simultaneous circulation of all sorts of coins gave raise to another significant 'space' – that of the 'money market'. The circulation of coins was a mediated phenomenon; it was often achieved through the agency of money changers or shroffs. Implicit in this phenomenon was the fact that all coins were not of a standard or one single value, even if they purported to be of the same denomination. Each inherently had differing silver contents, and depending on how long each coin had been in circulation, it lost its weight in wear as it circulated and concomitantly also lost some of its value. Even a cursory glance at papers of an eminent banking family like the Dikshit-Patwardhan or the Tulshibagwale, which operated in the city of Pune, the nerve centre of the Peshwa's political domains, is sufficient to get an idea of how elaborate this space was and how wide reaching its 'transactional domain' was. The bankers would often make vast amounts of money available on credit to their clients, effect trans-regional transactions with instruments such as Hundis and, most importantly for our purpose, even farm mints. A verse by Prabhakar, a balladeer (*Shāhir*) of the late eighteenth century mentions the names of various banker families in Pune.[4] The Peshwas established matrimonial relations with more than one banking house, presumably to bring in the availability of liquid cash within the familial ambit to make it more accessible.

In the geographic environment of money, the place(s) where a mint is located proved to be 'anchoring points' within the monetary space. In eighteenth-century Maharashtra, there were many mints producing silver coins. The most prominent were those located in large urban centres such as Pune or Nasik or those operating in garrison or *Jagir* towns like Miraj, Chandwad and Mulher. Smaller market towns like Talegaon, Chinchwad or Rahimatpur also had mints from time to time. In the Nizam's territories, the main mints were located at Aurangabad and Daulatabad. Nagpur, the capital of the Bhonslas, was also the site of their most productive mint. The Chhatrapatis of Kolhapur and Satara ran mints in both these towns, and so did the Savants of Wadi in South Konkan. The Angreys of Colaba (Alibaug) and the Sidis of Janjira had their own mint, too, located at their respective headquarters. The British established their own mint at Bombay in 1672. After a few decades of producing coins with Latin inscriptions, they finally got permission to strike coins in the name of the Mughal emperor in 1715. The Bombay mint remained functional through 1760 when production was given over to the mint at Surat. In the early nineteenth century, the 'Surti' rupee began to be struck at Bombay.

The monetary space of the Peshwa heartland

The Peshwa heartland largely constituted Western Maharashtra, a relatively thin strip of land covering the present-day districts of Nasik, Pune, Satara, Sangli and Solapur. It was bounded on the west by the Western Ghats and the Konkan strip and on the east by territories of the Nizams. It was a prosperous and fertile tract, watered by the Godavari-Bheema-Krishna river systems and populated by three prominent urban centres, namely Pune, Nasik and Satara. Of these two (Pune and Satara) were centres of polities, of the Peshwa and his nominal Master, the Chhatrapati; in the second half of the eighteenth century, the Chhatrapatis were largely eclipsed by the Peshwas. A number of mints for silver rupees functioned at various junctures over the eighteenth century; they were located at Pune, Chinchwad, Chakan (both close to Pune), Talegaon, Chandwad, Wafgaon and Nasik.

Pune was the nerve centre of the financial affairs of the Marathas, and this is where the main secretariat or *Phad* was located. The mint at Pune produced two kinds of rupees – the 'Hali Sikka' and the 'Ankushi'.

Figure 5.1 The 'Hali Sikka' rupee, struck at Pune.
Source: Photos by Shailendra Bhandare.

Figure 5.2 The 'Ankushi' rupee, struck at Pune.

The latter was named after the symbol of an elephant goad or *Ankush* that it carried on the reverse.

The rupees of Chinchwad had the symbol of a battleaxe or *Furshee* on them.

The issues of Chakan had the letter 'Shri' impressed upon them, while the coins struck at Nasik had the symbol of the Maratha pennant or *Jaripatka*.

These coins constituted a hierarchy in circulation and created 'authoritative domains' of their own. These hierarchies were essentially functional,

Figure 5.3 The rupee of Chinchwad with the symbol of a battleaxe or *Furshee*.

Figure 5.4 The Chakan rupee with the letter 'Shri' impressed on it.

Figure 5.5 The Nasik rupee the symbol of the Maratha pennant or *Jaripatka*.

and they resulted from governmental intervention. Thus, the Peshwa paid his troops in 'Hali Sikka' rupees but collected revenue mainly in *Ankushi* rupees. In fact, there were specific coins nominated for revenue collection and they were known as '*Potechal*' (from *Pota* पोता in Marathi meaning 'treasury'.[5]

However, the state was not the sole interventionist in such matters. Consumers too followed suit. Sometimes only a certain kind of rupee would be demanded to effect a transaction. This is well exemplified by instances of remarks such as 'converted into Chandwad (rupees) for (buying) butter' (लोण्याकरिता चांदवड केले) that we encounter against a record of commission paid when coins were exchanged.[6] For larger purchases, sums could be paid in mixed coins. When two bankers, namely Sadashiv Tambwekar and Naroba Tambwekar, bought a house in Kothrud, they paid a sum consisting of 875 Daulatabad rupees, and 500 *Potechal* rupees for it.[7] The shroffs or money changers created their own hierarchies that enabled them to charge exchange commissions or *Batta*. As mentioned earlier, the coins in the circulatory regime were worth their real metallic value. As they suffered wear in circulation, some of the metal was lost and so the value depreciated. Exactly how much depreciation occurred due to circulatory wear was decided by a shroff, who would then apply a suitable discount to devalue the coin. This was logical, although not always legitimate – the government tried to clamp on excessive devaluation through arbitrary commission charging. However, there were other mechanisms through which the shroffs intervened into the 'transactional domain' of circulating currency. Private coining meant that the coins were less trustworthy as far as standards were concerned. The licensees who bought the lease to run the mint from the government tended to produce substandard coins, both in terms of weight and purity, to make illicit profit. Often, mints were closed because of such malpractice. The charter given to a representative of Tukoji Holkar in 1774 to operate the mint at Chandwad makes clear mention to the fact that the mint had ceased to operate because the previous contractor struck coins that were not correct in purity and weight.[8]

The possibility of coins being debased beyond what the purity standard permitted meant that they had to be attested from time to time. Shroffs were also involved in the business of checking coins for their purity, and after a coin was attested, it was often stamped with a small 'shroff mark' to indicate that it had undergone the testing process. The number of such marks on a coin indicated its age in circulation – the more the attestation marks, the longer the coin had been in circulation and as such was less valuable. Depending on the extent of these marks, the shroffs assigned the coins a 'circulatory grade'. The commission for changing coins as well as the discount applied to correct the value of the coin corresponding to the wear both depended on which 'circulatory grade' the coin was physically in. All these hierarchies meant that there were many exchange rates in existence. They depended not only on the kind of coins but also on their physical condition and whether or not they carried certain characteristics, like a date of issue.

All these dynamics contributed to the intricacies of the 'monetary space' and the interaction of various domains within it. Evidently, this was a 'mediated' space – there were more than one agency operational within it to help money circulate. These agencies contributed to and benefitted from the dynamics within this space. However, it is interesting to note that the interventions imposed on circulatory regimes, either by the state or by other agencies, led to certain coins being more accepted than others, and that is what created a 'monetary zone of circulation'. A good example of the creation of such a circulatory space for one kind of coin is the one generated by circulation of the *Ankushi* rupee.

The 'circulatory zone' of the *Ankushi* rupee

After the Peshwa's rule ended and the British took over in 1818, a number of governmental 'projects' were undertaken, first by the newly constituted 'Deccan Commissionerate' and then by the government of the Bombay Presidency to appreciate the workings of the old order. Also, since the mid-1820s, the goal of the colonial government was to establish a uniform coinage in all its constituent presidencies, doing away with regionalism of any kind in circulatory currency. In the intervening period, stock was taken of the currency requirements of various regions, the Deccan being one of them. As a transitional measure, some mints in Maharashtra, which had been active under the Peshwas, were kept functioning after making appropriate changes to the design, like addition of a date.[9] Among many memoranda and reports that were compiled towards this effect, there was one submitted by Captain John Clunes that described the currency of the Peshwa's territories in the Deccan.[10]

From Clunes' memorandum, it becomes apparent that during the early nineteenth century, the *Ankushi* rupee, which was initially struck in Pune, had come to be extensively copied across the Deccan at mints located at many other places. The fact that the Peshwa's government had designated it as the main currency in which taxes could be paid made it a sought-after coin. Although initially it was struck at Pune, the demands on it to make payments must have been quite high. So it is plausible that its design was imitated by mints located at places which were in the same commercial zone as Pune and had strong transactional networks with that city. Clunes mentions *Ankushi* rupees as being struck at Bhatodi, Belapur, Chambhargonda, Tembhurni, Kamalgarh, Phulgaon, Mendurgee (Maindargi) and Alibagh. Some of these mints were run officially, like the one at Phulgaon, which was started at the behest of the Peshwa, when he took a fancy to the place because of its pristine riverside location and attempted to create a pleasure-village there. Some were exigent, like Kamalgarh, where coins were struck during the rebellion of Tai Telin, a concubine of the Pant Pratinidhi. Some like Bhatodi and Chambhargonda were short-lived operations initiated by the economic needs of localized market spaces. The mint at Belapur appears to have been started 'when the Poona Ankoosy became current in Konkun'; Clunes mentions that there were eight or ten other places in the region which also undertook the production of *Ankushi* rupees but does not name them. All these mints operated for only about two years (1805–1806) and then were prohibited by the Peshwa. Mints located at Wai or Tembhurni were run by influential Brahmin barons who were also Peshwa's acolytes and/or relatives. The mint at Wai was run by the 'Rastias' (Raste) and that at Tembhurni was operated by 'Sudaseo Bhow Mankesur' (Sadashiv Bhau Mankeshwar).

It is worthwhile to note that while all these mints produced *Ankushi* rupees, they were each of a differing purity. According to the information provided by Clunes, the alloy in the Ankushi rupee struck at Pune was about 7%, in that struck at Bhatodi was 9%–11%, Kamalgarh was 13%–14%, Phulgaon was 8%–9% and so on. Accordingly, their transactional values differed, and they each had a different exchange rate when compared with the 'Poona Halli Sicca'. The mint at Maindargi appears to be the worst – it struck very debased coins, worth only 10 Annas each and thus 160 Maindargi rupees passed equal to 100 Poona Halli Sicca.

The circulation of all these coins and the information we get from Clunes' memorandum can be neatly seen in context of how a monetary 'zone' or 'bloc' can be visualized when a particular kind of currency gains acceptance for a particular purpose through consumer intervention. Primarily, in this zone, circulated only the *Ankushi* rupees, but as mints located in more than one place began to strike it, a need to differentiate them became apparent. The coins, although all carrying the 'Ankush' mark, also had other more or less prominent symbols incorporated on them. Some were very conspicuous: Phulgaon incorporated a *hibiscus* flower in its design.

Figure 5.6 The 'Ankushi' rupee struck at Phulgaon with an additional symbol of a *Hibiscus* flower.

Some were inconspicuous: as per Clunes' mention, the rupees of Kamalgarh mint only had an extra dot at a particular place. Some of these are clear enough to be attributed, while others are not; however, the shroffs of the nineteenth century must have had some means to test and recognize them and apply an appropriate discount when presented for exchange.

The 'currency zone' created by the issue and circulation of various *Ankushi* rupees serves as a good example where the concepts of monetary geography as elucidated by Cohen can be applied. The 'territorial domain' of the currency can be defined by mapping the places that inhabit this circulatory space. The transactional hierarchies involved here are evident in exchange rates and pure metal/alloy contents as given by Clunes. The interventions, at various levels, by either the government or its representatives, or by consumers of currency, create a complex 'authoritative domain' for the *Ankushi* rupee. It is also interesting that coin design also plays its part in creating this space, and the features that are added in the design, apart from the most common attributive descriptor the 'Ankush' mark, can be all viewed as symbols of these interventions. The design thus also becomes an aspect of the 'authoritative domain' and plays a part in how conceptually such a space is envisaged.

Design modifications had cultural and political connotations, too. As mentioned above, the *Ankushi* rupees struck at Phulgaon incorporate a hibiscus flower in their design. Much as the 'Ankush' symbol, the hibiscus flower is closely associated with the god Ganesh. The Peshwas were ardent worshippers of this deity. However, the Marathi word for flower is '*phul*', and the additional symbol is a clever pun on the name of the place where the coins were produced.

The popularity of the *Ankushi* rupee meant that in its circulatory space were included areas which were not under direct control of the Peshwa, and other political authorities imitated the design too. A good example is the 'Hubshee' rupee struck under the authority of the Sidi Nawab of Janjira.[11]

Figure 5.7 The 'Ankushi' rupee struck at Janjira, known as the 'Hubshee' rupee.

The Sidis did not have their own mint to strike rupees and countermarked circulating coins with their own symbol, a Devanagari letter 'Ja' standing for Janjira. In the late eighteenth century, as the popularity of the *Ankushi* rupee grew, Janjira decided to issue its own rupee. The letter 'Ja' which was being countermarked was incorporated in the design of the coin, but it was placed inverted with respect to the rest of the Farsi inscription. The instance of *Ankushi* rupee being imitated at Janjira shows that the circulatory space of a particular coin was not limited to a single political authority at a time when the 'territorial domain' of money was not necessarily defined or limited by a government.

The monetary space of an urban money market

Markets are obviously the spaces where transactions happen, so in Cohen's scheme, they would constitute nerve centres of 'transactional networks'. The way that currency circulated in such a space would be another tool at our disposal to visualize such a space. Using Cohen's terminology, market space would be a 'space-of-flows' and thus primarily a 'transactional domain' of money; however, certain peculiarities contributing to it also help us visualize it as an 'authoritative domain'. Pune, the capital of the Peshwas, would serve as a good example as a market town to train our lens on.

There were at least three kinds of rupees struck in Pune, and perhaps two more. The 'Poona Halli Sicca' was the purest of the rupees struck at Pune, containing only 2.27% of alloy. It was the 'standard rupee of account' for bankers and was used to take comparative values of other coins (Clunes, 1). According to Clunes, it was struck first under the rule of 'Madhoo Rao, surnamed the great'. Clunes also makes reference to a story that prompted its issue – apparently a banker went bankrupt and a large number of rupees in his possession, which he had previously got issued from the Peshwa's treasury, turned out to be debased and substandard. It was then decided that the 'Halli Sicca' would be introduced as a new coin of Pune. The term itself means 'current coin', and there were other such 'Halli Sicca' rupees current in Pune, such as those of the Ujjain and Ahmedabad mints, as per Clunes' information. The 'Halli Sicca' had the name of Ali Gauhar impressed on it (this was an alternative, pre-accession name of the Mughal emperor Shah Alam II) and carried a peculiar symbol, sometimes described as 'scissors', or 'spectacles', but looking more like the markings on a cobra's hood. In the context of Ganesh worship, this probably alluded to a cobra which the deity is often showed carrying in one of his hands or worn as a girdle. The second popular local coin in the money market of Pune was the *Ankushi* rupee about which we just have had a discussion. According to Clunes, it was struck first at Chinchwad and then at Pune, during the reign of Narayan Rao Peshwa (3). Since the extant *Ankushi* rupees bear the twelfth year of Shah Alam II's reign, it is possible that they were first struck in 1772/1773 (which the year corresponds to), and then the regnal year was frozen or 'immobilized' in the design. The third coin struck in Pune was the *Furshee* or the 'battleaxe' rupee. This was initially struck at Chinchwad by the Dev of Chinchwad, who was a multifaceted personality, being an *Inamdar*, a cult-head associated with the god Ganesh, a hereditary incarnate of a seventeenth-century god-man, and a wealthy banker and moneylender. The mint at Chinchwad was transferred to Pune in about 1774.[12]

The fact that in the decades of 1760–1780, as many as three mints began operating in Pune points to an increase in the demand for coined specie in the Pune market. Monetization gradually increased as the eighteenth century progressed and turned into the nineteenth century, with the spread of the *Ankushi* rupee beyond Pune into its own circulatory zone or space. This increase in money use made the class of money changers proliferate. A number of bankers and moneylenders resided in Pune city. Their names can be easily discerned by the suffix 'Naik' they carried after their first name – e.g. Balaji Naik Bhide or Gopal Naik Tambwekar. Their distribution along various *peths* or local market-driven habitations of the city can be glossed over from *Pune Nagara Samshodhana Wruttanta*, a four-volume topographical, historical and ethnographic survey of Pune city done by the members of *Bharata Itihasa Samshodhaka Mandala* (see Appendix 1).

The bankers and their networks facilitated a range of mercantile and monetary transactions such as transfer of funds, brokering deals, making advances, changing money and exacting outstanding loans. A useful account of these activities can be found in the collection of papers titled *Peshwaichya Sawaleet* or 'In the Shadows of the Peshwa Epoch' by N.G. Chapekar. The collection draws from three eminent banking families of Pune, the Tulshibagwale, the Chiplonkar and the Khasgiwale. Papers from two other families, the Vaidyas of Wai and the Subhedars (Biwalkars) of Kalyan, are also included.

To transfer money, the bankers availed of the indigenous system of *Hundi* or bills of exchange that had differing conditions of encashment. The system allowed 'transactional domains' of money to be connected and help money flow across them. Depending on the way a Hundi could be encashed, there were several different types of *Hundis* – Chapekar mentions *Bhalāwan*, *Shahā Wyāpāri jog*, *Jāgā hundi*, etc. (138–139). Most hundis also contained a period of validity. *Hundis* payable at sight could be sold before encashment – there is a mention of a *Hundi* drawn from Paithan to be payable at Satara, being sold at Pune (134). *Hundis* could be drawn from one office and then transferred to another: a note of AD 1788 mentions a *Hundi* drawn for one Balkrishna Appaji for Aurangabad, with an instruction to the office that it should be drawn for Ujjain when presented at Aurangabad. *Hundi* transactions involved a commission, which was usually 1% or 1.5% on the amount transferred. Chapekar's data shows *Hundi* transactions occurring between Paithan, Satara, Srirangapattan, Pune, Mumbai, Kashi (Banaras), Aurangabad and Ujjain.

The bankers of Pune made huge cash advances and the figures in receipts published by Chapekar are a testimony to that (120–122). Among the debtors of the Tulshibagwale are important statesmen and barons like the Gaekwars of Baroda, the Pant Sachivs of Bhor, the Bhonsles of Nagpur, the Patwardhans and so on. In one month alone, the Tulshibagwale office is recorded to have issued *Hundis* worth 1,42,502 rupees (122). Occasionally, a *Hundi* was refused and then money in cash had to be physically sent (148 – 'सरकारी पोतेचालाची हुंडी पाठवली ती न पटे म्हणून सिका करून पाठवले'). In many instances, there are mentions of security deposits made against cash advances. These could be anything from a weapon to cloth to a valuable ornament or metal or even a stable of horses. In one case, a female slave (कुणबीण) is placed as a security deposit for an advance of 20 rupees.[13]

How money travelled between parties through the banker was a complicated affair. Money was transferred through pay orders or *warāts* or by forward accounting or *hawālā*. In most instances recorded by Chapekar, a middleman is involved. For the Tulshibagwale banking firm, this was a person by the name Keshavbhatt Karve, ostensibly a Brahmin by his name. Some accounting papers reproduced by Chapekar record complex transactions of sums being transferred between various accounts, for example, towards payment in the government treasury, against advances made previously, charging commissions applicable for encashing the pay orders, deducting interest and other expenses like *Darbar Kharch* ('court expenditure'). This last term was a euphemism for an expense incurred for 'oiling' the encashment processes such as payments rendered for execution of the transfer transaction (71–75) so that it proceeds smoothly. To pay a sum for what otherwise would be only a procedural matter appears to be a malpractice; however, as per Chapekar's records, it was evidently institutionalized because a fixed rate per cent is quoted for it in the expense statement! (See Appendix 2 for a couple of entries from the Tulshibagwale papers published by Chapekar. They exemplify the way such transactions were carried out and recorded.)

The banking houses had to change money for a number of reasons while conducting their business. When a bill of exchange like a *Hundi* was encashed, the money in which it is to be paid was often mentioned in its text, and the sum was paid in that coin. Sometimes, the sum was received in a coin different from that which was promised. In such cases, an appropriate commission or *Batta* was charged. An entry in the Tulshibagwale papers shows a debit of 156.25 'new Rahimatpuri' rupees, which were received in lieu of 125 'Mirji' rupees. Therefore, a commission of 31.25 rupees was added to the amount. This was based on a commission rate of 25%

between 'Mirji' and 'Rahimatpuri' rupees (100 'Mirji' rupees were equal to 125 'Rahimatpuri' rupees). The papers indicate that the commission rates were of two kinds – a prescribed or governmental rate (*Sarkari dar* सरकारी दर / बटा) and a market rate (*Sarafi* सराफी or *Bazar dar* बाजार दर / बटा). A commission was paid at various stages in the circulation of coins. As mentioned earlier, as they circulated coins lost their value and had to be tested. As value was lost, the coins changed their status from one circulatory grade to another. So when a new circulatory grade was assigned, a suitable discount was added and the coin depreciated. Sometimes, coins of an inferior grade were exchanged for those of a better grade, so a premium had to be paid for such a transaction. There is a curious charge mentioned in some entries in which the coins are said to have been 'brightened' (144). This appears to be a figure of speech for having changed them to a superior circulatory grade. Exchange rates were applicable when fractions of a particular coin were required and full rupees were changed for them and also when coins were exchanged across the metallic regime, i.e. when gold mohurs were exchanged for silver rupees and vice versa. (See Appendix 3 for a chart of exchange rates of some coins.).

A part of the transactional domain of money was occupied also by 'criminal space'. Coins would often be forged using innovative techniques. Some criminals struck in an opportunistic manner, in places like a Bazar. We find a mention in the *Pune Nagara Samshodhana Writtanta* (PNSW) that a person who was trying to peddle Malkapuri rupees 'filled with lead'. When he was apprehended, spurious coins were found on him. An entry in the Chiplonkar family's ledger shows a loss of one rupee because it was made of copper (142). There were a number of other ways by which circulating currency could be sabotaged, such as tampering with design features that distinguished the coins into grades of purity, or by diverting particularly pure coins into making those which were comparatively more debased, or by removing metal illicitly from coins. I have described these malpractices elsewhere.[14]

The linguistic space of money

An interesting aspect of the authoritative domain of money, which is not discussed by Cohen, is the language money generates as it circulates. In eighteenth- to nineteenth-century Maharashtra, there appear to be many words and names that are related to money, its consumption and practices involved in it. Some of them had already gone arcane and out of use by the time Chapekar authored his compilation in the mid-twentieth century. He, therefore, grapples with the meaning of certain terms like 'Chhapi' छापी or 'Panchmel' पंचमेल / पंचमेळ which are encountered in the banking houses' financial papers that he publishes. The explanation for such terms is given in the discussion below.

Coins were usually identified by names. These could be classified into six categories.[15] They were:

1 Named after the inscription on the coins, particularly the name in which they were struck. Examples: *Muhammadshahi/Ahmadashahi* (struck in the name of Muhammad Shah or Ahmad Shah, both Mughal emperors), *Achyutarayi* (bearing the name of Achyuta Deva Raya, the king of Vijayanagar).
2 Named after the place of issue. Examples: *Dilli Sikka*, *Kasi Sikka*, *Chandwadi*, etc., ostensibly named after where they were struck.
3 Named after the person who struck them, either a political authority or the licensee. Example: *Malharshahi*, named after Malhar Bhikaji Raste, the banker and moneyer operating mints at Wai in Maharashtra and at Bagalkot, Athni and Bijapur in Karnataka.
4 Named after a numismatic feature, such as a symbol. This was perhaps the most common way to name coins. Examples: *Ankushi* (symbol of Ankush), *Jaripatka* (with a symbol of a pennant), *Shri Sikka* (from the letter 'Shri' added as a differentiating symbol).
5 Named after particular circulatory conditions that the coin fulfilled. Chandwadi rupees accepted in or changeable at markets in Vasai would be called *Vasai-chal Chandwadi* rupees. The suffix '*-chalnee*' in a name often indicated the circulatory grade of the coin. Hence, '*Peth-chalnee*' would mean a coin of a grade usually acceptable in a *peth* or market. Clunes mentions 'Kurdee Parikh' (करडी पारख in Marathi) or 'rigorous testing/assessment' as a pre-requisite for differentiating coins in various circulatory grades (1–2). Thus, the 'Ankushi' rupee would usually be differentiated in three grades, *viz. Kora* or 'Numbree', *Madhyam* and *Naram*; however, after 'Kurdee Parikh', two more grades, namely *Rahat Saul* and *Sulakhi*, were distinguished, the former between *Kora* and *Madhyam* and the latter being the lowest below *Naram*. This distinction was important because the grades decided how much discount would be applied when these coins were changed or remitted.

It would be worthwhile at this juncture to return to Chapekar's misapprehension regarding the term '*chhapi*', by which he obviously took to mean bearing a 'stamp'. But being 'stamped' between dies is an essential feature of any coin, though Chapekar wonders what it might specifically mean. The verb form, 'to make / render *chhapi*' छापी करणे confuses him even more. The word no doubt comes from the verb that means 'to impress or imprint' but in the particular context of circulating currency, it refers to getting the coin 'impressed' with a mark, i.e. to make known that it has been tested for its genuineness, weight and purity. *Kora* refers to a coin fresh out of the mint, while it is rendered *chhapi* as it circulates and receives attestation marks. Since the value of a 'fresh' coin was higher, it was important to designate a coin that had been in circulation as such, because it would lose its value through being circulated. Chhapi is thus a circulatory descriptor and since the practice of testing coins as they circulated had virtually been unknown in the twentieth century, the word too had lost its meaning, thus leading to Chapekar's confusion.

6 General terms and names – included in this category are names which denoted a general category or group of coins, rather than particular issues. A term like *potechal* has already been referred to and would serve as a good example. The other term that confounded Chapekar was *panchmel* and that too is a general term. Chapekar's confusion appears to have resulted from the fact that he took the word in its literal meaning, which is 'an aggregate made of five different things'. Chapekar wonders if such a coin was made with an alloy of five metals. But in fact, the term is listed in the Marathi dictionary of Molesworth to mean, figuratively 'any heterogeneously composed assembly'. Thus, the term is ostensibly used as a synonym for 'assortment', in many instances a group of coins which can either be treated as an aggregate for a single exchange rate. Sometimes, the word is also used in the sense of 'non-specific'.

Judging from the description above, we see that money circulation in pre-modern Maharashtra was a complicated affair. It was controlled through several nexuses – the State often abrogated or outsourced its right to coin to private parties who would buy a licence. These private entities were also engaged in rendering the coins 'circulatable' and keeping money flowing through instruments of credit and transfer. The consumers of coins were often at the mercy of these entities. They also created and fostered elaborate systems out of they could make money as it was issued, circulated and recycled.

Epilogue

In the foregoing discussion, I have attempted to highlight how money worked, in its authoritative and transactional domains, in eighteenth- to nineteenth-century Maharashtra in the context of 'place' and 'space'. Within the authoritative domain of money, we can envisage a 'monetary space' that can be defined by more than one character. In a circulatory context, such a space can be envisaged by areas in which particular coin types circulated, going through the cycle of issuance, consumption and recycling. Places like towns where mints producing the coins were located could well be visualized as markers for the extent of this circulatory space, but as they were often producing coins of a particular type, the numismatic identity of the coinage also contributed to defining the space. Various factors, such as circulatory realities, practices and interventions of entities like the government or other agencies which rendered the coins 'circulatable' significantly altered the dynamics between places and the space they populated and contributed to. Administrative protocols or political conditions also played their role in the emergence and articulation of these dynamics. Language often reflected these practices and thus created its own 'space' in the various domains and dynamics money operated in.

An interesting insight in a conceptual manner into the place-space interactions so far as money circulation is concerned is the fact that money created spaces which were unifying as well as fragmenting. With one predominant type at its heart, the monetary space, even though inhabited by many places (which struck coins of that type), could be seen as a 'unifying' space. But the complexities involved in the circulation of money meant that 'uniformity' was not a virtue of currency in eighteenth- to nineteenth-century Maharashtra. It was produced only after colonial intervention after the end of the Maratha rule. It was not a smooth process; it meant a thorough reworking of the precolonial monetary order. It was eventually achieved through curtailing the rights and privileges held by the moneyed elite with regard to coinage, by clamping down on the practice of discounting coins, and by the advent of mechanised coinage, which was uniform, standardized and trustworthy, and satisfied the demand for coined currency needed in a monetary space that had effectively and extensively been monetized. However, that is a subject for another paper! In this chapter, I have shown how money circulation in pre-modern Maharashtra can be viewed in terms of 'places' and 'spaces', both from a conceptual and a physical point of view.

Notes

1 Benjamin Cohen, *The Geography of Money*, Ithaca: Cornell University Press, 1998.

2 Arjun Appadurai, 'Disjuncture and Difference in the Global Cultural Economy', *Public Culture* 2, no. 2 (Spring), 1990, p. 8. See also Appadurai, *Modernity at Large: Cultural Dimension of Globalization*, University of Minnesota Press, Minneapolis/London, 1998, pp. 33–35.

3 V. P. Pingulkar, *Sawantwadi Sansthancha Itihasa*, Sawantwadi, 1911, p. 139.

4 Y. N. Kelkar, *Kahi Aprasiddha Aitihasika Charitre*, Pune, 1967: 25, p. 16.

विपुल त्या रास्त्यांच्या घरी आजवर संतत संपत्ती
इचलकर्जीकर बारामतीकर सोयऱ्यांत धनपती
पहा कृष्णराव चासकर साजणी
कोंकणचे कोल्हटकर साजणी
दीक्षित-पेठे-साठे-ओक-ओंकार सभाग्यामधी
फाटक-थत्ते-बर्वे-देवधर-पेंडशांची रीत सुधी

5 Chapekar, N. G., *Peshwaichya Sawaleet*, BISM-sponsored series no. 34, Pune, 1937, p. 34.

6 Chapekar, *Peshwaichya Sawaleet*, p. 139.

7 Pune Nagara Samshodhana Wruttanta, ed. C. G. Karve, vol. 2. BISM, Pune, 1943, p. 155.

8 Shailendra Bhandare, 'More about the Maratha Mint at Chandor and Its Coinage', *Numismatic Digest*, 23–24, 1999–2000, p. 121.

9 For a detailed discussion of these coins, see Paul J. E. Stevens, 'The Coins of the Bombay Presidency: Transitional Mints of the Deccan', *Journal of the Oriental*

Numismatic Society, no. 181, 2004, pp. 21–30 and Paul J. E. Stevens, 'The Coins of the Bombay Presidency: The Transitional Mints of the Southern Maratha Country', *Journal of the Oriental Numismatic Society*, no. 183, 2005, pp. 20–22.

10 J. Clunes, *List of Rupees Most Current in Poona, with the Relative Value of Each Per Centum at This Date, to the Poona Hallee Sicca or Standard Rupee of Account among the Sahukars &c. Memorandum*, India Office Library, Vol. 1 of tracts, 1829, pp. 1–8.

11 S. Bhandare, 'Coinage of the Habshi Rulers of Janjira', *Oriental Numismatic Society Newsletter* 178, 2004, pp. 28–35.

12 Lawrence P. Preston, *The Devs of Cincvad: A Lineage and the State in Maharashtra*, Cambridge University Press, Cambridge/Hyderabad, 1988, pp. 128–135.

13 This sum seems too low to be equivalent for a human deposit; perhaps it is a printing mistake for 200 rupees.

14 S. Bhandare, 'Peshawekaleena Nanepaddhati', *Samshodhak*, Quarterly of the Rajwade Samshodhan Mandal, Dhule, Year 65, parts 1–2, 1996–1997, December 1996, pp. 20–21.

15 Bhandare, 'Peshawekaleena Nanepaddhati', pp. 6–8.

References

Appadurai, Arjun. *Modernity at Large: Cultural Dimension of Globalization*. University of Minnesota Press, Minneapolis/London, 1998.

Appadurai, Arjun. 'Disjuncture and Difference in the Global Cultural Economy', *Public Culture* 2, no. 2 (Spring) 1990: 1–24.

Bhandare, S. 'Coinage of the Habshi rulers of Janjira', *Oriental Numismatic Society Newsletter* 178, 2004: 28–35.

Bhandare, S. 'Peshawekaleena Nanepaddhati', *Samshodhak*, Quarterly of the Rajwade Samshodhan Mandal, Dhule, Year 65, parts 1–2, 1996–1997, published December 1996: 3–25.

Chapekar, N. G. *Peshwaichya Sawaleet*, BISM-sponsored series no. 34, Pune, 1937.

Clunes, J. *List of Rupees Most Current in Poona, with the Relative Value of Each Per Centum at This Date, to the Poona Hallee Sicca or Standard Rupee of Account among the Sahukars &c. Memorandum*, India Office Library, Vol. 1 of tracts, 1829.

Cohen, Benjamin. *The Geography of Money*. Cornell University Press, Ithaca/London, 1998.

Kelkar, Y. N. *Kahi Aprasiddha Aitihasika Charitre*. Continental Prakashan, Pune, 1967.

Pingulkar, V. P. *Sawantwadi Sansthancha Itihasa*, Sawantwadi, 1911.

Preston, Lawrence P. *The Devs of Cincvad: A Lineage and the State in Maharashtra*. Cambridge University Press, Cambridge/Hyderabad, 1988.

Pune Nagara Samshodhana Wruttanta. Ed. C. G. Karve, vol. 2. BISM, Pune, 1943.

Stevens, Paul J. E. 'The Coins of the Bombay Presidency: Transitional Mints of the Deccan', *Journal of the Oriental Numismatic Society*, no. 181, 2004: 21–30.

Stevens, Paul J. E. 'The Coins of the Bombay Presidency: The Transitional Mints of the Southern Maratha Country', *Journal of the Oriental Numismatic Society*, no. 183, 2005: 20–22.

Chapter 6

Architectural continuity across political ruptures

Early Marathas and the Deccan sultanates

Pushkar Sohoni

Introduction

In the late sixteenth and early seventeenth centuries, the sultanates of the early modern Deccan resisted the Mughals. Of these, the sultanate of the Nizam Shahs of Ahmadnagar was conquered by the Mughals in the early seventeenth century and completely vanquished by 1636. The sultanates of the Adil Shahs of Bijapur and the Qutb Shahs of Golconda were not annexed by the Mughals till late in the seventeenth century, in 1686–1687. But the downfall of the Nizam Shahs did not mean that no other group in the northern and western Deccan resisted the Mughals. In the political vacuum created by the downfall of the Nizam Shahs, a new independent and sovereign kingdom of the Marathas was established by Shivaji Bhonsale (1630–1680). The Marathas had served the various sultanates as military commanders and small fief-holders for 200 years preceding this event. Thus, even as the Maratha kingdom served as a political rupture, a cultural continuum between the Nizam Shahs and the Maratha kingdom was retained. Shivaji's own father had been an important commander for the Nizam Shahs, as had both his maternal and paternal grandfathers.

In this essay, we will principally consider three buildings built by the early Marathas, two by Shivaji's maternal and paternal grandfather, respectively, and one commissioned under Shivaji himself, to highlight and argue for the connections and continuities with the architecture of the Deccan sultanates in the seventeenth century.[1]

Early Marathas and the sultanates

The Marathas emerged as an ethnic group in a period from 1350 to 1700, and several of their families claimed Rajpur genealogies.[2] Similar to the process of identity formation among the Rajputs in northern India a few centuries earlier, the Marathas became the indigenous warrior-elites of the Deccan sultanates.[3] They were important nobility at the Bahamani court and later at the courts of the post-Bahamani sultanates. They received land grants and revenue rights from several sultanates, and in practice operated as independent rulers over their fiefdoms, while professing loyalty to the various sultans of the Deccan. Their received martial tradition and land grants in the form of *inām*, *jāgīr* and *vatan* distinguished them as a new caste identity.[4] Over time, their cultural practices, because of their association with the sultanate courts, were heavily Persianized and they used names, titles and the administrative and military nomenclature. They formed the building blocks of the sultanates, and as James Laine noted, '[a]ll the rival sultans of that period necessarily courted powerful Hindu chiefs, who styled themselves "Rajas" and thought of themselves as both feudatory Ksatriyas and servants of the Muslim Shahs'.[5] The Nizam Shahs had employed large numbers of Marathas in their armies, and with the downfall of the sultanate, several of the nobility switched allegiance to the Adil Shahs or the Mughals. But Shivaji had different ambitions: punishing those who opposed him, and rallying the others who joined him, he rebelled against the Adil Shahs, under whom his father nominally served.

Yet, barring a few buildings, until 1700 the early Marathas leave behind very few architectural markers of their power, other than military fortifications. Their patronage of architecture and art is curiously absent, and the reason for that may be the nature of their buildings, which were also built in the same mode as those of the sultanates. They most likely employed the same craftsmen and guilds who were commissioned for sultanate architecture, making sultanate and early Maratha architecture stylistically indistinguishable for the most part.

Arguably, the Mughals delayed annexing the sultanates of Bijapur and Golconda because they feared catalysing the emergence of more independent resistance movements like the Marathas, as it would cause a power vacuum in those lands. Aurangzeb annexed those two sultanates only after the death of Shivaji in 1680, after which the Mughals finally had the upper hand in the Deccan.

Shivaji and the later Marathas

Shivaji founded an independent kingdom in the territories where his father had received a fief after the distribution of Nizam Shahi lands between the Mughals and the Adil Shahs. For almost half a century, he battled the Mughals, and between campaigns, had little time to be a patron of architecture. Barring fortifications and military architecture, there were few other buildings constructed in his reign, many of them on Raigad, which he built as his capital. The Jagadīśvara temple at Raigad constructed in about 1674 is one such building that can be attributed to him.

The Maratha kingdom founded by Shivaji was in crisis after the capture and execution of his son Sambhaji (1657–1689), after which his family was taken into Mughal custody. Chhatrapati Shahu (1682–1749), the son of

Sambhaji and the grandson of Shivaji, was raised in Mughal custody and eventually acquired the Maratha throne only in 1708, after several struggles with other claimants from the family.[6] The Mughals had released him thinking that he would be sympathetic to their cause, but after the death of Aurangzeb in 1707, the Mughal court itself was in disarray, and several factions at court were being played against each other by king-makers such as the Sayyid brothers. In this turbulent period, in 1718, Shahu's Peshwa (prime minister) Balaji Vishwanath Bhat (1662–1720) negotiated a treaty with the Mughals, by which the Marathas received land rights to large areas of the Deccan. In return, the Maratha Chhatrapati acknowledged the nominal overlordship of the Mughal emperor.[7] From this period onwards, the artistic and architectural vocabulary of the Maratha state was fashioned by the visual culture of the Mughals who became their ceremonial masters. The Nizam ul-Mulk (1671–1748) of Hyderabad, who was the other token representative of the Mughals in the Deccan, also followed Mughal high fashion in his architecture in the eastern Deccan; though his state was also nominally under the Mughals, he ruled autonomously. Thus, as the Mughal state faltered and lost actual power in the Deccan, the *de jure* and normative empire of the Mughals comprised the territories that were under the control of the Marathas and the Nizam. Both of them adopted Mughal architecture, as they fashioned themselves as the new Mughals. Through the course of the eighteenth century, as the Marathas expanded into northern India and received revenue rights from the powerless Mughal court in Delhi, they further emulated the Mughal court in their patronage of architecture and art, competing with the Rajput courts who were well-entrenched in Mughal culture for over a century. Thus, as the Maratha confederacy became the most powerful force in India, it completely gave in to the architectural language of power, which in South Asia was derived from the Mughals. This essay is thus limited to a period before 1700. Just as political power was architecturally expressed in a Mughal visual language after then, it was the sultanates which defined the cosmopolitan and political aspirations of sovereignty before the eighteenth century.

Early Maratha architecture

Two of the earliest building sites for the Marathas are Sindkhed Raja and the village of Verul (Ellora). The settlements were the *jagir*s of the Jadhav and the Bhonsale families, respectively, awarded to them as important nobility of the Nizam Shahs. Both sites have several buildings, but are without inscriptions, and therefore, the evidence is largely anecdotal, circumstantial and visual. Yet the buildings at Ellora and Sindkhed Raja bear a striking visual semblance to the architecture of the Deccan sultans. In contrast, the temple of Jagadīśvara at Raigad, built by Shivaji around 1674, is a rare example of a firmly attributed and dated early Maratha building. This building too resonates with the architecture of the Adil Shahs, who were then in their last decade of architectural flourish.

Ellora (Verul)

The village of Ellora was the hereditary fief of the Bhonsale family, and they enjoyed the grant in perpetuity from the Nizam Shahs. Not only was it prestigious on account of being so close to Daulatabad and Khuldabad, it was also the site of an important temple, that of Ghrishneshwara. The present temple building dates from the eighteenth century, when Ahilyabai Holkar contributed to its renewal and construction, probably on the same site as the original. Ellora is just below the elevated plateau of Khuldabad, a famous necropolis of several hundred saints, and generally considered to be an important place with *barakat* (divine blessing).[8] Several important people and saints were buried here, including Malik Ambar (1548–1626), whose grand mausoleum is close to that of the Sufi saint Shah Muntajab ud-din Zar Zari Zar Bakhsh (died late fourteenth century CE). Malik Ambar served as the regent of the Nizam Shahs since around 1600 CE, and it was under him that Shahaji Bhonsale (father of Shivaji) served the Nizam Shah kingdom, particularly valorously at the battle of Bhatavdi.[9] The Bhonsales were the *de facto* and *de jure* patrons of the early Ghrishneshwara temple and leave behind some traces of their patronage of the site in the form of *chhatries* (funerary memorials) around the temple building. They are arranged around the temple much in the same way that the tombs of important people are situated about the *dargah* of a holy man. The latter is seen at Khuldabad, as in the tomb of Malik Ambar, and later the Mughal Emperor Alamgir Aurangzeb (1618–1707) who is buried in the vicinity of the Chishti saint Shaikh Zainuddin Shirazi. There are three memorials around the temple of Ghrishneshwara, of which the one to the south is identified as that of Maloji Bhonsale, grandfather of Shivaji Bhonsale. The one to the north is unidentified but does not have a cenotaph. The third *chhatri* is to the west of the temple and actually has a cenotaph inside. It is very likely a Muslim tomb. The spatial arrangement of these three memorials around the temple is not dissimilar to the pattern of tombs around that of a Sufi saint. Again, it is notable that the distance from Ellora to Khuldabad as the crow flies is barely two kilometres.

The ornamental details on the memorial buildings are like those on the tomb of Malik Ambar and also on buildings in Bijapur.

Sindkhed Raja

The Jadhavs or Jadhavraos served with distinction at the court of the Nizam Shahs of Ahmadnagar, and this village and surrounding lands were their fief. Emulating the court that they served, they built a large fortified mansion upon receiving the grant sometime around 1550.[10] This structure is now celebrated as being the birthplace of Jijabai, Shivaji's mother. Another fortified palace was left incomplete by the Jadhavs, possibly because they lost their lands in 1650 when an envoy of the Mughal emperor, Murshid Ali Khan, was displeased with his reception, and turned them over to a local *Qazi*'s family.[11] The fortified mansion is similar to several Nizam Shahi forts, and the Jadhavs would have tried to create their own smaller version of the ruling Nizam Shah's residence, including court ceremonials and rituals. Such emulation of architecture and ceremony was a strategy of legitimization, by which every entity in the nested hierarchy at court ultimately created a smaller image of the royal court.

In Sindkhed Raja are two dams built by the Jadhavs, and the one built by the Bada Talav has a resting chamber inside the thickness of the dam wall. This is similar to arrangements made by sultanate royal families, such as the Adil Shahs of Bijapur, who had conceptualized a similar arrangement at Naldurg. The lake called Chandani Talav has a pavilion built in its midst, which is accessible only by boat. Similar pavilions and palaces set in the midst of water bodies can be seen at Hasht Bihisht in Ahmadnagar built by the Nizam Shahs, and at Hauz Katora near Ellichpur, which was built by the Imad Shahs. But the most dramatic structure at Sindkhed Raja is undoubtedly the memorial dedicated to Lakhuji Jadhav, the father of Jijabai and grandfather of Shivaji. A large building built of stone, and about twelve metres on every side, it has a brick dome on top. It is decorated with a number of *kirtimukha*s and also bears depictions of lions triumphant over elephants, a motif commonly found across the Deccan in this period, and associated with royal and military architecture.[12] The bases of the cantoning pilasters on the building deserve notice, as they are similar to several buildings across the Deccan sultanates, including the Jal Mandir in Bijapur.

There are two artificial lakes around the village of Sindkhed Raja. In one of them, the Bada Talav, the masonry dam that creates the lake has a large resting chamber within its thickness. Similar to the set of rooms within the dam at Naldurg fort which was built by the Adil Shahs, such a space would have been used in the summers. The second lake, the Chandani Talav, has a pavilion in the midst of the water body, reminiscent of the lake pavilions of the Hasht Bihisht Palace at Ahmadnagar and the Hauz Katora outside Ellipur. The fortified mansion of the Jadhavs (Shivaji's maternal family) has several features that resonate with the pavilions of the Deccan sultanates, including triple-bayed loggias that can also be seen at various forts, tombs and palaces of the Adil Shahs, Nizam Shahs and Qutb Shahs.

The most striking building at Sindkhed Raja is the grand memorial built for Lakhuji Jadhav, the maternal grandfather of Shivaji. It is designed with a large brick dome on top of the building and is approximately sixteen metres in length on all sides. The walls all bear three blind arches, and on the eastern side is the entrance, placed centrally. Inside is a stone pavilion, about three metres square, within which is a *śivaliṅga* marking the actual location of the *samādhi*. This inner sanctum is entered from the south. In the four corners of the building are the *samādhi*s of the sons of Lakhuji. These too are marked by *śivaliṅga*s. There are several other smaller memorials to other members of the Jadhav family around Lakhuji's memorial. The site is in the proximity of Rameśvara and Nilakaṇṭheśvara temples, both associated with the Jadhav family.[13] The arrangement of the various memorials around that of Lakhuji is worthy of note and is expounded upon later. The ornament on the memorials is also comparable to that in Bijapur and Golconda, particularly the motif of rosettes on brackets in high relief.

Raigad

One of the few non-military buildings that can be firmly dated to the reign of Shivaji is the Jagadīśvara temple in the fort of Raigad. Built around the time of Shivaji's coronation (1674), it does not conform to any of the proportions of temples in medieval India.[14] Very clearly, the masons and artisans employed to work on this temple were used to making mosques and other buildings in the region. Architecturally, it is made up of two masonry cubes that comprise the sanctum and the enclosed hall in front of it. The massing is similar to several buildings from Bijapur, notably the entrance gate to the Ibrahim Rauza. Importantly, the dome and the finials are just like those on small mosques in the Bijapur sultanate, and reminiscent more of Islamic architecture than Hindu temples. Perhaps the composite nature of the Maratha-sultanate architecture is best encapsulated in the entrance doorway to the temple, which has over it a bas-relief in stone, bearing the motif of two minarets connected by decorative merlons. The architectural totality of the temple, in terms of elements and ornament, are completely related to the architecture of the Deccan sultanates and not with the early medieval temples built under the Yadavas. It is this coincidence of architectural forms that complicate the erroneous and simplistic narratives of Hindu and Muslim architecture, the former represented by the Marathas and the latter by the sultanates and Mughals.

Conclusion

The Maratha Empire ensured the survival of a sultanate idiom of architecture in the Deccan for over half a century in two ways. First, they kept the Mughal takeover of Bijapur and Golconda at bay, thus ensuring architectural patronage under those kingdoms as the latter constantly negotiated their status under Jahangir, Shah Jahan and then Aurangzeb. More importantly, they constructed in the same idiom as the Deccan sultanates thus carrying on the legacy of Deccan sultanate architecture. It might be imprudent to suggest that that the Marathas and the sultanates deployed an architectural strategy of resistance until the Mughals and their architecture swept through the Deccan in the early eighteenth century. A fair conclusion is that Maratha visual culture and polity were so deeply embedded in the court culture of the sultanate Deccan that there was no way to distinguish between their courtly and cultural practices, barring obvious religious ones. There has been a lot of recent scholarship on the popular religious culture and practices of the sixteenth- and seventeenth-century Deccan, which could not be neatly categorized into Hindu and Muslim binaries.[15] Similarly, the architectural patronage and practices of the early Marathas in the sixteenth and seventeenth centuries cannot be isolated from the sultanate culture in which they were entrenched. The eighteenth century would see the rise of a Mughal courtly and visual culture throughout the Deccan, as the sultanates came to an end, and the later Marathas under the Peshwas were reliant on their nominal vassalage to the Mughal emperor.

Notes

1 A version of this chapter was presented at the Maharashtra Studies Conference in Aurangabad in January 2016, and it has been published in the *Archives of Asian Art* in vol. 68, no. 1 (April 2018), pp. 33–46.
2 Stewart Gordon, *The Marathas: 1600–1818* (Cambridge: Cambridge University Press, 1993), p. 14.
3 Stewart Gordon, *The Marathas*, p. 17, 'The defining of Maratha as a new caste category continued throughout the period of the Maratha polity and into the nineteenth century, along the lines of the Rajput model …'.
4 Stewart Gordon, *The Marathas*, p. 15.
5 James Laine, 'Hindus and Muslims in the Age of Sivaji', in Sushil Mittal (ed.), *Surprising Bedfellows: Hindus and Muslims in Mediaeval and Early Modern India* (Lanham, MD: Lexington Books, 2003), p. 24.
6 Stewart Gordon, *The Marathas*, p. 101.
7 Stewart Gordon, *The Marathas*, p. 110.
8 Nile Green, 'Who's the King of the Castle? Brahmins, Sufis and the Narrative Landscape of Daulatabad', in *Contemporary South Asia*, vol. 14 no. 1, pp. 21–37.
9 A.R. Kulkarni, *Jedhe Shakavali-Karina* (Pune: Manasanaman Publishers, 1999), p. 43; James W. Laine and S.S. Bahulkar, *The Epic of Shivaji: Kavindra Paramananda's Śivabhārata* (Hyderabad: Orient Longman, 2001), Canto 4, pp. 76–84.
10 *Maharashtra State Gazetteers: Buldhana District* (revised edition) (Bombay: Gazetteers Department, Government of Maharashtra, 1976), p. 795.
11 *Maharashtra State Gazetteers: Buldhana District* (revised edition), p. 795.
12 Pushkar Sohoni, 'Old Fights, New Meanings: Lions and Elephants in Combat', in *Res: Anthropology and Aesthetics*, vol. 67/68 (2016/2017), pp. 225–234.
13 For basic information on these temples, see R.C. Agrawal, *Archaeological Remains in Western India* (New Delhi: Agam Kala Prakashan, 1989), pp. 81–85 *passim*.
14 Śrīnanda Lakśmaṇa Bāpaṭa, 'Rāyagaḍāvarīla Jagadīśvarācyā abhilekhāce punarvācana', in *Bharat Itihas Sanshodhak Mandal Quarterly*, vol. 86, nos. 1–4 (July 2009–April 2010), pp. 74–83.

15 Dušan Deák, 'Maharashtra Saints and the Sufi Tradition: Eknath, Chand Bodhale and the Datta Sampradaya', in *Journal of Deccan Studies*, vol. 3, no. 2 (July–December 2005), pp. 22–47; Pushkar Sohoni, 'Vernacular as a Space: Writing in the Deccan', in *South Asian History and Culture*, vol. 7, no. 3 (April 2016), pp. 258–270.

References

Agrawal, R.C. *Archaeological Remains in Western India*. New Delhi: Agam Kala Prakashan, 1989.

Bāpaṭa, Śrīnanda Lakśmaṇa. 'Rāyagaḍāvarīla Jagadīśvarācyā abhilekhāce punarvācana', in *Bharat Itihas Sanshodhak Mandal Quarterly*, vol. 86, nos. 1–4 (July 2009–April 2010), 74–83.

Deák, Dušan. 'Maharashtra Saints and the Sufi Tradition: Eknath, Chand Bodhale and the Datta Sampradaya', in *Journal of Deccan Studies*, vol. 3, no. 2 (July–December 2005), 22–47.

Gordon, Stewart. *The Marathas: 1600–1818*. Cambridge: Cambridge University Press, 1993.

Green, Nile. 'Who's the King of the Castle? Brahmins, Sufis and the Narrative Landscape of Daulatabad'. In *Contemporary South Asia*, vol. 14 no. 1, 2005, 21–37.

Kulkarni, A.R. *Jedhe Shakavali-Karina*. Pune: Manasanaman Publishers, 1999.

Laine, James W. and S. S. Bahulkar. *The Epic of Shivaji: Kavindra Paramananda's Śivabhārata*. Hyderabad: Orient Longman, 2001.

Laine, James. 'Hindus and Muslims in the Age of Sivaji', in Sushil Mittal (ed.), *Surprising Bedfellows: Hindus and Muslims in Mediaeval and Early Modern India*. Lanham, MD: Lexington Books, 2003.

Maharashtra State Gazetteers: Buldhana District (revised edition). Bombay: Gazetteers Department, Government of Maharashtra, 1976.

Sohoni, Pushkar. 'Vernacular as a Space: Writing in the Deccan'. In *South Asian History and Culture*, vol. 7, no. 3 (April 2016), 258–270.

Sohoni, Pushkar. 'Old Fights, New Meanings: Lions and Elephants in Combat'. In *Res: Anthropology and Aesthetics*, vol. 67/68 (2016/2017), 225–234.

Chapter 7

Blurred lines

Historical knowledge and the politics of statues

Daniel Jasper

Introduction

Chhatrapati Shivaji Maharaj, the seventeenth-century Maratha king[1] who reigned in Western India, remains a powerful cultural touchstone in the Marathi-speaking region. In the late 1800s, anti-colonial leaders rediscovered the memory and legacy of Shivaji Maharaj. With Shivaji Maharaj, they found a symbolic icon that could rally the people to challenge the British Raj.[2] Over the past 150 years, Shivaji has been commemorated in a number of ways and has been posited as the representative and/or protector of a number of different groups based on characteristics such as caste, religion, language, as well as occupation and nationality.[3]As Shivaji's legacy was celebrated, commemorative cues came to mark the urban and rural landscape of Maharashtra, the state of Western India established in 1960 during the linguistic reorganization of the Indian states to consolidate the Marathi-speaking population.

Statues commemorating Shivaji Maharaj serve as a point of departure for this chapter, where I explore the politics of history, focusing on the social and cultural conditions that lead to the construction and unveiling of statues. In this way, I focus on the functions that statues play in symbolizing and sanctifying social groups. In particular, I seek to use statues of Shivaji Maharaj to think broadly about statues as spaces of knowledge. What are the conceptual frameworks that make memorials a meaningful space for making sense of the past? Why does it make sense to direct one's material and political resources towards statues? I suggest that statues, memorials, and other commemorations are specific ways of engaging with the past. Statues are socially and culturally situated, encoding particular ways of knowing the past, discerning the relevance of the past for the present day and authorizing particular meanings of the past. In addressing the social functions of statues, I also reflect on how statues are sites where boundaries are established and maintained, demarcating the lines separating those included in the social group from those who are excluded. Using statues of Shivaji Maharaj to provide examples, I show how the boundaries of social inclusion and solidarity have shifted and blurred alongside the politics of creating statues.

Shivaji in the Arabian Sea

On 24 December 2016, Indian Prime Minister Narendra Modi laid the foundation stone for a new statue of Shivaji Maharaj off the coast of Mumbai in the Arabian Sea. In Mumbai, formerly Bombay, all of the major transit gateways are named after Shivaji – both the international and domestic airport terminals are named after him; the majestic train station in south Mumbai, once known as Victoria Terminus, is now called Chhatrapati Shivaji Terminus; and beyond the gateway of India, built to welcome the arrival of King George V in 1911, lies a large equestrian statue of Shivaji Maharaj, which sits at the end of Shivaji Marg (Road). Symbolically, in order to arrive in the cosmopolitan city of Mumbai, one must pass by, or through, a portal celebrating regional greatness as marked by the Maratha King Shivaji Maharaj.

A new statue in the Arabian Sea, as proposed, will stand a total of 192 metres tall, making it the tallest statue in the world. Situated on a small island off the coast of a major commercial city, the statue is often compared to the Statue of Liberty, which, by comparison, is a mere ninety-three metres tall. This proposed monument to commemorate Shivaji is tall, but it is also expensive. The state government has already allocated Rs. 360 crore ($530 million) for the project.[4]

One of the intriguing aspects of this particular monument to Shivaji Maharaj is how long it has taken for the construction to begin. The proposal to build a monumental statue of Shivaji in the Arabian Sea was first floated in the middle of the 1980s. From that time until today, nearly all political leaders and political parties have supported the proposal. Indeed, it would be political suicide to speak in opposition to celebrating the great Shivaji. Instead, politicians seem to compete to see who can praise Shivaji the most.[5] Renaming public works after Shivaji Maharaj and erecting statues to celebrate his life and kingdom seems a sure-fire way to eradicate any bureaucratic red tape that might slow down development. Under these circumstances, I find it interesting that this particular proposal has taken so long to get started.

While politicians over the past three decades might all see the benefits of spending more than half a billion dollars to build a colossal statue on a man-made island in the Sea, not everyone is in agreement.[6] Months before the foundation stone was laid, hundreds of fishermen held a 'Sea Rally', sailing their boats with black flags in protest. It is important to note that 'The fishermen clarified that they were not against the construction of the memorial per se but the site which they said will "jeopardise" the livelihood of 3500-odd fishermen'.[7] The fishermen, however, did not hold a scheduled protest on the day the Prime Minister visited to lay the foundation stone.

The fishermen were concerned about the construction upsetting their livelihoods but also willing to forego any direct confrontation with the dominant narrative that celebrates the greatness of Shivaji Maharaj. In this case, we see the common social conflicts over symbols as signs of social cohesion and social division. On the one hand, memorials serve to symbolize a shared heritage or experience. The mere existence of a commemorative statue is meant to trigger feelings of attachment, connection and pride: attachment to the collective and connection with one's fellows who share the same past, along with pride about these connections and collective past. On the other hand, memorials are sites where conflicts around defining legitimate membership in the social collective takes place. Debates about which statues are placed where, whether certain images should be included or removed from extant statues are ways of demarcating the boundaries of the social collective. The protesting fishermen were claiming their membership in the collective that reveres Shivaji Maharaj but were also willing to question whether their own livelihoods should be put at risk. In the end, by calling off their protest of the Prime Minister, cultural belonging seems to have won out over claims for material resources.

Fisherfolk are not the only ones who have questioned the legitimacy of spending such a large sum of money on another memorial to Shivaji Maharaj. Concerns have been raised on a number of internet sites, including the social media site Twitter,[8] on the crowd-sourced question and answer site Quora,[9] and through an online petition campaign that has garnered over 50,000 signatures.[10] In online posts, critics have questioned whether the costs of building the memorial are justified and offered alternative ways to allocate the funds. Some have suggested that the funds should be spent to restore some of the many forts associated with Shivaji Maharaj that are currently in states of disrepair. Whether for or against the construction of the statue in the Arabian Sea, many posts speak of the greatness of Shivaji Maharaj and how more people around the world should know of his story.

As should be expected, participants express a wide range of viewpoints in the multi-vocal realm of social media and the internet. What is interesting, rather than the range of viewpoints, is the fact that people are engaging in discussion and debate about the statue and its cost. Within these 'debates', it is clear that the vast majority of participants are not questioning the legitimacy of celebrating Shivaji Maharaj. Indeed, whether they are for or against this particular construction project, participants tend to mention the importance of Shivaji Maharaj on the global stage. Instead, it is primarily the cost of the project that is being questioned. It seems to me that this questioning of whether this is money properly spent is also a questioning of the necessity for a new statue. In other words, this is really a debate about whether there is a functional need for a statue of Shivaji Maharaj in the Arabian Sea. In the next section, I will review Dipesh Chakrabarty's analysis (2015) of the development of scientific history in India in order to explore the functions of statues, and the role that they play in historical understanding.

Making sense of statues in the Indian context

In recent years, scholars have shown a renewed interest in the distinction between popular and academic or 'scientific' history. An insightful contribution to this discussion is Dipesh Chakrabarty's recent book, *The Calling of History: Sir Jadunath Sarkar & His Empire of Truth* (2015). In this work, Chakrabarty reads the letters between Sir Jadunath Sarkar and Rao Bahadur Govindrao Sakharam Sardesai as a lens through which to understand the development of 'scientific' history in India, which Chakrabarty argues, emerges through a tension and dialog between 'popular' and 'cloistered' history. His terms are significant, as they point to both the locations and the functions of different modes of historical writing. Public, or popular, history is meant to be easily accessible and has a populist function, helping the masses to better understand both the past and why knowing about the past matters. Cloistered history, on the other hand, is secluded within the confines of the archives, the academy and other similar institutions. The function of the cloistered history practiced by Sarkar is to place the Indian past on a parallel intellectual plane with the European past. Chakrabarty argues that Sarkar's concern with European historiographic conventions reflects his greater concern that his work be validated as equal to professional European writing on the past; in this reading, Sarkar is less concerned with having his work validated by a popular Indian readership who might find the narratives meaningful and relevant for their own lives.

Sarkar and Sardesai were brought together by their shared fascination with the history of medieval India. Their letters provide a sense of their extensive collaboration, their common front against the 'Poona' historians associated with the Bharatiya Itihas Samshodhak Mandal, and their disagreements with each other over the purpose of history. Chakrabarty reads their correspondence, especially their concern with methodology, as a means of understanding how new forms of historical research, historical thinking and historical argumentation were developed under conditions of colonialism in India.

In Chakrabarty's analysis, both forms of historical knowledge – the public and the cloistered – help to shape the development of professional history in India. In contrast, Partha Chatterjee argues that professional history came to supplant 'the old social history' and 'displaced it [the old social history] to a zone outside the authorized academy' (Chatterjee 2003). In contrast, Chakrabarty contends that 'the basic categories of the discipline—such as "research", "facts", "evidence", "archives" – can be molded by the interaction between history's cloistered and public lives' (8). He argues that amateur 'history of discussions in the public domain actually come to shape the fundamental categories and practices of the discipline's "cloistered" or academic life' (6). It is important to note here that Chakrabarty does not privilege the 'truth' produced through academic history; his use of the term 'cloistered' is meant to help show that the 'reach' of academic history might be quite limited while popular understandings of the past might be validated by alternative authorities and mechanisms.

Two additional elements of Chakrabarty's argument are worth noting. First, Chakrabarty looks at how Sarkar, though he did not always live up to his own understandings, sought to develop a 'scientific' approach to the validation of sources. He argues that Sarkar and Sardesai 'fetishized' documents, seeing value in them because they were 'original'. This was linked to Sarkar's understanding that sources should be freely and easily accessible to researchers, a fundamental point of disagreement with the Poona historians. History was conceived as part of the public sphere, and as such, the sources themselves needed to be public. Chakrabarty argues that neither 'the state reifying [n]or the market turning old papers into historically valued commodities and thus into historical records – was in operation on any significant scale' in India (109). Instead, a variety of factors determined whether and which documents would find their way into a publicly accessible archive. One of the key factors was the initiative of the document-hunting historians. In a similar vein, Prachi Deshpande (2014) shows how complex, and at times convoluted, were the processes that placed some documents in the public realm while withholding others for a variety of purposes.

Also worth noting from Chakrabarty's analysis is his reading of how Sarkar and Sardesai, despite their collaboration and united front against the Poona Historians, disagreed on the purpose of history. In Chakrabarty's telling, the 'nationalist' sentiment evident in Sardesai's work rankled Sarkar who believed that the purpose of history was to objectively record the past. This is not to say that Sarkar did not see history as contributing to a national sensibility. As Chakrabarty puts it, 'there was an emerging consensus that dissemination of historical and other forms of knowledge in public life was a crucial ingredient for building a nation' (41). But Sarkar felt that this must be secondary to telling the objective 'truth' of the past.

In sum, Chakrabarty makes a distinction between popular and academic history, claiming that these two distinct ways of knowing the past occupy two very different spaces. They produce different truths about the past, and they authorize these truths in different ways. Chakrabarty's analysis of these two distinct historiographies provides conceptual tools for making sense of commemorative statues. Statues of historical figures are positioned between these two spaces, occupying distinct spaces with their own way of producing and authorizing the truth about the past.

Statues between popular and cloistered history

Statues are clearly public expressions, which might indicate that they should be seen as part of the realm of popular history. I want to suggest, however, that statues of historic figures stand between the public and cloistered realms of history, overlapping with both. It is important here, I think, to return to Chakrabarty's discussion of the tension between sources and the historical 'truth' that can be discerned from them.

The authority of statues is not rooted in 'original sources', nor is it rooted in the 'realism' of the artistic representation. Nor is the authority rooted in a popular 'common sense' reading of the past. The authority of statues, I contend, actually results from them becoming historical sources, no different from the documents that historians such as Sarkar, Sardesai and the Poona group sought to collect. That is to say that the 'truth' about the past can be discerned by engaging with a statue, just as it can by closely reading documentary evidence. As Schwartz argues, equestrian statues are narrative texts that situate politics within the everyday.[11] But as a source for producing knowledge about the past, statues work differently than court documents, genealogies, chronologies and other written sources. With textual sources, the space between the source and historical knowledge is filled by interpretation and analysis, done by readers who have been specially trained to find the truth in the documents. When reading statues, this space between source and 'truth' is elided; the truth of the past is constructed as part of the image. In this way, statues perform an epistemic function that is at once theoretical and practical. Practically, they affirm what one already 'knows' and understands about the past; theoretically, they provide a guidepost for how one is to use this understanding in the present. In this way, statues also serve to reflect the self, providing a sense to the viewer of how they are to incorporate what is represented into their understanding of self within a shared social horizon.

As stated above, when fisherfolk and others raised questions about whether the statue of Shivaji Maharaj in the Arabian Sea was worth the expense, they were not questioning the value of statues. Instead, the protesting fishermen were focused solely on their livelihoods. On social media and other public fora where people have questioned whether erecting the statue is the best use of limited state resources, there is a near unanimous sentiment that Shivaji Maharaj is worthy of praise and that statues celebrating him are a means to do this. This embrace of the 'logic' of statues while also challenging this particular statue points to a deeper understanding of the social and cultural functions of statues. I now turn briefly to other moments where statues of Shivaji Maharaj were erected to highlight these functions.

Equestrian statues of Shivaji Maharaj

The model for the statue in the Arabian Sea calls for Shivaji Maharaj to be atop his horse, which is rearing up, perhaps about to launch into a jump, with both of its front hooves off the ground. There are many equestrian statues of Shivaji Maharaj throughout western Maharashtra. Political and military leaders atop a horse are a common motif of stately and military commemorations.[12] One of the most famous equestrian statues of Shivaji Maharaj sits at the end of Shivaji Marg (Road), just behind the Gateway of India. This statue was designed by the sculptor Sadashiv Sathe and unveiled on 26 January 26 1961, the first Republic Day after the establishment of Maharashtra as a unified Marathi-speaking state with Bombay as its capital.[13] The timing is important, as this statue was conceived, commissioned and constructed during an unsettled, perhaps even a liminal time.[14] Statues seem to make sense during such periods of time. This is perhaps because they provide a visual symbol of strength and stability. But more importantly, as indicated above, statues root one's self in the past by affirming particular readings of the past, and especially by providing a sense of how that past relates to the present. During unsettled times, statues are solid and stable points of reference that can serve as anchors. This sense of stability is created as the statue draws the viewer in, creating an intimate connection between the figure of the statue and the viewer. Even when surrounded by a protective fence, or buffered by vegetation, the purpose of a statue is to encourage a form of direct interaction between the viewer and the past that is being celebrated.

Equestrian statues have long symbolized political and military power. Reading the English and North American cases, Schwartz (1988) argues that the political meaning of equestrian statues underwent a shift in symbolic meaning – from upholding to subverting the traditional political order. Traditionally, 'The association of royal or aristocratic power with horses enabled the monarch or the lord to appear more "erect", more potent, more the rational and spiritual master' (657). During the revolutionary age of the seventeenth and eighteenth centuries, 'English and American revolutionaries alike used this logic dialectically to transform legitimating symbols of authority – equestrian symbols in particular – into their opposites' (655). Just as Chakrabarty sees Sarkar's historiographic concerns as functioning between European and Indian spaces, I suggest that equestrian statues of Shivaji Maharaj echoed the traditional authority of kingship while also subverting the traditional colonial authority, inherited by political elites in New Delhi.

The installation of the Shivaji Maharaj statue behind the Gateway of India served to provide a sense of stability, and historic inevitability, for the Marathi-speakers of the new state of Maharashtra. But the installation of this statue also represented the dawning of a new era, a clear break with an alternative reading of Mumbai's past. The area of South Mumbai where this statue is located is known as Kala Godha (Black Horse). This name became attached to the neighbourhood not with the installation of the statue of Shivaji, but instead because of a different statue known as Kala Godha. This statue was of Edward VII as the Prince of Wales, which was funded by David Sassoon, a prominent Baghdadi Jew and significant civic benefactor in Mumbai. *Kala Godha* was erected in the 1870s and symbolized the cosmopolitan elites who benefited from colonial policies. Located a few short blocks from where the Shivaji statue now stands, for a few years, the statues co-existed within a relatively close distance, serving as iconic representations of indigenous and colonial authority. Here, we see how statues of historic figures exist within Chakrabarty's realm of 'popular' history. The public could clearly see the parallels in how Edward VII and Shivaji Maharaj were represented, allowing all viewers to situate the local hero within a cosmopolitan understanding of political leadership and 'greatness'.

Statues, however, are not limited to the realm of popular history. They exist simultaneously within the realm of cloistered history. Statues operate in both the popular and cloistered registers at the same time. The specific popular past being celebrated is encoded in the clothing, armaments and other local features that directly place the figure within the local region. Yet there is also a formal, art-historic register that attaches particular meanings to the tilt of the horse's head and the lifting of its hoof. One must be specially trained in the cloistered world of academic history to be able to properly interpret these elements of the statue as source material depicting the kingly realm.

It is because equestrian statues of historic figures indicate power, stately authority and military might that this form was a preferred model for statues after the contentious movement to establish the state of Maharashtra. But this stately reading of equestrian statues always existed alongside the popular. In 1966, for example, an equestrian statue of Shivaji was installed in Shivaji Park in Dadar, a site that hosted many rallies in support of the Samyukta Maharashtra Movement. This statue was funded by contributions from local residents who were organized by Balasaheb Desai. The funding for this statue highlights the popular aspirations represented by the figure of Shivaji Maharaj.

Conclusion

Statues of historic figures are a significant space where people engage with the past. Statues tend to solidify the past into and onto the representations of an individual. Statues sit within and between the two realms of history that Chakrabarty argues shaped the development of academic history in India. In this way, statues are able to reflect popular sentiments and ideas about the past, while also placing these within more generalized and universal understandings of history. Statues encourage a particular type of interaction from the viewer, encouraging all to look upon them with reverence. Indeed, statues evoke a sense of reverence. The connection between statue and viewer, as indicated earlier, is intimate. But, alongside this intimacy, the statue demands a sense of respect and reverence. The viewer must look up, and they must circle around the statue if they are to 'see' it in its entirety.

Statues occupy public places; typically, they are a central, if not dominant, feature of the place, further enhancing the special quality of the statue. Statues provide a sense of stability, anchoring and affirming identity. In looking at statues of Shivaji, it seems to me that these reaffirm the local by placing the local within a larger cosmopolitan framework. (Even the comparisons between the Shivaji in the Sea and the Statue of Liberty is meant to evoke this global field.) One of the significant functions is to symbolize the social collective. The boundaries of the collective, demarcating who is included and who is excluded from the social group, are often blurry and contested. It is for this reason, I contend, that debates that surround statues of Shivaji in Maharashtra focus on the surrounding details of the statue – where it will be located rather than if it will be located; who will be with Shivaji, not whether there should be a statue.[15]

In conclusion, I want to return to the Kala Godha statue of Edward VII. I mentioned above that for a brief time, this statue and the equestrian statue of Shivaji Maharaj stood a short distance from each other in South Mumbai. In 1965, the Kala Godha statue was removed from its pedestal and relocated to the gardens of the Victoria and Albert Museum (now known as the Dr. Bhau Laji Dal Museum, situated within Veermata Jijamata Udyan). Removed from the imposing pedestal, one no longer needs to look up to fully view the statue. The sense of awe and reverence is diminished. But further, I would suggest that its location near a museum, with its title on a simple placard, in a garden that also houses a zoo, facilitates a particular way of looking at and interacting with the statue. In other words, Kala Godha no longer functions as a statue serving as a site of aspiration, projections and reflections of the self in relation to an understanding of nation and statehood. It is now a relic, an artefact of a colonial past.

Notes

1 On Chhatrapati Shivaji Maharaj, see Gordon (1993), Kulkarni (1996), Mehendale (2011), Pagadi (1993) and Sarkar (1979).

2 On the symbolic importance of Shivaji during the anti-colonial movement, see Samarth (1975) and Jasper (2003).

3 See Jasper (2002).

4 In Gujarat, the state directly to the north of Maharashtra, a 182-metre-tall statue of Shri Vallabhai Patel, an anti-colonial leader and the first Deputy Prime Minister of India, is under construction. The Noida-based sculptor, Ram Vanji Sutar, along with his son Anil, is responsible for designing and casting both of the statues. See the article by Dipti Singh in the *Indian Express*, 24 December 2016.

5 Many journalists and commentators see the competition between politicians in their praise for Shivaji as a means to appeal to various voting blocs ahead of elections. See, for example, the piece by Ashish Dixit for *The Quint*.

6 See, for example, the article by Manish Singh on *Mashable*.
7 As quoted in an article appearing in *Mid-Day*, 25 May 2016.
8 On Twitter, see the hashtag #ShivSmarak.
9 One relevant Quora discussion can be found at: https://www.quora.com/What-are-your-thoughts-regarding-the-proposed-King-Shivaji-statue-in-Arabian-Sea-near-the-Indian-city-of-Mumbai#!n=12. Accessed 11 January 2017.
10 The petition, addressed to the Chief Minister of Maharashtra can be found here: www.change.org/p/devendra-fadnavis-stop-the-government-from-wasting-rs-3600-crores-on-building-the-shivaji-statue-in-mumbai. Accessed 3 January 2018.
11 Peter Hammond Schwartz, 'Equestrian Imagery in European and American Political Thought: Toward an Understanding of Symbols as Political Text', *The Western Political Quarterly* 41, no. 4 (1988): 653–673. doi:10.2307/448488. Accessed 6 November 2017.
12 On the role of equestrian statues in the US context, see *Art and Progress* (1913). Schwartz (1988) evaluates equestrian statues in the English and North American contexts. Dodd (1969) argues that the equestrian motif originates in the Islamic world.
13 The years following the establishment of the state Maharashtra on 1 May 1960 saw the construction of many statues and other memorials to celebrate Shivaji. Shivaji was a pivotal symbol during the Samyukta Maharashtra agitation that called for the creation of a unified Marathi-speaking state with Bombay as its capital. See Phadke (1979).
14 I am drawing on the work of Victor Turner (1966).
15 In recent years, there have been a number of debates of this sort. Significant examples include the removal of Dadaji Khondev, who some believe was a mentor to Shivaji Maharaj, from Lal Mahal, Shivaji's boyhood home in Pune.

References

Chakrabarty, Dipesh. *The Calling of History: Sir Jadunath Sarkar and His Empire of Truth*. Chicago and London: The University of Chicago Press, 2015.

Chatterjee, Partha. 'History and the Domain of the Popular'. *Seminar* 522. Rewriting History, 2003.

Deshpande, Prachi. 'Caste as Maratha: Social Categories, Colonial Policy and Identity in Early Twentieth-Century Maharashtra'. *Indian Economic & Social History Review* 41.1 (2004): 7–32.

Dikshit, Ashish. '337 Yrs After His Death, Shivaji Dominates Maharashtra Politics'. *The Quint*, 2017. N.p., n.d. Accessed 21 June 2017.

Dodd, Erica Cruikshank. 'On the Origins of Medieval Dinanderie: The Equestrian Statue in Islam'. *The Art Bulletin* 51.3 (1969): 220–232. doi:10.2307/3048627. Accessed 6 November 2017.

'Equestrian Statues'. *Art and Progress* 4.8 (1913): 995–998.

'Fishermen Organise Boat Rally with Black Flags to Oppose Shivaji Memorial'. *Mid-Day*. N.p., n.d. Accessed 29 December 2016.

Gordon, Stewart. 'The New Cambridge History of India. "Vol. 2, Part 4:" The Marathas, 1600–1818'. *New Cambridge History of India: The Marathas 1600–1818*, 1993.

Jasper, Daniel. 'Commemorating Shivaji: Regional and Religious Identity in Maharashtra, India'. Ph.D. Dissertation. New School for Social Research, 2002.

———. 'Commemorating the "Golden Age" of Shivaji in Maharashtra, India and the Development of Maharashtrian Public Politics'. *Journal of Political & Military Sociology* 31.2 (2003): 215–230.

Kulkarni, A. R. *The Marathas*. New Delhi: Books & Books, 1996.

Mehendale, Gajanan Bhaskar. *Shivaji His Life and Times*. India: Param Mitra Publications, 2011.

Pagadi, Setu Madhavrao. *Shivaji*. Third reprint. New Delhi: National Book Trust, 1993.

Phadke, Yashawant D. *Politics and Language*. Bombay: Himalya Publishing House, 1979.

Samarth, Anil. *Shivaji and the Indian National Movement*. Bombay: Somaiya Publications Pvt. Ltd., 1975.

Sarkar, Jadunath. *The House of Shivaji: Studies and Documents on Maratha History; Royal Period*. New Delhi: Orient Longman, 1979.

Schwartz, Peter Hammond. 'Equestrian Imagery in European and American Political Thought: Toward an Understanding of Symbols as Political Texts'. *The Western Political Quarterly* 41.4 (1988): 653–673.

Singh, Dipti. 'Father-Son Duo to Design Chhatrapati Shivaji Statue for Mid-Sea Memorial'. *The Indian Express* 24 December 2016. Accessed 20 June 2017.

Singh, Manish. 'India Is Spending $530 Million on a Statue Twice as Tall as Statue of Liberty'. *Mashable*. N.p., n.d. Accessed 11 January 2017.

Turner, Victor. *The Ritual Process: Structure and Anti-Structure*. New York: Aldine de Gruyter, [1966] 1995.

Chapter 8

Karle/Ekvira

Many places over time, and at once

Laurie Hovell McMillin

On Republic Day in 2004, I went to see the Buddhist caves at Karle. As a long-time admirer of Maharashtra's rock-cut caves, I travelled with my family and some local Buddhist friends. I had visited the place in 1982 as an American student in Pune, and I remembered the *leṇi* at Karle as exquisite: a beautiful 2000-year-old structure carved into the side of a mountain, centred on a *chaitya* with a stone *stupa*; this had once been the home of a sizeable monastic community, whose rock-cut cells lined the mountainside.

I expected a fairly quiet day. While I recalled having met some fishermen on holiday near a shrine for the smallpox goddess Shitalamata years ago, I wasn't prepared for the scene that met us. Pilgrims crowded the stairs up to the caves, and the entire way was lined with shops selling cold drinks, prasad and images of gods, saints and goddesses. Once we neared the caves, I was surprised by the sight of a bright and busy temple. A long line of worshippers snaked around the veranda, some of them with goats and chickens for sacrifice. The vast majority of the people gathered were not there to circumambulate the *stupa* at Karle like my companions and I, but rather to take *darshan* of the goddess known as Ekvira or Veherai. (Figure 8.1)

This project began from that initial impression – that initial surprise, shall we say, which I now admit was naïve and uninformed. For as I explored the Karle/Ekvira temple site, I began to see it as a contested space, a space that various people, over time, have construed as a number of very different places. In what follows I do not try to give an objective account of the Karle/Ekvira temple space but rather to evoke various ways of experiencing the space, to suggest what Edward Soja calls 'actually lived and socially created spatiality, concrete and abstract at the same time, the habitus of social practices'.[1] These lived and imagined places, which are inevitably tied to groups, communities, histories and memories, are often tied to different historical moments, but they are also sometimes simultaneous, and overlap and compete with each other.

My efforts to present such a complex space/place can only be incomplete, of course, but in exploring the space in this way, I want to move beyond

Figure 8.1 The entrance to Karle caves next to the Ekvira temple.
Source: Photo by Laurie Hovell McMillin.

discussions that aim to 'claim' the place for one group or another. Throughout this chapter, I use the shorthand term 'Karle/Ekvira' as a way to suggest the simultaneity of possibilities and ways of seeing the place, both in the present and historically. This chapter is interested in how various people, over time, have imagined this space, and also in moving us to see something of their interests in claiming and naming the space, for such claiming is never neutral.

A word on my position in this project. Much of my previous work has focused on the construction of place and on contested sites, in very different contexts.[2] When I have worked and travelled in South Asia, I have focused largely on Buddhist culture, particularly that of the Ambedkar community. At the same time, I have long been fascinated by lived religion and the experiential dimensions of religion. While I can't claim any kind of objectivity in regard to the phenomenon that is Karle/Ekvira, I hope that this focus on what I will call 'the one and the two' suggests the ways in which interpreters of any contested site can begin to move beyond their own favoured perspectives.

This chapter, then, is an effort to see Karle/Ekvira afresh. Both terms in the formulation 'Karle/Ekvira' refer to present discourses about the place, as well as to current debates around whose place it is. By putting the terms together in this way, by setting them side by side, I want to suggest an entity that is both singular and dual (or multiple). For example, sometimes people treat it as one place, as when patrons built the Buddhist structure 2000 years ago, and as when Son Kolis treat the chaitya as adjoining the temple, with the *stupa* as an image of the mother goddess.[3] Some British travellers around the turn of the nineteenth century also tended to see it as one place, the home of a set of caves (variously identified as Buddhist and Jain) that they referred to as Ekvera.[4] Others have seen two places there: in 1845, James Fergusson complained about a crowd of Shaivites that prevented him from sketching the caves, which he understood as Buddhist[5] – for him there was both the present Shiva temple and the ancient Buddhist caves. When an American Buddhist describes the site as 'co-opted by local Hindus',[6] this viewer sees it as two things that are in distinct contrast with each other – there are the Buddhist caves and the Hindu temple. Today, when Ekvira worshippers treat the *stupa* as a place to make wishes and toss coins at it, they treat the site as part of two different places – one sacred, one something else – but they don't see the same two things that some Buddhists today do. When I went to the place in 2004, I was going to *Karle*, and I was surprised because I wanted to see one thing (the Buddhist cave) and I saw two (the cave and a temple). And when some visitors claim the Buddhist site as part of a greater Indian heritage, they are claiming as one something that others insist are two.

As we look into the history of Karle/Ekvira, we will find that it has repeatedly moved from being one place to being two and back again. And whether the viewer sees one or two places in relation to Karle/Ekvira depends on where one stands, what one's interests are and what powers are at work. For example, there has long been goddess worship at Karle/Ekvira site. Is Ekvira continuous with ancient goddess worship, as some suggest,[7] or is the autochthonous image found in the rock different from the gold-faced goddess of the temple? Are they one or are they two? Two thousand years ago Buddhists lived at Karle/Ekvira; are these Buddhists different from Ambedkar Buddhists and other Buddhist communities today, and if so, how and why? Are they one, or are they two or are they many?

Any answer to these questions depends upon one's point of view, one's framework, the categories one has available for making sense of the world. And these categories don't exist benignly – they connect to discourses and structures of power. In this chapter, I want to use the idea of 'the one and the two' to help frame the discussion. As we move through the history of the site, first by looking at the development of the Buddhist caves and then at the evolution of the Ekvira temple, I will call attention to the moments of one and of two. And what's interesting is that even when we try to focus only on one – the caves, say – we are inevitably pulled into a discussion of two – the caves *and* the goddess. Similarly, as we shall see, when we explore the temple and the goddess who inhabits it as part of one thing, we are drawn into the Buddhist site – into two. At first glance, then, though the space of Karle/Ekvira appeared to me as two, there are moments in its history that challenge that perspective, and in that way, perhaps, give us a way to move beyond dualistic approaches to the site today. Looking at Karle/Ekvira as a space/place reveals a great deal not only about the actors in the space and their particular perspectives, it shows us something about the limits of our own scholarly categories, and the challenge of bringing them into conversation with people from very different perspectives.

The history of the Karle caves and the Ekvira temple

To begin this study, let me first pry apart the terms and take them as describing two things – the Karle caves and the Ekvira temple. First the caves.

Rock-cut Buddhist caves (*leṇi*) in the Western Ghats began to be built around 2000 years ago; caves such as Bhaja, Bedse and Karle were all situated along trade routes from ports to inland cities and linked to each other.[8] These routes likely followed ancient tracks established by humans and animals that avoided the swampy or forested valleys and moved along a broad path that followed mountain passes.[9] Scholars debate the exact dates of the construction at Karle, but most place the date between 75 and 120 CE. The cave at Karle was built by the support of donors from many levels of society; inscriptions indicate that donors included tradespeople, a banker, a carpenter, 'a great warrior', 'a perfumer', a mother of monks, nuns and *bhikkhus*.[10] Some donors gave whole villages, tribute from which would help to sustain the monastery. Although the *vinaya* forbids monks from handling money, individual monks and the monasteries themselves had a fair amount of wealth at the time, as they accepted patronage and engaged in moneylending.

At this moment in history, Buddhist identity was constructed in opposition to Brahmanical and Vedic traditions – they were two. One of the donors mentioned at Karle was Ushvadata, son-in-law of the Kshatrapa king Nahapana;[11] these Scytho-Parthians were foreigners to the region and would have been considered *mlechcha* by Brahmans. As Walter Spink notes, 'if they were at once invaders and outcastes, they must have found political and psychological advantage in patronizing [Karle]'.[12] During the era of cave building, the Kshatrapas were involved in prolonged conflict with the Brahmanical Satavahanas over dominion in the region. In this period of conflict, patronage for Buddhism waxed and waned.[13]

The site at Karle includes sixteen rock-cut structures. In its heyday, Karle housed monks (maybe as many as 100)[14] in its many-roomed *vihara*; it is likely that lay people and monastics interacted there, especially in rituals surrounding the great rock-cut *stupa* in the *chaitya* hall. *Stupa*-worship was a Buddhist ritual dating from the early days after the Buddha's death/*para-nirvana*, and, initially, open-air *stupas* contained relics of the Buddha. The magnificent *stupa* at Karle stands at the end of a *chaitya* hall that is forty-five metres long and fourteen metres high and is framed by thirty-seven stone-cut columns. As a solid stone structure, there are no relics inside Karle's *stupa*; instead, the space in front of the *stupa* was likely used by both the laity and monastics for collective gatherings led by 'ritual mediators'; in addition, worshippers could circumambulate the *stupa* following a pathway outside the columns and remain unseen by those in the assembly hall (Figure 8.2).[15]

Figure 8.2 Inside the Karle *chaitya*, in view of the main *stupa*, 2004.
Source: Photo by Laurie Hovell McMillin.

It is not clear how long the Buddhist community at Karle was active or when the site ceased to be occupied by Buddhist monks. Buddhism was only one of several religious groups competing for ascendancy during the first millennium, vying with (1) the Brahmanical tradition with its adherence to the Vedas, (2) religious orders devoted to local deities or the more encompassing devotions to Shiva, Vishnu and Devi, as well as with (3) other the anti-Vedic groups such as the Jains and Ajivakas (107–108). As elsewhere, the fate of the Buddhist community at Karle depended on patronage and protection, but with the rise of Kushan rulers with Brahmanical ideologies, Buddhism in the Deccan was sorely tested. Kali Age literature from this period indicates a strong 'Brahmanical hostility towards the *sramanas*' or Buddhists; by the early fifth century, as documented by Faxian and others, 'in the new kingdoms of the Deccan this hostility turned into a cleansing policy' (18). Rather than collapsing from lack of patronage, then, as is sometimes suggested, Buddhist communities may have also declined under more violent circumstances. And when the monastic community at Karle disappeared, it would have had devastating effects on the local lay Buddhist population. As Giovanni Verardi argues in graphic terms: 'Buddhism was structured in such a way that the devastation or forced abandonment of a monastery meant the beheading of the Buddhist community at a local level' (102).

The story I have told so far is about the single site of Buddhist Karle, constructed and maintained by a community and by rulers who placed themselves in opposition to Brahmanical traditions and powers, among other things. Yet the very choice for the site of Karle may have arisen out of such an oppositional approach. We have noted how the Buddhist caves of western Maharashtra were built along trade routes, which themselves followed paths worn by humans and animals long before the use of iron tools and agriculture. Writing in 1960, D.D. Kosambi argues that these ancient tracks are marked all along with images of the mother goddess, who appear particularly at crossroads. These pre-Vedic (Kosambi called them 'non-Aryan') goddesses were not 'images in iconic form [but were] represented by shapeless little stones daubed with minium, or by red marks on the side of a tank, or on a rock, or on a tree by the water'.[16]

> The Buddhist monks who penetrated the wilderness to preach ahimsa and peaceful social behaviour would naturally follow the same tracks in order to reach the greatest number of savages [sic]. Their religion insisted upon the cessation of blood sacrifices, and the cult-spots were the most likely places for their preaching. So these cults and the major Buddhist caves which are obviously at the junctions of great trade-routes should have some demonstrable connection. In fact, this is just what we find. (II, 136)

It appears then that the goddess predates the Buddhist site; in some sense, she is the very reason for it. The iconic image of Ekvira today is built around a *swayambu* image of the goddess in the rock, which is just to the right of the *chaitya* entrance. It seems likely that the Buddhist construction was deliberately chosen for this site. Kosambi again: 'The monks ... chose such spots from the proximity of savage [sic] cults, because it was a principal mission of their Order to put an end by persuasion to all ritual killing. The primeval cults returned when the caves were deserted' (II, 137–138).

In this way, when we try to look at one thing at a certain point in history – the Buddhist caves at Karle – we are forced to consider two – the caves *and* the goddess. And though some may want to claim primacy for the Buddhist site (as I once did), the history of the space is more complex than that.

When Karle ceased to be a Buddhist monastery, local people likely found other uses for the structure. Among other possibilities, some may have seen the *stupa* as a womb symbol of the mother goddess. And if so, how do we think about this – would that be a *resumption* or an *initiation* of goddess worship at the site? Is the goddess always one thing, or is she, in this case, two? (Figure 8.3)[17]

After the site's early history, accounts of the place are scanty until the nineteenth century, leaving many centuries and understandings of the site unaccounted for. By 1809, a British writer describes people living in the *vihara*,[18]

Figure 8.3 Photo of poster at Karle, with an image of Ekvira superimposed on the site, January 2016.

Source: Photo by Laurie Hovell McMillin.

and other writers describe how the *stupa* was worshipped as a Shiva *lingam*, a phenomenon that occurred with other *stupas* and Ashokan pillars. Writing in 1845, James Fergusson describes the 'Hindoo' priests who live there:

> Though all the cave-temples in India have long been desecrated, and although the Buddhist religion is now extinct there, a few years ago, if not at the present time Karli could boast a very large attendance of Brahmins, who derived their support from pensions granted them by the Peishwa [sic]. Buddha having gone out of fashion, the Hindoos of the more orthodox creed have disfigured the entrance of this splendid excavation by erecting a mean temple to Mahadeva [Shiva] in the front; and they are further accused of altering the figures to suit their own peculiar notions.[19]

Fergusson's account presents a site that is two – both Buddhist (extinct) and Shaivite or 'Hindoo'. He sees conflict there, and contrast. Travelling in 1809, Maria Graham saw something different. She understood the caves as Jain, referred to them as 'Carli', spoke about 'priests' she met there [without identifying them with any religious group],[20] mentioned the village of Carli which has 'a large tank and a good bazar', as well as another village in 'melancholy decay' below the caves. 'It is named Ekvera, and the cave is often called by the same name'.[21] For Graham, there are the different villages of Carli and Ekvera [sic], but also the one site of Carli/Ekvera.

So far, then, when I tried to separate the caves and the temple and focus only on what was apparently 'Buddhist', I found myself inevitably in complex terrain. In order to further explore it, I will turn (again) to Ekvira and then to her temple.

The mother goddess who started all of this was a *swayambu*, autochthonous, non-Brahminized figure who resided in the open air. (Is she same as present-day Ekvira, or is she different?) As the mythology of mother goddesses evolved and became Sanskritized, Ekvira appeared as part of a cluster of powerful goddesses. Ekvira is described in both the *Renuka Mahātmya* and the *Markandeya Purāna* of the fourth and fifth centuries CE, the latter of which states that when the goddess Bhavani is enshrined in the Sahyādri she's known as Ekveera Ai.[22] Both Bhavani and Ekvira are connected to Durga, Mumbadevi[23] and Renuka, who all demand blood sacrifice and are known to possess their devotees.

Although the roots of the goddess are ancient, the *name* Ekvira seems to have been a later development. Indeed, writing in 1960, Kosambi does not use this name at all for the goddess at Karle but rather refers to Yamai, Amba-bai and Veher-ai, this last which Kosambi glosses as 'Mother-at-the-caves'.[24] In this formulation, the 'caves' refer to the *vihara*, the monks' living quarters: the goddess then is 'Vihar-Ai'. Phonically, if not etymologically, it is a short step from 'vihār' to 'Veher', and from there to the more Sanskritic 'Ekvira'.[25] Two things (goddess, Buddhist site) link up as one (the name Ekvira derived from vihara) and then turn back to two (the Buddhist caves and the Ekvira temple).

Today, Ekvira Ai with her iconic golden face is attended by Brahmin priests in a temple. But just when the temple was built is unclear. Accounts of local informants dating back to at least the early nineteenth century maintain that the temple was built by the Pandavas.[26] (This is what worshippers at the site told me in 2016 as well.) In this story, the Pandavas visit this location, where Ekvira Mata appears before them. In order to test their devotion, Ekvira demands they build her a temple in one night.[27] This story is not in the Mahabhārata but gains legitimacy by linking to it.[28] It also echoes the ways in which the goddess was Sanskritized – taken out of the open air and placed in a temple.

The earliest historical evidence I have found for the temple dates from the late eighteenth century. The Scottish artist James Wales travelled throughout the Maratha Empire and apparently visited the caves in 1792 and made drawings.[29] After Wales' death, in 1803 his friend Thomas Daniell created aquatints from them. In one that shows the entrance to the *leṇi* along with the single lion capital, there is a small structure, perhaps three to four metres cubed, that stands at the present site of the Ekvira shrine.[30] Interestingly, although the aquatints focus on the Buddhist *chaitya*, the images are titled 'Ekvera'.

Subsequent accounts describe or depict the temple, but though they refer to the name 'Ekvera', there is no mention of goddess worship until the latter half of the nineteenth century.[31] Writing in 1845, Fergusson described an active Shaivite community situated in the caves. As he notes, he could not sketch the Buddhist caves as planned because

> there was a fair going on, and a festival in honour of his Hindu godship .... [E]very corner was occupied by pilgrims or devotees of some sort or other, who, though they did not actually prevent my entering or sketching, were extremely clamorous for alms, and annoyed me a good deal by their curiosity and impertinence.[32]

Fergusson notes that 'strangely enough [the cave's] inhabitants are now Sivites [sic], and the cave is considered a temple dedicated to Siva, the Daghopa [*stupa*] performing the part of a gigantic Lingam, which it must be confessed it resembles a good deal' (29).

In the historical accounts so far we have the *name* 'Ekvera', we have Buddhist caves, Shaivites and a temple, but no mention of a goddess. That doesn't preclude the possibility that the goddess was worshipped there, of course. She is associated with Shiva and also with Khandoba. But it's interesting how the name Ekvera has split from the goddess in these accounts:

what would seem to be one (her name) is treated as two (the caves and the goddess as yet accounted for).

The first explicit link between the temple and the goddess Ekvira that I have identified appears in *The Gazetteer of Bombay* of 1885, which notes that an inscription found on the temple refers to it as 'Shri Ekviri Bhavani's' temple[33] and claims that this inscription states that the temple was built in 1866.[34]

> According to the local story an older temple stood for four generations on the same site. The people know that the worship of the goddess dates from much earlier times. They do not know whether it is older than the Pandavas and the great rock temple. (454)

The Gazetteer also notes that the musicians who play there four times a day were first placed there by a Peshwa 'four generations earlier' (454). In this way, by 1866, Ekvira, Bhavani and the temple all come together, and worship of the goddess is projected back into the past. Ekvira – the name and the temple become one again.

Let me sum up the story so far, using the idea of one and two to explore different moments. I do so not to try to be clever, but rather because I think it says something important about this place and contested places in general: this approach helps us grapple with the complexity of different discourses and perspectives that come to bear on Karle/Ekvira. I would note that I am trying to get not just at how I myself perceive the place at different moments but also at how it might have been perceived by different actors.

So we begin:

- A *swayambu* goddess image on an ancient track is worshipped. There is one thing there: a goddess.
- The site of her shrine is selected by Buddhists because they want to discourage blood sacrifice. They see themselves as opposed to the goddess: there are two things there.
- When the Buddhist community abandons – or is pushed out – of this place, local people reclaim the site, worshipping the *swayambu* image and perhaps reclaiming the *stupa* as an image of the mother goddess. From the point of view of goddess worshippers, we are back to one.
- In the late eighteenth and early nineteenth centuries, some British travellers refer to the whole site as Ekvera, even when their focus is on the caves. There is one thing there, from their point of view, and it's a different one from what local people might see.
- By the nineteenth century, the *stupa* was serving as a Shiva lingam for an active group, the Peshwas have supported the construction of a temple at the site, and priests reside at the site with their families.

Fergusson sees all this as an example of 'Hindoo' religion – he sees this all as part of one thing, but he wants to see the Buddhists caves. To him, there are two things there. A secular scholar looking at the same thing, however, might construe not only one or two entities, but perhaps three, if not four things vying for the space.

- In 1866, the earlier temple – which dates back 'four generations' – is replaced by another Peshwa-sponsored temple and dedicated to 'Ekviri-Bhavani'. The dedication and Peshwa ideology makes the site one again.
- The name of this goddess, also known as Veherai, seems to be rooted in the word vihara, for the Buddhist site. What appears to be one can be seen as two.
- Writing in 1960, Kosambi describes how 'Bombay Koli fisherman' perform the ritual circumambulation about the great *stupa*. 'The Kolis take the stupa as the goddess herself, though unable to explain this ... It is natural, as has happened elsewhere, to take a stupa (trimmed suitably, if necessary) as Shiva's symbol; but to take it as a mother-goddess is extraordinary'.[35] The Kolis see one, according to Kosambi, while he himself sees two, if not three different things and traditions coming together.

As I hope this shows, despite its basis in stone, the site of Karle/Ekvira has not stood still. Over time, it has developed in a dynamic way, and it is precisely because of this dynamism that sorting out contemporary discussions about the site is so challenging. But once again, as we move into the present, we will turn to the idea of the one and the two (or the multiple) to help frame the discussion.

Karle/Ekvira today

These days the overwhelming majority of visitors to Karle/Ekvira come for *darshan* of the goddess. Ekvira is the *kuladevi* of the Chandraseniya Kayastha Prabhu caste (CKP), the main goddess for Mahadev Kolis, and the tribal clan goddess of the Son Kolis. Worshippers sometimes bring chickens and goats to sacrifice to the goddess. They do so at some distance from the image itself, which, as Kosambi suggests, may be a remnant of the site's Buddhist past (II: 138). Such sacrifices are understood as reviving and restoring the mother who gives so much of herself. A larger temple and other structures have grown up around her image, and today, the names of donors to the temple etched in granite line the paths around it. (Indeed, the area changed a great deal even over the twelve years between 2004 and 2016, when I visited it.)[36]

The Son Kolis have developed a special affinity to the goddess at Karle, as Vicziany, Bapat and Ranade argue. These scholars maintain that Son Kolis have appropriated devotional forms into their practices, such that today the 'quintessential Son Koli pilgrimage is from Bombay to the Ekveera

Devi Mandir', where pilgrims go to ask her blessings, especially at a child's first haircut or before marriage.[37] There, as Vicziany, Bapat and Ranade describe it, '[t]he Son Kolis have also appropriated the stupa inside the main hall of the Karle Buddhist cave by circumambulations, to make up for their inability to walk around the Ekveera Devi image' (243).

Vicziany et al. note that some Son Kolis connect Ekvira Devi to Renuka, but for most 'she is really the goddess Bhavani, a ferocious avatar of Parvati, Shiva's consort' (234). Bhavani has a special relationship with the Maratha ruler and warrior Chhatrapati Shivaji – so close, in fact, that he named his sword after her. Ekvira is also known to possess her devotees; in 2016, at a small temple near the top of the stairs I witnessed five *devi* possessions in a short period. The play of twos and ones here is dizzying but not at all unusual in the case of goddesses.

- Ekvira and Bhavani – are they one or are they two?
- The *devi* and the person she possesses – are they one or two?

Not only is Ekvira important to the Son Kolis, she is also the kuladevi of CKPs. A famous CKP was Bal Thackeray, founder of the Shiv Sena, who worshipped Ekvira as his family goddess and travelled to the site for her *darshan*.[38] His wife had a dharamshala built there. In 2011, Uddhav Thackeray launched a website for Ekvira, and both Uddhav and his brother Raj, founder of the Maharashtra Navnirman Sena, have helicoptered in for *darshan* of the *devi*, as covered by local television news.

In addition to the Thackerays' family and caste connection to Ekvira, the Shiv Sena has had a particular affiliation with the goddess and the site. In November 2015, Uddhav Thackeray took all sixty-three of Shiv Sena's newly elected MLAs on a tour, first to visit his father's memorial in Mumbai and then to the shrine of Ekvira.[39] When I was there in 2016, there were many visible reminders of the close association of the temple and the Shiv Sena, including images of Anant Tare, a Son Koli and Shiv Sena notary who was serving on the temple board. The prominence of Shiv Sena symbols at the Ekvira site encourages visitors to associate the goddess and the political party.

These days, other visitors to Karle/Ekvira include Ambedkar Buddhists, who tend to see the site quite differently from devotees of Ekvira. With the *dhikshabhumi* led by Ambedkar in 1956, sites such as Karhave taken on a new importance. Ambedkar was inclined to rationalism and egalitarian ideals; he did not place faith in elaborate rituals or religious structures, and he did not believe that Buddhist monasticism would liberate the Scheduled Castes. Nonetheless, Buddhist followers of Dr. Ambedkar look to sites such as Karle, Bhaja, Bedse and the Auranagabad caves as evidence of Buddhism's ancient roots in the region. Indeed, because of this connection, politically-minded Buddhists have called repeatedly for the 'liberation' of the caves from Hindu occupation.[40]

Writing in 1996, Munshilal Gautam condemned the way that visitors to Ellora wore shoes: he describes how one visitor stood in the lap of the sitting Buddha there to get his photo taken, while another used the Kanheri caves as a toilet; 'the mindless lot', he writes, 'behave in the meanest possible ways'.[41] Today, a number of groups actively lobby against the presence of the Ekvira temple at Karle. They see two communities – two very different entities at work at Karle/Ekvīra.

That some Buddhists today feel affronted by the presence of the Ekvira temple at Karle is tied to their sense of being part of a larger and continuous tradition. Some critics may want to distance ancient Buddhists from Ambedkar Buddhists – they are two groups, not one; this seems to be the stance of Vicziany, Bapat and Ranade, who repeatedly refer to the latter by the term 'neo-Buddhist dalits' (242–244). But Ambedkar posited a connection – they are one – that more recent scholarship has begun to confirm. In short, Ambedkar argued that the idea of untouchability stemmed from the Dalits' original identity as Buddhist. He hypothesized a group he called 'the Broken Men', and argued that 'these Broken Men were Buddhists. As such they did not revere the Brahmins, did not employ them as their priests and regarded them as unpure'.[42] Not only was this group steadfastly Buddhist during Buddhism's flourishing, according to Ambedkar, they remained devoted Buddhists even after the monastic community collapsed and others around them succumbed to Brahmanical pressure or worshipped other gods now identified as Hindu.[43]

This may seem a bit of reconstructive history on Ambedkar's part, an ideological effort to assert the continuity – the oneness – of a community. But Ambedkar seems to have anticipated recent research in this area. This research suggests that in Buddhism's early days, as when the caves were built, the religion grew because it was open to populations outside the *varna* system – people who were otherwise anathema to Brahmans: these included Brahman apostates, tribals, people from low castes and foreigners. But when the Buddhist monastic community collapsed, lay people suffered; as Verardi suggests, the Buddhist community at the local level 'was beheaded'[44]: in effect, Ambedkar argues that this abandoned community was the Broken Men, whose continued opposition to Brahmans was reinforced by the Broken Men's practice of eating meat, particularly beef. And, for Ambedkar, it was this practice of eating beef that 'completely mark[ed] off the Touchables from the Untouchables'.[45]

So while some want to see two different Buddhist communities, there is historical evidence to suggest that perhaps they were one. In any case, the discourse of the Broken Men posits a connection between early Buddhists and Buddhists today that should not be dismissed out of hand and is certainly meaningful for many members of that community today.

But if Ambedkar Buddhists tend to see two different kinds of things at Karle/Ekvira, there is another line of thought that would render the whole site 'Indian'. One of the thrusts of Hindu nationalism is to bring many things under its banner – to bring what is 'Indian' and what is 'Hindu' under one encompassing ideology. And Buddhist sites, if not Buddhism itself, are part of this. As Verardi writes:

> *Hindutva* preaches that being Hindu means having one's sacred sites in India, unlike foreigners and unlike those Indians – Muslims and Christians – who have their main places of worship, and thereby frames of reference elsewhere. The Buddhists are, therefore, Hindus (an old if crudely expressed construct).[46]

In some forms of Hindu nationalism, what many see as two – Hindu and Buddhist identities/religions – becomes one: Hindu/Indian. By the same token, what is some see as multiple – Hinduism and Buddhism, on the one hand, and Christian, Muslim, etc., on the other – is construed as two.

While some viewers tend to collapse Buddhism into a reified Hinduism, for Ambedkar and many of his followers, Brahmanism (and by extension Hinduism) is explicitly opposed to Buddhism (as Brahmanism was for the early Buddhists in the Deccan). Ambedkar created twenty-two vows for his followers, and the nineteenth is this: 'I renounce Hinduism which is harmful for humanity and impedes the advancement and development of humanity because it is based on inequality, and adopt Buddhism as my religion'.[47] For Ambedkar, Hinduism and Buddhism are clearly two different religions. Indeed, elsewhere in the twenty-two vows, Ambedkar specifically addresses and rejects another way that Buddhism is sometimes subsumed within Brahmanical religion. Rejecting the idea that the Buddha is the ninth incarnation of Vishnu as argued in the *Vishnu Purana*, this vow affirms: 'I do not and shall not believe that Lord Buddha was the incarnation of Vishnu. I believe this to be sheer madness and false propaganda'.[48]

The Ambedkar Buddhist community is not unified, of course – it does not speak with one voice. Some Buddhists who spoke to Vicziany et al. saw Ekvira as the mother of the Buddha and thus accommodated the temple within a single vision. But for many Ambedkar Buddhists, there is a Hindu site and there is a Buddhist site. Given this orientation, many Ambedkar Buddhists can only see the sacrifices of chickens and goats – so very near to the historical site of Buddhist Karle – as an affront, a misguided gesture, reverence paid to a deity that works on behalf of caste and 'superstition'.

Despite or alongside these different discourses about Karle/Ekvira, the way that the site is organized today encourages particular narrative frames or motifs. Today, the site is managed by the Archaeological Survey of India. If you go there, you will pass by a ticket booth and pay a small fee before you are allowed to enter the terrace from which the Buddhist structure towers and on which the Ekvira temple stands. Visitors to the temple must slip off their shoes before entering the gates that are designed to help manage the hundreds of people who queue for *darshan* of the deity. No photos are allowed. Passing from the temple to the *chaitya*, visitors must buy an entrance ticket at a metal gate manned by a uniformed person from the

Archaeological Survey. They keep their shoes on. Photographs are allowed. In this way, visitors moving through the space are told a certain story about it: one is set aside as sacred space and the other as something secular. According to this construction, the temple is holy (or at least not ticketable), but the *chaitya* is not (and thus demands a fee). The temple is a site of worship, and the *chaitya* is a tourist attraction. They are two different places.

Visitors who follow this construction of the space take *darshan* of the goddess, and, if they do decide to pay the admission fee and come to see the *chaitya*, they change their behaviour – seeing the *stupa* is not the same as seeing the goddess. Maybe they'll pose for a photograph in front of the *stupa*. They may throw coins at the *chattri* for good luck. Some run around inside it and play games. They see the temple and the *chaitya* as two different things – one is sacred and the other not.

Others treat the *stupa* as a sacred symbol; they smear *kumkum* on it, the way they might anoint a *lingam*. Such visitors may see the site, then, as either one holy place (Hindu, with Ekvira and Shiva perhaps as a stand in for Khandoba) or as two holy places (Ekvira and Shiva).

Still others may see a Buddhist *stupa*, a goddess temple, and a Shiva *lingam*. Depending upon their orientation, the three could be examples from one great godhead, three different examples of a generic religious expression or three examples from two different religions, among other things.

As I have suggested, Ambedkar Buddhist visitors to the temple today see still other things. Some may accept the Ekvira temple as part of one Buddhist site, with Ekvira as the mother of the Buddha.[49] But others see two different entities: they see a Hindu temple encroaching on the doorstep of the Buddhist site. For some, the Buddhist site is sacred; but for others who adopt Ambedkar's 'rational' view of religion, the *chaitya* is something to be respected, and the temple is a symbol of 'superstition'. They are definitely two.

This play of ones and twos was enacted in an encounter I had in the *chaitya* in 2016.

I travelled with some Ambedkar Buddhist friends, one of whom had become a Buddhist in 1956 in Nagpur when Dr. Ambedkar led the conversion to Buddhism. We were in the *chaitya*, and a handful of people who'd come over from the temple were with us; three men were throwing coins at the stone *chattri* on top of the *stupa*, their laughter echoing through the hall. As the coins hit the stone, my friends and I cringed, imagining each one chipping a bit of rock away from the ancient structure.

In a friendly way and in Marathi, we asked one young man why he was throwing coins. The man's face changed suddenly from boisterous to somber: 'We are Ambedkar Buddhists', he said, 'and we do this for good luck'. Soon a small group gathered, and another of the throwers joined our circle.

'You're Buddhist?' I asked the newcomer.

'No', he shook his head. Then the first man dropped his Buddhist story. 'No, we're Hindu. We just do it for good luck'.

The newcomer went on: 'The *stupa* is hollow, you see', [it isn't] 'and if we can get a coin to fall inside it, we will have good luck'.

What I want to highlight about this story is the way in which the coin-thrower seems aware of different discourses about the *stupa* and the site. He first suggests that, as a Buddhist, he is connected to the *stupa*: I'm a Buddhist – I have a connection to the *stupa* – and 'we do this for good luck'. At the same time, by claiming he is Buddhist, the man implicitly acknowledges that, to his mind, Buddhists differ from Hindus – they are two. By switching identities, he aligns himself with the *stupa* – their identities are connected. When the deceit is revealed, however, and he admits that he is 'a Hindu', he apparently loses that connection to the *stupa* and feels a bit of shame: they become two. The reason for throwing the coins doesn't change – it's for good luck – but the throwers seem to understand that their licence to throw coins and their relationship to the *stupa* changes depending on their identity as Hindu or Buddhist.

As I hope is clear by now, we cannot finally resolve the conundrum that is Karle/Ekvira – the one and the two. And perhaps that is the point. We should not settle on a single narrative about the place, because, as I hope this work suggests, any narrative, any story, any version of the place is motivated, can be linked up with power, can lead to the silencing and oppressing of others. In saying that, however, I don't want to suggest that all stories and discourses about the site – all the claims for one and two and the many – are relative. Instead, we need to look and look again at these discourses and at ourselves with a critical eye. The point is not to resolve the paradox of Karle/Ekvira, of the one and the two — but to seek a way out of hatred and violence, and to resist it wherever we find it.

Notes

1 Edward Soja, *Postmodern Geographies: The Reassertion of Space in Critical Social Theory*. London: Verso, 1989, p. 18.
2 See *Buried Indians: Digging up the Past in a Midwestern Town*. Madison: University of Wisconsin, 2006 and *English in Tibet, Tibet in English: Self-Presentation in Tibet and the Diaspora*. New York: Palgrave, 2001.
3 Kosambi, D. D. 'At the Crossroads: Mother Goddess Cult Sites in Ancient India: Part II', *The Journal of the Royal Asiatic Society of Great Britain and Ireland*, no. 3/4 (October 1960), p. 135 and Vicziany, Marika, Jayant Bhalchandra Bapat, and Sanjay Ranade, 'Ekveera Devi and the Son Kolis of Mumbai: Have the Buddhists Appropriated the Karle Buddhist Chaitya?' *Conceiving the Goddess: Transformation and Appropriation in Indic Religions*, eds. Bapat and Ian Mabbett (Clayton: Monash, 2016).
4 See, for example, Maria Graham, Journal of a Residence in India (New Delhi: Asian Educational Services, 2000 [1812], p. 65 and 'Ekvera', Coloured aquatint by Thomas Daniell after James Wales. Plate 5 of [Antiquities of India], published by T. Daniell, London, 1803). British Library www.bl.uk/onlinegallery/onlineex/apac/ /other/019pzz000000178u00000000.html. Accessed 28 December 2017.

5 James Fergusson, *Illustrations of the Rock-Cut Temples of India*, London: John Weale, 1845, p. 29.
6 'Ambedkar's Children: Indian Buddhism Reborn Among the Untouchables', www.clearviewproject.org/indiabuddhismrising.html. Accessed 16 October 2017.
7 Vicziany, et al. suggest this when they argue on behalf of Son Kolis' sense of entitlement to the site. 'Ekveera Devi and the Son Kolis of Mumbai', p. 243.
8 Vidya Dehejia, *Early Buddhist Rock Temple: A Chronology*, Ithaca: Cornell University Press, 1972, p. 30. For much of the historical background, I have relied on Giovanni Verardi, *Hardships and Downfall of Buddhism in India*. New Delhi: Manohar, 2011.
9 D. D. Kosambi, 'At the Crossroads: Mother Goddess Cult Sites in Ancient India: Part I', *The Journal of the Royal Asiatic Society of Great Britain and Ireland*, no. 1/2 (April 1960), pp. 30–31.
10 *Gazetteer of the Bombay Presidency*, ed. Sir James M. Campbell. Bombay: Government Central Press, 1885, pp. 460–461.
11 *Gazetteer*, p. 461; Verardi, p. 91.
12 Walter Spink, 'On the Development of Early Buddhist Art in India', *The Art Bulletin*, vol. 40, no. 2 (June 1958), p. 98.
13 Upinder Singh, *A History of Ancient and Early Medieval India*, Delhi: Pearson Longman, 2008, p. 383.
14 This is B. G. Gokhale's estimate. *Buddhism in Maharashtra: A History*. Bombay: Popular Prakashan, 1976, p. 51.
15 Lars Fogelin, *An Archaeological History of Indian Buddhisn*. New York: Oxford, 2015, p. 134.
16 Kosambi, Part I, p. 21.
17 Kosambi notes that the effect of Buddhism still lingers in some such sites, where blood sacrifice is not tolerated, and, specifically in the case of Karle, where sacrificial animal is shown to the goddess but is killed some distance away (Kosambi, Part II, p. 138).
18 Graham, p. 65.
19 I follow Vicziany et al. in attributing this to Fergusson, though no author is listed. Fergusson, 'Cave-Temples of India', *The Asiatic Journal and Monthly Register for British and foreign India, China, and Australasia*, London: W. H. Allen, vol. 18, 1835, pp. 47–48.
20 Graham mistakenly took the structures for Jain; compounding her mistake, Vicziany et al. accept Graham's mention of 'priests' as evidence that there were Jain priests living there. Vicziany et al. (2016, p. 239).
21 Graham, 65 and 68.
22 Punekar sites the *Markandeya Purana* 13–40: 179–217 as the source for this information. Vijaya Punekar, *The Son Kolis of Bombay*. Bombay: Popular Book Depot, 1959, p. 160.
23 Marika Vicziany and Jayant Bapat, 'Mumbadevi and the Other Mother Goddesses in Mumbai', *Modern Asian Studies*, vol. 43, no. 2 (March 2009), p. 525.
24 Kosambi, Part II, p. 135.
25 This idea was brought to my attention by Shailendra Bhandare. I was pleased to discover Kosambi's matter-of–fact account of this after the fact. Incidentally, the village below the Karle site is known as Vehergao – 'veher village'.
26 Rev. Stevenson, who was interested in deciphering the inscriptions at Karle, reports that while visiting the site, he asked locals about the caves and they reported they 'were builts by the sons of Pandu' (cited most likely by Fergusson in 'Inscriptions of the Caves at Karli', *The Asiatic Journal and Monthly*, vol. 18, 1835, p. 79).
27 'Ekvīra', Wikipedia. Accessed 27 December 2015.

28 The Ramayana scholar Paula Richman has suggested that the tendency to incorporate local goddesses through the Pandavas is quite common. See Paula Richman, 'Why Did Bhima Wed Hidimbaa?' In *Reflections and Variations on the Mahabharata*, Ed. T. R. S. Sharam. New Delhi: Sahitya Akademy, 2009, pp. 172–200.
29 www.bl.uk/onlinegallery/onlineex/apac/other/019pzz000000179u00000000.html. Accessed 26 December 2015.
30 See 'Ekvera'. Coloured aquatint by Thomas Daniell after James Wales. Plate 5 of [Antiquities of India], published by T. Daniell, London, 1803). British Library www.bl.uk/onlinegallery/onlineex/apac/other/019pzz000000178u00000000.html. Accessed 28 December 2017.
31 See Graham, pp. 65–68.
32 Fergusson, p. 29.
33 *Gazetteer*, p. 454.
34 The inscription runs: 'Shri Ekviri Bhavaani's old temple built for religious sake by Naaga Posu Varlikar and Harippa Charnaavir, Fajandar of Bombay, in consultation with Baburav Kulkarni on Maha Shud 5th, S. 1788 (February–March 1866), *Gazetteer*, p. 454.
35 Kosambi, Part II, p. 136. See note 6 above. Vicziany et al. suggest that Son Kolis may feel 'a sense of entitlement [to the hill at Karle], as the worship of Koli mother goddesses long predates the evolution of Buddhism in India' (p. 243).
36 On 3 October 2017, gold-plated ornamentation from atop the Ekvira temple was reported stolen. www.thehindu.com/news/national/other-states/theft-at-ekvira-devi-temple/article19792362.ece. Accessed 4 January 2018.
37 Vicziany et al. (2016), p. 231.
38 Vaibhav Purandara, *Bal Thackeray and the rise of Shiv Sena*. Roli Books Private Limited, 27 February 2013, 1st p. of Chapter 5 (unpaginated).
39 www.dailypioneer.com/nation/uddhav-hints-at-healthy—shiv-sena-bjp-alliance.html. Accessed 7 December 15.
40 Johannes Beltz, *Mahar, Buddhist and Dalit: Religious Conversion and Socio-Political Emancipation*. New Delhi: Manohar, 2005, p. 156.
41 Munshilal Gautum, *Bapusaheb Rajbhoj: In Search of Buddhist Identity*, Aligarh: Siddharth Gautam Shikshan and Sanskriti Samiti, 1995, pp. 226–227.
42 B. R. Ambedkar, 'Origin of Untouchability', *The Essential Writings of B. R. Ambedkar*, ed. Valerian Rodriguez. New York: Oxford, 2002, p. 401.
43 Christophe Jaffrelot. *Dr. Ambedkar and Untouchability: Fighting the Indian Caste System*, New York: Columbia University Press, 2005, p. 40.
44 Verardi, p. 102.
45 Ambedkar in Rodrigues, p. 404.
46 Verardi, p. 57.
47 www.ambedkar.org/impdocs/22Vows.htm. Accessed 26 December 2015.
48 Ibid.
49 Vicziany, p. 243.

References

Ambedkar, B. R. 'Origin of Untouchability', In *The Essential Writings of B. R. Ambedkar*, pp. 396–405. Ed. Valerian Rodrigues. New York: Oxford, 2002.

Beltz, Johannes. *Mahar, Buddhist and Dalit: Religious Conversion and Socio-Political Emancipation*. New Delhi: Manohar, 2005.

Dehejia, Vidya. *Early Buddhist Rock Temple: A Chronology*. Ithaca: Cornell University Press, 1972.

Fergusson, James. 'Cave-Temples of India', In *The Asiatic Journal and Monthly Register for British and foreign India, China, and Australasia*, vol. 18, pp. 41–28. London: W. H. Allen, 1835.

———. *Illustrations of the Rock-Cut Temples of India: Text to Accompany the Folio Volume of Plates*. London: John Weale, 1845.

Fogelin, Lars. *An Archaeological History of Indian Buddhism*. New York: Oxford, 2015.

Gautam, Munshilal. *Bapusaheb Rajbhoj: In Search of Buddhist Identity*. Aligarh: Siddharth Gautam Shikshan and Sanskriti Samiti, 1995.

Gazetteer of the Bombay Presidency. Ed. Sir James M. Campbell. Bombay: Government Central Press, 1885, pp. 460–461.

Gokhale, B. G. *Buddhism in Maharashtra: A History*. Bombay: Popular Prakashan, 1976.

Graham, Maria. *Journal of a Residence in India*. New Delhi: Asian Educational Services, 2000 [1812].

Jaffrelot, Christophe. *Dr. Ambedkar and Untouchability: Fighting the Indian Caste System*. New York: Columbia University Press, 2005.

Kosambi, D. D. 'At the Crossroads: Mother Goddess Cult Sites in Ancient India: Part I', *The Journal of the Royal Asiatic Society of Great Britain and Ireland*, no. 1/2 (April 1960), 17–31.

———. 'At the Crossroads: Mother Goddess Cult Sites in Ancient India: Part II', *The Journal of the Royal Asiatic Society of Great Britain and Ireland*, no. 3/4 (October 1960), 135–144.

Punekar, Vijaya. *The Son Kolis of Bombay*. Bombay: Popular Book Depot, 1959.

Purandara, Vaibhav. *Bal Thackeray and the rise of Shiv Sena*. New Delhi: Roli Books Private Limited, 2013.

Richman, Paula. 'Why Did Bhima Wed Hidimbaa?' In *Reflections and Variations on the Mahabharata*, pp. 172–200. Ed. Sharma T. R. Srinivasa. New Delhi: Sahitya Akademy, 2009.

Singh, Upinder. *A History of Ancient and Early Medieval India*. Delhi: Pearson Longman, 2008.

Soja, Edward. *Postmodern Geographies: The Reassertion of Space in Critical Social Theory*. London: Verso, 1989.

Spink, Walter. 'On the Development of Early Buddhist Art in India', *The Art Bulletin*, vol. 40, no. 2 (June 1958), 95–104.

Verardi, Giovanni. *Hardships and Downfall of Buddhism in India*. New Delhi: Manohar, 2011.

Vicziany, Marika, Jayant Bhalchandra Bapat, and Sanjay Ranade. 'Ekveera Devi and the Son Kolis of Mumbai: Have the Buddhists Appropriated the Karle Buddhist Chaitya?' In *Conceiving the Goddess: Transformation and Appropriation in Indic Religions*, pp. 225–256. Eds. Jayant Bhalchandra Bapat and Ian Mabbet. Clayton: Monash, 2016.

Vicziany, Marika and Jayant Bapat. 'Mumbadevi and the Other Mother Goddesses in Mumbai', *Modern Asian Studies*, vol. 43, no. 2 (March 2009), 511–541.

Part III

Religious spaces and places in Western India

Chapter 9

The significance of place in early Mahānubhāv literature

Anne Feldhaus

One of the most striking impressions one gets upon a close and extensive reading of early Mahānubhāv literature is of the care, precision and depth of its attention to geography. Some of this attention is paid on the macro-level, to Maharashtra as a whole and to various subregions within it. For example, one of Cakradhar's commands recorded in the 'Ācār' section of the *Sūtrapāṭh* is 'Stay in Maharashtra' (*mahārāṣṭrīṃ asāveṃ*) (*Sūtrapāṭh*, 'Ācār' 24). This simple command may seem a bit paradoxical coming from someone whose body was born in Gujarat,[1] and the *Sūtrapāṭh* does not really explain it. The text does, however, place this command immediately after another, 'Do not go to the Kannada land or the Telugu land' (*kānaḍadeśā telaṅgadeśā na vacāveṃ*) (*Sūtrapāṭh*, 'Ācār' 23), which it does explain: 'Those lands are full of sense pleasure. Ascetics are considered worthy of honor there' (*te vīṣaebahaḷa deśa. tetha avadhūta mānya*). In other words, Maharashtra is a good place for ascetics because it has few sense pleasures and ascetics do not get much respect there – two conditions that are advantageous for the practice of asceticism. Later Mahānubhāv literature transforms this simple and somewhat backhanded compliment into elaborate praises of the glory of Maharashtra.[2]

Beyond such references to a large region named Maharashtra, the early Mahānubhāv biographical texts – most importantly, the *Līḷācaritra* (Kolte 1982), the biography of Cakradhar, the Mahānubhāvs' 'founder'; *The Deeds of God in Ṛddhipur* (Kolte 1972; Feldhaus 1984), the biography of Cakradhar's guru, Guṇḍam Rāüḷ or Govindaprabhu; and *Smṛtisthaḷ* (Deśpāṇḍe 1939; Feldhaus and Tulpule 1992), the account of the early years after the departure of these two divine incarnations, when the group of their followers was led by Cakradhar's appointed 'deputy', Nāgdev or Bhaṭobās – portray Cakradhar and his disciples as travelling back and forth repeatedly between two subregions of the Marathi-language world: Vidarbha and what they call 'Gaṅgātīr' or the 'Gaṅgā Valley', the valley of the Godāvarī river. A vivid illustration of the linguistic aspect of what seems to have been an important geographical contrast for these early Mahānubhāvs is found in Chapter 88 of *The Deeds of God in Ṛddhipur* (Feldhaus 1984: 74–75):

> One day Māhādāïseṃ asked the Gosāvī, 'Lord, Gosāvī, I'll give you a *dhīḍareṃ* today. Don't go out to play, Gosāvī'.
>
> The Gosāvī accepted her offer. He was delighted, and said, 'Oh, drop dead! She'll give me a *dhīḍareṃ*, I tell you!' He didn't go out at all to play. 'Oh', he said, 'she'll give me a *dhīḍareṃ*, I tell you. I should eat it … I shouldn't eat it, I tell you'.
>
> Then Māhādāïseṃ prepared a *dhīḍareṃ* and put it onto a plate. She prepared a seat. The Gosāvī sat on the seat, and Māhādāïseṃ offered him the *dhīḍareṃ*. She poured ghee into a metal cup.
>
> Then the Gosāvī looked at the *dhīḍareṃ*. And he said, 'Hey, this isn't a *dhīḍareṃ*, I tell you. This is an *āhītā*, I tell you. Come on! Bring me a *dhīḍareṃ*! Bring me one, I tell you!' And he acted angry.
>
> 'Lord', said Māhādāïseṃ, 'in the Gaṅgā Valley, where I come from, they call it a *dhīḍareṃ*. Here in your Varhāḍ they call it an *āhītā*'.
>
> 'Oh, bring me a *dhīḍareṃ*', he said. 'Bring me one! Bring me one, I tell you!' And he acted angry.
>
> Māhādāïseṃ began to think, and suddenly she got an idea. So she put some fine wheat flour into milk. She mixed it up. She sponged some ghee onto the earthen griddle. She poured [the batter] onto it in a phallic shape. (According to some, she poured it in the shape of a conch.) On top she sprinkled powdered cardamom, black pepper, and cloves. When one side was done, she turned it over and took it off. She put it onto his plate.
>
> It looked different to him, and he said, 'This is what I want. Now it's right, I tell you. Oh, it's good, I tell you'. So Māhādāïseṃ, delighted, served him more.
>
> In this way, the Gosāvī accepted the meal.

Although the broader regional consciousness displayed in the literature created by the early Mahānubhāvs is a fascinating topic,[3] the present chapter will examine a kind of geographical awareness that is more important to Mahānubhāvs themselves: their attention to smaller places, to particular villages, tanks, temples, houses, fields, trees and other finely specified locations. After presenting some of the evidence of early Mahānubhāvs' interest in places, I will consider the reasons for that interest in terms of Mahānubhāv theology. I will also, finally, show some of the non-sectarian scholarly uses to which Mahānubhāv place literature has been put and ways in which it can advance our understanding of the broader religious history of Maharashtra. Through attention to the places that were important to the early Mahānubhāvs, we get a glimpse of the remarkable dynamism that characterizes that history.

Attention to place in early Mahānubhāv literature

Whereas the Mahānubhāv biographies appear to be rather cavalier about chronology, they are scrupulously precise about geography. Some of the Mahānubhāv biographical texts (though not the *Līḷācaritra*) are even named for the principal place where their primary subject lived: the verse text *Sahyādrī Varṇan*, for example (Kolte 1964), is about Dattātreya, who is for Mahānubhāvs a divine incarnation connected with Māhūr, a pilgrimage place in Nāndeḍ District located on a mountain considered to be a spur of the Sahyādrī range. The text that Kolte published under the title *Govindaprabhucaritra* (Kolte 1972) is better known as *Ṛddhipurcaritra*,[4] naming it not for Guṇḍam Rāüḷ or Govindaprabhu, the divine incarnation whose deeds it narrates, but rather for his home town: the village of Ṛddhipur in Amrāvatī District, Maharashtra.

Internal evidence in the Mahānubhāv texts also demonstrates abundantly their interest in particular places. Some of this evidence takes the form of stories in which people (the main, divine protagonists or others) decide where to go, or whether to go to some particular place or other. For instance, during the early part of the *Līḷācaritra*, the part sometimes called 'Ekāṅka' ('The Solitary Period') because it tells about the part of Cakradhar's life in which he travelled around alone, without (yet) a group of disciples accompanying him, Cakradhar begs his Gujarati parents to let him go to Rāmṭek (Kolte 1982: 13. 'Pūrvārdha' 20). At the transitional point between 'Ekāṅka' and 'Pūrvārdha' ('The First Half', proper), he decides *not* to go to Tryambakeśvar during the Siṃhastha period (Kolte 1982: 87–89. 'Pūrvārdha' 106).[5] Most striking in this regard is a series of episodes in *The Deeds of God in Ṛddhipur* in which Guṇḍam Rāüḷ sits on a stone called his 'Thinking Rock' (Vicār Cīrā) and decides where to go next. For example, take *The Deeds of God in Ṛddhipur*, Chapter 263 (Feldhaus 1984: 139):

> The Gosāvī used to sit on his thinking rock and say to himself, 'Shall I go to Dhāmaṇeṃ, or shall I go to Māüreṃ? Oh, shall I go to Nāṇaurī or shall I go to Sonaurī?'
>
> He would talk to himself this way; then he would go where he wanted to go.

Other evidence of the biographies' interest in geography is more purely formal. Most of the more than 1,000 chapters (*līḷā*s) of the *Līḷācaritra* begin by stating where Cakradhar (whom the text calls 'the Gosāvī' or 'the Omniscient one') was when the episode to be narrated in the *līḷā* took place. For example, 'Pūrvārdha' 190:[6]

> He stays in a cell in the Kedār [temple] in Pāṭavadhā for less than a fortnight.

> The Gosāvī went to Kedār's temple in Pāṭavadhā. To the east of the temple was a cell that faced north. The Gosāvī was sitting on the verandah next to the western wall. Bāïseṃ washed his feet. He went to sleep inside. Bāïseṃ prepared something to eat. The Gosāvī woke up. He ate his meal. He rinsed his mouth. He chewed pan. He went back to sleep.
>
> He stayed [there] this way for less than a fortnight.

As in this *līḷā*, not just the first sentence but also the heading of the chapter often includes the name of the village or town where the *līḷā* took place. Most notably, some chapters of the *Līḷācaritra* are missing, lost when the original manuscript of the *Līḷācaritra* was carried off by highway robbers and the text had to be reconstructed from the memories of disciples who had learned it by heart.[7] For many of these missing chapters, all that remains is the heading. And in many cases, this heading consists of only a word or two, one of them indicating the place where the *līḷā* happened. For example, the two chapters preceding the one just cited consist of one line each:

> 188. He stays overnight at the Mairāḷ [temple] in Pālī.
> 189. He stays overnight in the outer temple at Nimbā.

Furthermore, because the original manuscript of the *Līḷācaritra* was lost, and the text was reconstructed by a number of different disciples who had memorized it, manuscripts and editions of the *Līḷācaritra* retain records of the points of divergence among the disciples' memories. Thus, the text itself includes words, sentences, and sometimes paragraphs introduced by words like 'Hīrāïsā version', 'Rāmeśvarbās' or 'Paraśarāmbās'. In addition, the text of the *Līḷācaritra* includes within itself the results of subsequent research by unnamed editors whose views are introduced by the term '*śodh*', '*vāsanā*' or '*ekī vāsanā*'. Quite often these variants have to do with questions of place: *where* exactly the Gosāvī was sitting when such-and-such happened or when he spoke some particular words, or in *which* village a particular event took place. For example, *līḷā* 'Pūrvārdha' 304[8] has towards its end the parenthetical comment, '(According to Hīrāïsā's version, this līḷā [took place] at Hīvaraḷī.)'. 'Pūrvārdha' 225[9] ends with the note, 'Rāmeśvarbās: This *līḷā* took place in the Nāgnāth [temple] in Paiṭhaṇ'. In some cases, such as the Hīrāïsā statement about Hīvaraḷī, these notes about place serve as a kind of corrective to the chronology of the text. Thus, although, as I have said, the biographies appear to be uninterested in chronology, it may in fact be the case that the chronology is pegged to the geography. That is, the chronology that is significant for those who composed and reconstructed the text is the itinerary of Cakradhar's wanderings, the order in which he went to the various places where he is remembered to have visited or lived. Thus, when the text includes a note indicating that Hīrāïsā or Rāmeśvarbās or someone else suggests a variant location for a particular *līḷā*, this is a way of saying that the episode should be placed earlier or later in the text.

In addition to the biographies, the Old-Marathi literature of the Mahānubhāvs also includes a text that is almost purely geographical in nature. This text is the *Sthānpothī*, a text that I will discuss later in this chapter.

Understanding the significance of place for the Mahānubhāvs[10]

Why are these Mahānubhāv texts so interested in, and so precise about, places? I think it is because even these early texts were composed and edited within the context of a lively Mahānubhāv pilgrimage tradition that persists to this day. What may well have been the first Mahānubhāv pilgrimage is portrayed at the very beginning of *Smṛtisthaḷ* (Deśpāṇḍe 1939; Feldhaus and Tulpule 1992), a text that tells of the actions and thoughts of Cakradhar's followers after his departure and, fourteen years later, the death of Guṇḍam Rāüḷ. Griefstricken at Guṇḍam Rāüḷ's death, Nāgdev (Cakradhar's 'deputy', also called Bhaṭobās) sets out from Ṛddhipur with a number of other disciples. They travel along the Godāvarī river, from Rāvasgāv (downstream from Paithan) to Ḍombegrām (upstream from Paithan), a total of more than 100 miles. Along the way, they bow 'to the river bank' at a number of places (*Smṛtisthaḷ* 5, Feldhaus and Tulpule 1992: 71):

> Thus, after many days, in the Saṃvatsar year Vyaya, on the fourth day of the dark half of the month of Māgh, Śrīprabhu Gosāvī also died. Bhaṭobās and the devotees were very sad.
>
> Then, because of that grief, Bhaṭobās came to the Gaṅgā Valley.[11] With him were Lakṣmīdharbā, Bāïdevobā, Māhādāïseṃ, Kothaḷobā, Pomāïseṃ, and Sādhe, and others as well. They bowed to the river bank from Rāvasgāv to Ḍombegrām. They spent five nights in Pratiṣṭhān [Paithan]. They all circumambulated the town and bowed to it. Then they went from Vṛddhāsaṅgam and Jogeśvarī to Chinnapāp. They bowed to Chinnasthaḷī and to all the other holy places (*sthāns*). They sat for a while at Chinnasthaḷī. Then they left.

In subsequent generations, Mahānubhāvs began not only bowing to the *sthāns* but also marking them with large concrete blocks or pedestals called *oṭās*. They decorate some of the *oṭās* with shiny satin and ruffles, and in some cases, they inscribe above them references to what happened at the places the *oṭās* mark. Modern times have brought guidebooks helping pilgrims to find the *sthāns*,[12] and the internet age has introduced a burgeoning of websites[13] and mobile apps[14] documenting them. In the decades during which I have been observing Ṛddhipur and other Mahānubhāv holy places, Mahānubhāv monks and pious lay people have engaged in contests to build ever more elaborate arches, shrines and temples over the *oṭā*s.

But to say that places are important because people go on pilgrimage to them is almost redundant. We must probe a bit more deeply, asking what it is that motivates the Mahānubhāv pilgrimage tradition and thus explains the importance of place in Mahānubhāv literature as well. So far I have found three theological explanations.[15]

The first explanation is based on hints in Mahānubhāv texts and more elaborate statements that contemporary Mahānubhāvs have made to me. According to these hints and statements, the divine incarnations deposited *śakti* in things they touched and places they visited. The *Sūtrapāṭh* justification of this idea is found in *sūtra* 'Vicār' 171 (Feldhaus 1983: 105, 187): *vastusambandhe śaktinikṣepu*, '*Śakti* is deposited through contact with the Absolute'. This *śakti*, or power, is helpful in solving worldly problems and in making one a better person, a more likely candidate to attain liberation from rebirth and the permanent presence of God. I have also heard some Mahānubhāvs use the concept of *śakti* to explain how subsequent generations could find the places mentioned in the divine incarnations' biographies and in the *Sthānpothī*.

Another explanatory concept is found in a term that some contemporary Mahānubhāvs use in talking about their holy places. The term is *pavitra*, and it means some combination of what the English words 'holy' and 'pure' express. Here, as with the concept of *śakti*, the idea is most often that the touch of the feet of a divine incarnation is what makes the places *pavitra*. This concept goes a long way towards explaining the elaborate precautions that previous generations of Mahānubhāvs are said to have taken to avoid polluting Ṛddhipur, as well as the inclusion, among the many *oṭā*s that Mahānubhāvs bow to today, of a sizeable number marking places where the divine incarnations are remembered to have urinated or defecated.[16]

My sense is that explanations involving the terms *śakti* and *pavitra* are almost post facto rationalizations for Mahānubhāvs' pilgrimages to the places visited by Cakradhar and the other incarnations of Parameśvar. More basic, I believe, is a concept that is even more central to the kind of *bhakti* the Mahānubhāvs practice. This is the concept of *smaraṇ*, recollection. Short of enjoying the liberating presence (*sannidhān*) of a divine incarnation, Mahānubhāvs living in a time (like the present) when there is no incarnation physically available on earth try to bridge their separation from God by the practice of *smaraṇ*. According to the *Sūtrapāṭh* ('Ācār' 27–32, 'Ācār Mālikā' 138, etc.), Cakradhar commanded his followers to practice *smaraṇ* of him and the other divine incarnations: their names, their appearance, their actions.

The connection between *smaraṇ* and pilgrimage becomes clear as early as the *Smṛtisthaḷ*. Here, in Chapter 115, Nāgdev tells an ascetic who is setting out to wander how to perform the 'constant wandering' (*nityāṭan*) that Cakradhar commanded of his disciples. Instead of being aimless, the wandering should aim at visiting places where Cakradhar and the other divine incarnations are remembered to have lived or visited at some time in the past (Feldhaus and Tulpule 1992: 106):

> Once when Bāïdevbās set out to wander, Bhaṭobās [that is, Nāgdev] said, 'Bāïdev, you should direct your wandering to the holy places (*sthāns*). You should bow to all the places'. He made this rule.
>
> Then Bāïdevbās set out to wander, bowing to the holy places as he went.

Elsewhere in *Smṛtisthaḷ*, Nāgdev connects pilgrimage to the holy places with recollection, *smaraṇ*, of the things that were said and done at them (*Smṛtisthaḷ* 39, Feldhaus and Tulpule 1992: 79):

> One day Bhaṭobās said, 'Go to holy places and recollect the divine deeds (*līḷās*) that were done at them. That is the way one practices recollection (*smaraṇ*) there'.

For Mahānubhāv pilgrims today as well, the places they visit and bow to are important because the divine incarnations were there before them. Not all pilgrims are always aware of the specific things that were done at the places they visit. When I ask people what *līḷā* was done at a spot they are bowing to, they often are unable to tell me: '*kāhītarī kele*' ('He did something or other'), they say. But they know, or trust, that the *oṭā* they bow to marks a place made special by the former active presence there of a divine incarnation.

The *Sthānpothī*

Besides these indications of the early Mahānubhāvs' interest in geography, the early Mahānubhāv literature also includes several specifically geographical texts. A number of these are Māhātmyas, sectarian versions of a kind of text found widely in Hindu traditions of pilgrimage and religious geography, texts whose purpose is to praise particular places in terms of the Purāṇic events that occurred at them and in terms of the places' power to bestow merit on pilgrims who visit them. The geographical text I want to focus on here, though, is of a different kind – unique, as far as I know, in world literature. This is the *Sthānpothī*, an early Marathi prose text that lists, locates and describes places where the divine incarnations, especially Cakradhar and Guṇḍam Rāüḷ, stayed, visited, stood, sat, slept, ate, spoke and excreted.[17]

The *Sthānpothī* is something like a guidebook for Mahānubhāv pilgrims. As we have seen, Mahānubhāvs have a highly developed pilgrimage tradition whose main theological justification is Cakradhar's command that his followers practice *smaraṇ*, recollection, of not just the names and appearance but also the deeds of the divine incarnations; going to places where Cakradhar and Guṇḍam Rāüḷ said and did things is understood as a stimulus to *smaraṇ*. The *Sthānpothī* identifies and lists the places made holy by the former presence of the divine incarnations. The text describes the places' locations in terms of nearby buildings and other landmarks in the villages and towns where the places are found. Frequently, it gives the total number of holy places (*sthāns*) in a particular village or town. It tells about the buildings, gates and doorways that the divine incarnations used and refers briefly to the deeds, or *līḷā*s, that they performed at the *sthān*s. The order in which the *Sthānpothī* deals with the places it covers and the choice of titles for the divisions of the text ('Pūrvārdha Sthāneṃ', 'Uttarārdha Sthāneṃ', 'Ṛddhipur Sthāneṃ', etc.) indicate the *Sthānpothī*'s dependence on the Mahānubhāv biographies. (As I have indicated, the *Līḷācaritra* has divisions named 'Pūrvārdha' and 'Uttarārdha', and the biography of Guṇḍam Rāüḷ is often called *Ṛddhipurcaritra*.) Besides, the brevity of the *Sthānpothī*'s references to episodes in the *Līḷācaritra* and the *Ṛddhipurcaritra* indicates that the author of the *Sthānpothī* assumed its readers' familiarity with the episodes narrated in the biographies.

To speak of 'the author' of the *Sthānpothī* is to oversimplify. The history of this text, like that of much Mahānubhāv literature, is quite complex.[18] First of all, assuming that there was a single author of the text, the only written version of it too is said to have been lost, along with the manuscripts of the *Līḷācaritra* and some other early Mahānubhāv texts. Like these other texts, the *Sthānpothī* was then reconstructed based on the recollections of early Mahānubhāvs who had memorized it. Where different disciples' recollections disagreed, variants were marked, as in the *Līḷācaritra*, by giving the name of the disciple from whom the variant comes: Hīrāïseṃ, Paraśarāmbās and so on. In addition, similar to what we have seen for the *Līḷācaritra*, there are variants marked by the words *śodh* or *tathā*. In the case of the *Sthānpothī*, some of these seem to indicate the findings of a subsequent editor or editors who made revisions based on on-site observations at the places.

Conversely, just as the text itself has been subjected to a series of editings based on visits to the places made by a series of editors, so the *Sthānpothī* has been used by pious Mahānubhāvs intent on discovering the exact location of the holy places and by an increasing number of monastery abbots and other religious entrepreneurs who are building, rebuilding and putting roofs and shrines and temples over more and more *oṭā*s. Mahānubhāv tradition tells, for example, of a fourteenth-century monk called Munivyās/ Munibās Koṭhī who used the *Sthānpothī*, among other resources, as a way of discovering and then marking the holy places (Feldhaus 2003: 204).

Religious archaeology

Besides the *Sthānpothī*'s usefulness in the development of Mahānubhāv pilgrimage traditions, it also turns out to be an excellent resource for what I call 'religious archaeology'. In the process of identifying the places where Cakradhar and Guṇḍam Rāūḷ lived and visited, the *Sthānpothī* provides a detailed survey of the deities who had temples 700 years ago in the parts of Maharashtra now called Marāṭhvāḍā and Vidarbha. It tells us the directions in which the temples faced and sometimes on which side of a town or village they were found. Frequently, it also names the deities whose temples were clustered together and describes the configurations of the clusters in terms of the directional relationships of the temples to one another. It thus gives us a good deal of information about religious architecture and directional orientation in thirteenth-century Maharashtra. This information is by-and-large coincidental to the original biographical and devotional intentions of the *Sthānpothī*.

As another byproduct of the text's own intentions, the *Sthānpothī* gives us a baseline from which to measure the rise and fall of cults, sects and even religions in the Deccan by helping us to see the changes in the use and configuration of buildings at particular places. We find examples of new gods, cults and religious traditions that have arisen or become more prominent since the time of the *Sthānpothī*, old gods whose cults have waned or disappeared and temples that have changed their religious function and meaning but have retained their old names.

Two scholars who used the *Sthānpothī* to conduct such religious-archaeological research in the second half of the twentieth century are Setumādhavrāv Pagaḍī and Aruṇcandra Pāṭhak. Pagaḍī, an historian who carried out his research in Auraṅgābād District in the early 1950s, published his findings more than thirty years later (Pagaḍī 1985). Pāṭhak, an archaeologist, carried out similar research in the 1980s at fifty-five sites, mostly along the Godāvarī river; he too published the results of his observations three decades after making them (Pāṭhak 2013). Pāṭhak's emphasis is on discovering the early- and pre-Yādava history of places described in the *Sthānpothī*, but he too, like Pagaḍī, indicates the current state and uses of the buildings he found in the twentieth century on sites the *Sthānpothī* describes at an earlier stage.

Together, these authors' works provide numerous examples of a type of change that has occurred again and again as cults have risen and fallen in popularity or in political favour and as buildings have collapsed, their stones later being used to construct new buildings at or near the same site.[19] In many cases, a temple of one god has come to be dedicated to another. For example, there are some cases in which temples of Śiva have replaced those of various forms of Viṣṇu. Pagaḍī found a Śiva temple at Pūrṇagāv on a site where there had been a Nārāyaṇ temple at the time of the *Sthānpothī*

(Pagaḍī 1985: 4; cf. Pāṭhak 2013: 265), and Pāṭhak found a Marāṭhā-period Śiva temple on the site of, and making use of the stone doorway of, a Hemāḍpantī-style (that is, Yādava-period) Viṣṇu temple at Kācarāḷe (now called Kājaḷā, Jālnā Taluka, Jālnā District; Pāṭhak, 306). On the other hand, in Ambaḍ Taluka, Jālnā District, Pāṭhak found a fallen-down temple that he believes the *Sthānpothī* identifies as a temple of Somnāth (a form of Śiva), which is now called a Mahalakṣmī temple (Pāṭhak 2013: 312).

In three places in Auraṅgābād Taluka, Auraṅgābād District (Sāvkheḍā, Nāgaṃṭhāṇ and Āvaḷ), Pagaḍī found that there were or had until recently been temples to Śiva on the sites of what the *Sthānpothī* describes as temples of the sun-god, Āditya (Pagaḍī 1985: 5, 6, and 7).[20] Including these three places, Pāṭhak counts a total of twenty-nine places where the *Sthānpothī* refers to Āditya temples, most of them, apparently, no longer extant or no longer dedicated to Āditya (Pāṭhak 2013: 116–117). An important exception is Bhiṅgār, where Pāṭhak found an eighteenth-century Āditya temple built on top of the Yādava-period temple to that god (Pāṭhak 2013: 249).[21] To explain the waning of the cult of Āditya since the thirteenth century, Pagaḍī suggests that over time Āditya has come to be called Śiva (Pagaḍī 1985: 5), or that Śiva temples were called 'Āditya' temples at the time of the *Sthānpothī* (Pagaḍī 1985: 7). However, it seems more likely that the cult of Śiva has continued to rise in popularity as that of Āditya has almost completely died out or has been transformed into that of another god identified with the sun: Khaṇḍobā, also known as Mārtaṇḍa Bhairava.[22]

Another cult that seems to have risen in popularity since the thirteenth century is that of Viṭṭhal/Pāṇḍuraṅga/Viṭhobā, the god of Paṇḍharpūr.[23] As V.B. Kolte (1976: 21), the editor of the *Sthānpothī*, points out, the *Sthānpothī* mentions no temples of Viṭhobā, who now has numerous temples all over Maharashtra. Kolte interprets the absence of Viṭhobā in the *Sthānpothī* as evidence that the cult of Viṭhobā was not particularly widespread when the *Sthānpothī* was composed – or, for that matter, at the time when Cakradhar was wandering around visiting temples. However, it is also possible that Cakradhar's antipathy towards the cult of Viṭhobā – as recorded, for example, in his derogatory explanation of the cult in *Līḷācaritra*, 'Uttarārdha' 519 (Kolte 1982: 659) – would have led him to avoid any Viṭhobā temples that he came upon in the course of his travels. Since the places where Cakradhar did *not* go are generally *not* included in the *Sthānpothī*, its failure to mention Viṭhobā temples does not necessarily mean that there were no temples of this god in the villages and towns that Cakradhar visited. Still, I think it quite likely that Kolte's deduction is correct. Kolte also notes the strong predominance of Śaiva deities among those in whose temples Cakradhar sat or stayed (Kolte 1976: 20–21).[24]

Finally, the greatest number of changes that the *Sthānpothī* helps reveal are the transformations of temples with *mūrti*s of Hindu gods into Mahānubhāv temples with aniconic *oṭā*s. For example, Pagaḍī (1985: 7) shows that, in Cakradhar's time, the large Mahānubhāv monastery now found in the 'Old Jālnā' neighbourhood of Jālnā city (Jālnā District) was a Narasiṃha temple (a Rājmaḍh)[25] in a village called Hīvaraḷī (Pagaḍī 1985: 7–8). Here too, as in the temple still called 'Rājmaḍh' in Ṛddhipur,[26] there is no trace of Narasiṃha to be found. In Ṛddhipur, there are a number of Mahānubhāv shrines and temples that retain more or less concrete reminders of the Hindu gods that once were (or in some cases still are) housed in them.[27] For instance, a Mahānubhāv temple on the site of a goddess's temple in which Guṇḍam Rāüḷ used to play has inside it two Mahānubhāv *oṭā*s and an image of Kṛṣṇa holding a flute; however, the name of the temple is still that of the original goddess: Mahākālī. Another example is Bhairav Buruj, which was a Bhairava (that is, Śiva) temple when Cakradhar lived there for ten months; it is now a Mahānubhāv temple, complete with *oṭā*s. Outside the temple, towards the back, are a Śivaliṅga and a Nandī, not obviously objects of worship, but decently preserved nonetheless.[28]

Similar patterns of change are also found in other places where Cakradhar is remembered to have stayed for a long period. For example, Pāṭhak points out that there is a Mahānubhāv monastery on the site of what an inscription edited by V.B. Kolte shows was the Bhogārām temple in Paiṭhaṇ (Pāṭhak 2013: 277). Pāṭhak also describes a newly built Mahānubhāv temple next to a hillock full of medieval architectural remains that he identifies as having been the Jogeśvarī temple at Gevrāī (Pāṭhak 2013: 343), and he states that Mahānubhāvs have 'renovated' the whole area around Pāñcāḷeśvar (on the southern bank of the Godāvarī, in Bīḍ District, across the river from Āpegāv) to the point where there are no Yādava-period buildings left (Pāṭhak 2013: 305–306). Finally, showing that change can occur in both directions, in the village of Kānaḍī (present-day Kānad, Gaṅgāpūr Taluka, Auraṅgābād District), Pagaḍī learned that 'four or five years' before his 1952 visit there, a Śivaliṅga had been installed in the hall (*sabhāmaṇḍap*) of the Siddhanāth (Śiva) temple, replacing a Mahānubhāv *oṭā* that had been moved outside the doorway of the temple; Mahānubhāvs had installed that *oṭā* in the temple only ten years or so before it was moved outside (Pagaḍī 1985: 17–18).

Thus, not only has the text of the *Sthānpothī* been involved for centuries in a dialectical process of interaction with the places it describes – being corrected on the basis of visits to the places and being used in the process of identifying the places – the *Sthānpothī* can also serve as a tool that gives us access to the fluid and ongoing process of change in the identities and meanings of significant places and to the rise and fall of important gods, cults and religious traditions. As we come to know more and more about the history of places that are important to the Mahānubhāvs, it becomes increasingly clear that places like these can change their identities more easily than they can lose their significance.

Notes

1 Cakradhar is understood to be the person who resulted when Cāṅgdev Rāüḷ of Dvārāvatī, an incarnation of Parameśvar, was harassed by a female ascetic and gave up his body, entering the corpse of Haripāḷdev, the son of a royal minister (*pradhān*) in Gujarāt.

2 I trace this development in some detail in Anne Feldhaus, 'Maharashtra as a Holy Land: A Sectarian Tradition', *Bulletin of the School of Oriental and African Studies, University of London* 49, 1986, pp. 532–548.

3 See Feldhaus, 'Maharashtra as a Holy Land', 1986. See also Anne Feldhaus, *Connected Places: Region, Pilgrimage, and Geographical Imagination in India*. New York: Palgrave Macmillan, 2003, pp. 185–194 and 206–210.

4 This is the text that I have translated as *The Deeds of God in Ṛddhipur* (Feldhaus 1984).

5 The Siṃhastha is the thirteen-month period, occurring once every twelve years, in which the planet Jupiter is considered to be situated in the constellation Leo (the Lion, or Siṃha). Still today, this period is an important time to go on pilgrimage to Tryambakeśvar, a temple town at the source of the Godāvarī river. The Siṃhastha is considered part of the twelve-year cycle of Kumbha Melā pilgrimages, the most famous of which is the one to Allāhabād (Prayāg), at the confluence of the Gaṅgā and Yamunā rivers in North India.

6 This is the number and text of this chapter in my forthcoming translation of the *Līḷācaritra*, which is based on the edition by H. N. Nene (Nene 1936–1950, in which the chapters of 'Pūrvārdha' are not sequentially numbered). The corresponding number of this chapter in Kolte's edition (Kolte 1982: 199) is 'Pūrvārdha' 324, and in Tulpule's edition (Tuḷpuḷe 1966) it is 'Pūrvārdha' 138.

7 See the introduction to Kolte's edition of the *Līḷācaritra*, Kolte 1982: (66)–(74). See also Feldhaus 1983: 12–16.

8 See note 6 above. This *līḷā* appears as 'Pūrvārdha' 226 in Tulpule's edition (Tuḷpuḷe 1966, Part 2: 17); it is 'Pūrvārdha' 482 in Kolte's edition, which does indeed place the *līḷā* in the context of others set in Hīvaraḷī (Kolte, *Mhāïṃbhaṭ Saṅkalit Śrīcakradhar Līḷā Caritra*, 1982, p. 282).

9 See note 6, above. This *līḷā* is 'Pūrvārdha' 165 in Tulpule's edition (Tuḷpuḷe 1966, Part 1: 78–79) and 'Pūrvārdha' 360–361 in Kolte's (Kolte 1982: 212–213).

10 This section draws on my discussion in Feldhaus, *Connected Places*, 2003, pp. 185–210.

11 The valley of the Godāvarī river. See Feldhaus, *Connected Places*, 2003: pp. 178–181.

12 An early example of this sort of text is Dattarāj Śevalīkar, *Sthān-Mārga-Darśak*. Ghogargāv, Tāluk Śrīgondā: Mahant Śrī. Dattarāj Śevalīkar, Mahānubhāv, 1970.

13 For example, www.youtube.com/watch?v=sVA2nyRSup4, accessed 8 October 2017.

14 For example, https://play.google.com/store/apps/details?id=com.softgen.sol.mynewproject&rdid=com.softgen.sol.mynewproject, accessed 8 October 2017.

15 The discussion that follows draws upon the somewhat more extensive ones in Anne Feldhaus, *Connected Places*, pp. 201–205 and Anne Feldhaus, 'The Religious Significance of Ṛddhipur', in Milton Israel and N.K. Wagle (eds.), *Religion and Society in Maharashtra*, Toronto: University of Toronto, Centre for South Asian Studies, 1987, pp. 68–91, pp. 69–73.

16 See Feldhaus, *Connected Places*, pp. 202–203.

17 The discussion that follows is based on the more extensive one in Feldhaus, *Connected Places*, pp. 196–198.

18 For more detail, see the discussion in Feldhaus, *Connected Places*, pp. 203–205 and pp. 260–261.

19 For a fascinating discussion of the repurposing of buildings and architectural elements in the history of the Deccan, see Richard M. Eaton and Phillip B. Wagoner, *Power, Memory, Architecture: Contested Sites on India's Deccan Plateau, 1300–1600*, New Delhi: Oxford University Press, 2014. For an example from Ṛddhipur, see Viṣṇu Bhikājī Kolte, 'Tārīkhe Amjadī āṇi Mahānubhāv', in *Mahānubhāv Saṃśodhan: 1*. Malkāpūr: Aruṇ Prakāśan, 1962, pp. 146–159, pp. 158–159.

20 In the case of Sāvkheḍā, what Pagaḍī found in what he believed to be the former Āditya temple was in fact not a Śivaliṅga but a Mahānubhāv *oṭā*. Older citizens of the village told him that the temple had been a Śiva temple until fairly recently, when villagers had moved the Śivaliṅga to another location.

21 Pāṭhak points out that most of the Yādava-period Āditya temples mentioned in the *Sthānpothī* were likely to have been subsidiary temples within a *pañcāyatan* (five-temple) complex of temples (117). The implication is that the deities in the four subsidiary temples of a *pañcāyatan* complex would more easily be replaced than would the deity in the central temple.

22 This suggestion is supported by Pānse (1963: 115), cited in Pāṭhak (117).

23 Gaṇeś/Gaṇapati too is by no means as prominent in the *Sthānpothī* as in present-day (post-Peśve) Maharashtra. I am grateful to Vijaya Chitre for this observation.

24 This seems to me to confirm the fundamentally Śaiva character of most Maharashtrian Hindu traditions, prior to – and still today, in spite of – the Vaiṣṇava-Kṛṣṇaite overlay of the Vārkarī tradition. See Charlotte Vaudeville, 'The Shaivite Background of Santism in Maharashtra', in Milton Israel and N.K. Wagle (eds.), *Religion and Society in Maharashtra*, Toronto: University of Toronto, Centre for South Asian Studies, 1987, pp. 32–50.

25 Rājmaḍh or Rājmaṭh is an old name for a Narasiṃha temple (Ḍhere 1971: 48–50).

26 See Feldhaus, 'The Religious Significance of Rddhipur'.

27 I first published the following information in Feldhaus, 'The Religious Significance of Rddhipur', 1987, p. 77.

28 In some places in Ṛddhipur, as in the temple of the Measure-Breaking Gaṇapati, the original Hindu image is itself the object to which Mahānubhāvs do homage – because it was touched by Guṇḍam Rāüḷ or Cakradhar. The gods most central to typical village life are bowed to in Ṛddhipur both by Mahānubhāvs and by non-Mahānubhāv Hindu villagers. In the case of the village's largest Māruti (Hanumān), non-Mahānubhāv villagers worship him from the front, while Mahānubhāvs go around to the back. Many people in Ṛddhipur say that the principal goddess of the village is Kolhārāī ('Jackal-Lady'). At her temple, Mahānubhāvs and non-Mahānubhāvs do their puja and/or make their prostrations side by side.

References

Deśpāṇḍe, Vāman Nārayaṇ, editor. *Smṛtisthaḷ*. 2nd edition, Puṇe: Venus Prakāśan, 1939.

Ḍhere, Rāmcandra Cintāmaṇ. *Loksaṃskṛtīcī Kṣitije*. Puṇe: Viśvakarmā Sāhityālay, 1971.

Eaton, Richard M. and Phillip B. Wagoner. *Power, Memory, Architecture: Contested Sites on India's Deccan Plateau, 1300–1600*. New Delhi: Oxford University Press, 2014.

Feldhaus, Anne. *The Religious System of the Mahānubhāva Sect: The Mahānubhāva Sūtrapāṭha*. New Delhi: Manohar, 1983.

———. *The Deeds of God in Ṛddhipur*. New York: Oxford University Press, 1984.

———. 'Maharashtra as a Holy Land: A Sectarian Tradition'. *Bulletin of the School of Oriental and African Studies, University of London* 49, 1986: 532–548.

———. 'The Religious Significance of Rddhipur'. In *Religion and Society in Maharashtra*, edited by Milton Israel and N.K. Wagle. Toronto: University of Toronto, Centre for South Asian Studies, 1987, pp. 68–91.

———. *Connected Places: Region, Pilgrimage, and Geographical Imagination in India*. New York: Palgrave Macmillan, 2003.

Feldhaus, Anne and Shankar Gopal Tulpule. *In the Absence of God: The Early Years of an Indian Sect*. Honolulu: University of Hawaii Press, 1992.

Kolte, Viṣṇu Bhikājī. 'Tārīkhe Amjadī āṇi Mahānubhāv'. In *Mahānubhāv Saṃśodhan: 1*, edited by V. B. Kolte. Malkāpūr: Aruṇ Prakāśan, 1962, pp. 146–159.

———. editor. *Ravalobās-kṛt Sahyādri-Varṇan*. Puṇe: Puṇe Vidyāpīṭh, 1964.

———. *Mhāīṃbhaṭ-Saṅkalit Śrī Govindaprabhu Caritra*. Malkāpūr: Aruṇ Prakāśan, 1972.

———. *Sthān Pothī*. 2nd edition, Malkāpūr: Aruṇ Prakāśan, 1976.

———. *Mhāīṃbhaṭ Saṅkalit Śrīcakradhar Līḷā Caritra*. 2nd edition, Mumbaī: Mahārāṣṭra Rājya Sāhitya-Saṃskṛti Maṇḍaḷ, 1982.

Nene, Hari Nārāyaṇ. *Mahārāṣṭrīya Ādya Caritrakār Mahindrabhaṭṭa-saṅkalit Līḷācaritra*. 5 volumes. Nāgpūr: Nārāyaṇ Mudraṇālay, 1936–1950.

Pagaḍī, Setu Mādhavrāv. 'Mahānubhāv Sāhityātīl Bhūgol āṇi tyācā Itihās'. *Pañcadhārā* (Quarterly of the Marāṭhī Sāhitya Pariṣad of Andhra Pradesh) 27/28, 1985: 1–22.

Pānse, Murlidhar Gajānan. *Yādavkālīn Mahārāṣṭra, i. sa. 1000 te 1350*. Mumbai: Mumbai Marāṭhī Grantha Saṃgrahālay, 1963.

Pāṭhak, Aruṇcandra Śaṅkar. *Sthānpothī: Ek Purātattvīya Abhyās*. Mumbaī: Mahārāṣṭra Rājya Sāhitya āṇi Saṃskṛtī Maṇḍaḷ, 2013.

Śevalīkar, Dattarāj. *Sthān-Mārga-Darśak*. Ghogargāv, Taluka Śrīgondā: Mahant Śrī. Dattarāj Śevalīkar, Mahānubhāv, 1970.

Tuḷpuḷe, Śaṅkar Gopāl. *Līḷācaritra*. 5 volumes. Nāgpūr/Puṇe: Suvicār Prakāśan Maṇḍaḷ, 1964–1967.

Vaudeville, Charlotte. 'The Shaivite Background of Santism in Maharashtra'. In *Religion and Society in Maharashtra*, edited by Milton Israel and N.K. Wagle. Toronto: University of Toronto, Centre for South Asian Studies, 1987, pp. 32–50.

Chapter 10

Seven Sufi brothers

Dargah vernacular narratives and Konkani Sufi-Muslims

Deepra Dandekar

This chapter outlines relationships between Sufi-Islam and present-day worship at Sufi *dargahs*[1] in coastal Maharashtra (Konkan), based on locally assembled Sufi oral hagiographies from the Ratnagiri district.[2] I have attempted a historically layered reconstruction of vernacular Sufi-Muslim piety in the Konkan, examining mutual associations between Sufism and Konkani *dargahs*. I am especially interested in the institution of Sufi-Muslim 'brotherhoods' and its vernacular Konkani version, which is interstitially located between a widespread acceptance of Sufi-Islam and its tenets, and an everyday, quotidian expression of Muslim religiosity and Sufi piety. To that end, I begin my argument with a discussion on Sufi-Islam, and the Sufi-Muslim idea of 'brotherhood' and *dargahs* in the Konkan, followed by oral hagiographies from the Ratnagiri district. My argument seeks to juxtapose accepted ideas of Sufi-Islam, with the vernacular Muslim notion of the same, as I aim to deconstruct universalizing notions about Islam and religion. To achieve this goal, I promote a vernacular hermeneutic of Sufi-Islam that formulates a quotidian subtext for written Sufi hagiographies that first became popular in the nineteenth century in Bombay with the emergence of the printing press.[3]

Sufi-Islamic ideas of 'brotherhood'

Nile Green has outlined some basic principles of Sufi-Islam – *Tasawwuf* and its origins – that may prove useful for this chapter.[4] While *Tasawwuf* or 'being Sufi' is derived from the word *sūf* or wool, the term Sufi connotes the wearers of 'wool', which considered an uncomfortable and coarse cloth associated with asceticism. Sufis were considered *awliyā*, or Allah's friends, whose powers of intercession with the latter on behalf of the suffering alleviated their sorrows, illnesses and misfortune.[5] *Awliyā* or Sufis, who were deemed holy, especially gained social status if they claimed direct descent or claimed a shared blood-line with the Prophet's family or his companions. Their bodies were believed to be infused with *baraka*, a miraculous power that allowed them to intercede with Allah, and to affect miracles (*karāmāt*).

The power of these miracles evidenced in their friendship with Allah, helped Sufis in missionizing Islam by initiating novices as member-adherents of their mystical traditions. And ritual initiation or the *bayat* of novices often included the physical transfer of *baraka* to the novice *murīd*, by the *dargah*'s leading Sufi (variously known as *sheikh*, *pīr* or *khalifā*).[6] As Green demonstrates, Sufis came to be organized in various networked conglomerates that propagated specific methods of intellectual and mystical traditions, such as prescribed meditation techniques, by the thirteenth century. These conglomerates known as *silsila* (chain) or *tarīqa*s (path)[7] have often been likened to Christian 'brotherhoods' organized around the veneration of particular saints.[8] Sufi lodges in South Asia are associated with the burial-places of important Sufi saints, whose *baraka* is said to bless people even after their disappearance from the worldly domain. The belief that the saint is not dead but existing in a veiled, pure and powerful state within his grave is common and often produces the building of his burial, known in South Asia as *dargah*, as a precinct suffused with *baraka*.[9] The longevity of the *tarīqa* and Sufi-Islam, therefore, hinges on ritual initiation or *bayat*, a process that recruits new members and adherents into the brotherhood and expands it geographically into other regions, where new *dargahs* are built. As Sufis travelled to different parts of the world, establishing new *dargah*s and initiating local novices, their piety and achievements generated hagiographies that further increased the power of their brotherhoods.[10]

Sufi-Islam spread across Africa, Asia, South Asia and South East-Asia as a result of the pioneering achievements of Sufi Sheikhs from different law schools.[11] And *tarīqa*s from the Arabian Peninsula such as the *Qādiriyya*, *Aydarūsiyya* and *Rifāiyya* became prominent in the Konkan, due to the presence of Arab trading groups in Coastal Maharashtra and Southern Coastal Gujarat.[12] Proliferating brotherhoods, accompanied by travelling Sufis were, therefore, geographically specific, even as they spread to the Deccan. Their presence combined the principles of Sufi-Islam with vernacular piety, enabled by the patronage of local rulers.[13] The relationship between earthly and other-worldly dominions of political control (*wilāyat*)[14] shared between rulers and Sufis is exemplified through their burials; kings and Sufis often share common burials at many *dargah*s, such as at the *dargah* of Sheikh Zaynuddīn at Khuldabad shared by Aurangzeb.[15] It is also well known that Shivaji, claimed as the progenitor of a Hindu-Marathi empire in the Deccan,[16] patronized the Sufi Yaqūb Sarvari (with his *dargah* at Kelshi) in the seventeenth century, consulting the latter regularly on political matters, such as the conquest of Konkan. Vernacular Konkani Sufi-Islam rooted in Maharashtra traces its descent to the Arabian Peninsula, to Konkani-Arabic activities of trading and sailing across the Arabian Sea. Konkani Sufi-Islam is, therefore, considered dissimilar to North Indian, Urdu-Persianate Islamic traditions by Konkani Muslims themselves. Due to this dissociation, Konkani Muslims, who mostly follow the *Shafi'i* Islamic law school and adhere to the *Qādirī* and *Rifāī tarīqa*, are also differentiated from the Deccan Sultanates or Bijapuri traditions bearing origin in North India, characterized by the *Hanafi* law school, and accompanied by brotherhoods/*tarīqa*s such as the *Chishtī*, *Suhrāwardi*, *Madāri* or *Junaydī*.[17]

Before proceeding to the subject of vernacular Konkani Islam and Sufism, it is important to mark alleged cultural differences between Konkani Muslims and North Indian Muslims as politically coloured. The Shiv Sena has commonly labelled Konkani Muslims 'autochthonous', in comparison to North Indian Muslims, who are considered migrant outsiders and infiltrators.[18] During my fieldwork with Konkani Muslims in Raigarh and Ratnagiri districts, I observed their precarious and marginal existence. Many among my Konkani interlocutors reported that Konkan had gradually become depopulated of Muslims in postcolonial times. Half the original population had left India for Sindh after the 1947 partition, and the other half had left for jobs in the Gulf in recent times. Those who remained behind were considered residual and old-fashioned. They were alleged to cling to their ethnic-religious community-identity today in an effort to influence local electoral politics. Those Konkani Muslims who return regularly from the Gulf, on the other hand, were increasingly influenced by Wahhabi reformism that decried Konkani Sufi traditions as decadent, Hindu-istic and non-Islamic.[19] On the other hand, many Hindu nationalists, chiming in with Wahhabis in an unusual alliance, proclaimed that 'real' Muslims did not have graves or graveyards.[20] In a bid to push even these residual Konkani Muslims out, they claimed that Konkani *dargah*s and graveyards represented Muslim land-grabbing strategies. Besides, there were Brahmanical rationalists, who carried out secret raids at *dargah*s, claiming that rituals here exploited women and the downtrodden. According to my interlocuters, no *dargah* ever stopped non-Muslims from praying there; but despite this, local Sufi adherents were blamed for Hindu superstitions practiced at *dargahs*.

Finally, the oxymoronic and hyphenated category of autochthonous Marathi-Muslims locates Konkani Muslims awkwardly.[21] According to my informants, the Shiv Sena's claim of Konkani Muslims being Marathi and autochthonous to Maharashtra has two repercussions. While Konkani Muslims confront religious isolation for being a small Muslim minority, they also enjoy better social integration as Maharashtrians. Their fragmentary position is increasingly utilized as an exemplar of 'Indian-Muslimness' that discriminates against North Indian Muslim migrants, who are labelled Pakistani or Bangladeshi infiltrators. Based on the Shiv Sena's attempts to launch 'Marathi' as an ethnic identity, Konkani Muslims have become closely associated with Hindu majoritarian discourse, with Marathi serving to erase their experience of being Muslims in the public domain. Muslim erasure affected by and through prescribed conformity with a vernacular state is symbolized by the *dargah* – a crumbling public symbol of vernacular Islam in Maharashtra, an ambivalent and dilapidated edifice expressing discomfort with indigeneity, excluded but still indirectly allied with Indian national and transcultural relations. Konkani Sufi-Islam as transcultural religiosity, with its history in Indian Ocean networks, therefore, declines increasingly in an age of nation states.

Extending Sufi brotherhoods to Konkani *dargahs*

There was a sense of 'history being destroyed' among many of my Konkani Muslim respondents who were Sufi adherents. For them, Konkani Sufism was neither an eminent Delhi-based tradition, nor a result of their geographical proximity with Bijapur.[22] Instead, according to them, powerful Muslim traders from Arabia (*Arabastān*), who once served local Konkanis, became transformed here into souls revered as Sufi saints, who were worshipped as Muslim village deities by Hindus.[23] In discussions about Sufi brotherhoods or *tarīqa*s, my interlocutors pointed to present-day *dargahs* in the Konkan as all-encompassing of brotherhoods operative in the past, promoting Sufi learning, meditation, initiation and healing. Although there was no historical evidence that present-day *dargah*s ever functioned as Sufi lodges and *tarīqa*s in the past, my respondents pointed to the existence of *dargah*s (and miracles effected at the Sufi's grave) as proof for thriving and powerful Sufi institutional settlement here in the past. And this evidence of greatness in the past, indeed local Muslim history, according to them, was gradually being destroyed by Wahhabis, rationalists and Hindu nationalists. It was said that Konkani Muslims travelled to old *dargah*s on pilgrimage to not just pray for the saint's divine intercession but to behold their heritage in the region, a heritage that provided them political validation in the present. While my respondents argued for the past, making its evidence contingent on the present, this present was also projected backwards – 'it is so now, because it was so in the past'. By doing so, however, they also erased the opportunity for acknowledging the transformative role played by present-day Sufism in bolstering Muslim society. Instead, they viewed it as static and residual. I understood such opinions to be reflective of postcolonial Muslim identity-building in the Konkan. By positing present-day *dargah*s and Sufi traditions as all-encompassing, my respondents expressed their identity as ancient regional Muslims with political claims to the Konkan. According to them, *dargah*s today were facilitated by saintly souls of Sheikhs from the past, whose Sufi institutions of learning were international and who shared discourse and contact with travelling Sufis from all over the world. While they were buried within these institutions, in graveyards surrounding it, Sufi *tarīqa*s and spaces housing such institutions from the past became transformed into *dargah*s, where Sufis belonging to a hoary tradition were buried and worshipped by devotees. As for this moment of transformation, my respondents remained divided. Again, projecting their current political situation backwards, one variety of viewpoint stated that Konkanis had intermittently forgotten and relinquished their *dargah*s due to colonial oppression.[24] Only after independence were these *dargah*s revived as identity-markers for Konkani Muslims. And now, they crumbled again as Konkan became depopulated of Sufi adherents, becoming replaced by Wahhabis and Hindus.

The other variety of viewpoint was more interesting, promoting a composite interpretation. According to this view, current-day *dargahs*, encompassing historical remnants from the past, promoted a concealed variety of Sufism in the present that remained, as yet, thriving and vibrant. My respondents explained that Sufi-Islamic principles from the past had transformed into present-day *dargah* rituals through a concealment of the transformative process that produced a continuity in tradition. For example, if *dargah*s had functioned as translocal Sufi-Muslim lodges/institutions housing different *tarīqa*s from the past, they were still doing so by retaining direct involvement with modern Muslim institutions that housed orphans or promoted Islamic teaching (*yatīm khāna*s and *madrasa*s). However, this process of continuity had remained largely unrecognized, as *dargahs* today continued to house the poor and destitute, and the ill and praying. Devotees continued in their learning of spiritual practices at *dargahs*, enabled by trances facilitated by the Sufi, who instructed disciples from inside the grave. Travelling *dervishes*, *fakirs* and mendicants still arrived at the *dargah* and lived here, like before. But this continuity was now, instead, marked by the absence of Muslim adherents and the increasing influx of Hindu-Marathi majoritarianism. The non-evident continuity that had now gone undercover (as *zāhir* that had become *bātin*) instead highlighted renewed Hindu-Marathi participation within a transformed Sufism, especially after the partition of 1947. Since Wahhabis considered Sufis as mortal and dead within their graves, *dargah*s represented grave-worship to them, though the Sufi heart of the matter indicated the opposite. The concealed knowledge of a transformed Sufi had emerged ever stronger in modern times, as he was now like a foreigner, surrounded by Hindus, who considered him a Muslim deity, while the Sufi remained a *Zindāpīr* (eternally alive) and a *Jihādī* (warrior for the faith) within his grave.

My respondents applied the same argument of concealed transformation in postcolonial Hindu majoritarian Maharashtra to *baraka* (the Sufi's power of miracles), *bayat* (ritual initiation) and *tarīqa*s (Sufi brotherhoods). Though the Sufi's *tarīqa* had in many ways passed away, it had not died. Instead, it had become concealed behind a veil, as the saint existed in a meditative state in his grave (variously described as *tap* or *jhikīr/zikr̥*). The Sufi's ever-powerful *baraka* now flowed out and seeped into the body of his grave, and into the floors, walls, pillars, and ceiling of the *dargah*. Through this concealed transformation, the Sufi who had once lived in the *dargah* became infused with the *dargah*'s body, his power imbuing every brick.

The *dargah*'s traditional caretaker (*mujāwar*), whose forefathers had once cared for the Sufi, now cared for the Sufi's transformed physical state and the *dargah*, soaked with *baraka*. The *mujāwar*'s body, therefore, also absorbed the Sufi's *baraka* due to his constant proximity with the grave. And this meant that the passing away of the *tarīqa* no longer mattered, and that there was no longer any formal requirement of *bayat*. The *mujāwar* received the Sufi's *baraka* directly and carried out his orders by communicating through divine visions (*bashārat*). According to my respondents, *bayat* had concealed-transformed itself, and instead of abating with the *tarīqa*, it now proliferated by enlisting Hindu adherents to Sufism. Since the Sufi was now surrounded by Hindus, he summoned the latter to the *dargah* through *bashārat* and dreams, under the pretext of healing illnesses. Hindus, in addition to various other treatments, performed healing rituals at the *dargah*. Unknown to them, however, these healing rituals constituted taking *bayat* from the Sufi. The absence of knowledge about *bayat* or mistaken healing rituals was convenient for most Hindus, as they misidentified the glory bestowed on novices by Sufis during *bayat* as the healing power of deities. While *bayat* or healing rituals at *dargah*s mostly involved eating ash from the Sufi's graveside-incense (*udī*), drinking water used to wash the Sufi's grave (*ghusl*) and breathing in the Sufi's incense (*lobān*),[25] the corporeal ingestion of the Sufi's physicality led to the transference of *baraka* between devotees and the Sufi. The Sufi's *bayat* was hence rearticulated as healing for Hindus, and it is only after *bayat*, when novices continued to go into trances and receive *bashārat* from the Sufi, that their true and secret nature of inner transformation was achieved. The publicly known *zāhir* of healing was, hence, layered with the privately understood or secret, *bātin* world of the Sufi's *bayat*. According to my respondents, this transformation within *bayat* terminology was important, since Hindus could misunderstand *bayat* as religious conversion and might even attack *dargahs*. Especially, the un-initiated Hindu could be hardly expected to understand *bayat* as it was a parallel moral and spiritual universe that did not necessitate physical, professional or administrative conversion to Islam.

I had noticed that *mujāwar*s from different *dargah*s where I conducted interviews often replaced discussions about *tarīqa*s with descriptions of brotherly relations between Sufi saints. They typically related seven Sufi saints buried in *dargah*s from the surrounding region as seven brothers (*sāt-bhāū*). In our discussions, this brotherly fraternity of seven Konkani Sufis within the local region seemed to replace traditional *tariqa* bonds between novices. The replacement of brotherhood with brother-ship created a Sufi Muslim region, where Konkani Sufi-Muslims and Hindu-Sufi adherents (secret novitiates) became interrelated like a family that shared *baraka*. Therefore, though Hindu novitiates did not know that they had become novitiates through *dargah* rituals, they nevertheless became allied with Muslims as 'brothers' through the brother-ship of their Sufis – the recreated and secretly transformed *tarīqa*. I was to conclude that discussions about secret transformations within Sufism in modern Konkan pointed to a political cleavage between classical relationships of Sufism and Islam. While my respondents spoke of Islam as now relegated to Pakistan, Bangladesh or the Gulf, Sufism remained accessible as 'Indian', Marathi and Hindu, characterized by brother-ship, healing and the tutelary power of the *mujāwar*, who conveyed divine messages from inside the Sufi's grave to the public.

Konkani hagiography and brother-ship

I encountered descriptions of Sufi brother-ship quite regularly at *dargah*s in Raigarh and Ratnagiri, as I collected information from local *mujāwars* who enthusiastically explained how their Sufi was brothers with six or seven nearby others. Their favourite way of explaining this brother-ship was to claim that all *dargah*s belonging to the seven brothers had been built in a single night, after the Sufis had travelled together to the Konkan coast from *Arabastān*. The list of Sufi brothers provided by each *dargah* was, however, often subjective, since each *dargah* provided me with different names and a different list of Sufi brothers. I was unable to find many *dargah*s located within forests or on mountain-tops, but even when I did, not all corroborated their brother-ship with the shrine where I had first begun their search. Many Sufis, like those at the *dargah* of Akusarkhan at Pophli (Raigadh district), claimed uncorroborated brother-ships with *dargah*s at Kelshi, Dabhol, Alibagh, Khed and Chiplun. The *dargah* at Pophli also claimed brother-ship with the local village-goddess (goddess Kali) and celebrated this in an annual procession of the goddess (*chhabinā*). Realizing that the seven Sufi brothers was a trope that enlisted *dargah*s in the task of creating Sufi micro-regions, the arduous exercise of tracing brothers provided me with a visual Sufi map, internal to Raigarh and Ratnagiri.

In Ratnagiri, for example, I began with the *dargah* of Sufi Bābā Karāmuddīn at Bhatye, whose *tarīqa* was considered unknown by most devotees, but whom the *mujāwar* claimed belonged to the Qādirī *tarīqa* and Shafi'i law school. Bābā Karāmuddīn was known to have arrived by sea on the Konkan coast under Allah's and the Prophet's orders from *Arabastān* – somewhere from the direction of Mecca – accompanied by seven brothers and 1,24,000 Sufi followers.[26] The *mujāwar* explained that Bābā had no options but to travel by sea, since Konkan had no roads and was full of jungles in ancient times. Bābā's *dargah* was made on the sea coast by a follower who was a boatman and fisherman. This boatman-fisherman became a devotee after he was saved from drowning by Bābā. His boat suddenly sprang a leak in the middle of a storm at sea, and Bābā, realizing this leak while in meditation on the coast at a great distance, had proceeded to block the leak through his meditative powers. Bābā was so powerful that he could leave his body and travel elsewhere while meditating. Bābā had six other brothers: one was at Shirgaon (Pīr Jawān Shāh Walī), the second at Kalba Devi (Hasan Pīr), the third at Hatis (Bābar Sheikh) and the fourth at Lanja (Chānd Shāh Bukhārī). The *mujāwar* couldn't remember the last two brothers but was confident that I could find them by going to any one of these *dargahs* that he had listed. Though I found the *dargah*s he had named, I found very little reference to Bhatye and was instead directed to other nearby brother-*dargah*s. With the exception of Shirgaon and Lanja, I found no cross-mention to the Bhatye *dargah*. Therefore, though I continued to follow the Bhatye *dargah* track, one could hypothetically start with any one *dargah* in the Konkan and follow thousands of potential seven brother-ship routes branching out from it. According to the *mujāwar* at Bhatye, all brother-ship *dargah*s could be identified by certain unifying features, such as the story of being built together in one single night. Also, the proof of their brother-ship was evidenced in the date of their *urs* (annual celebration of the saint's anniversary) that coincided with the full-moon night of Māgh (January–February). I soon discovered that most *dargah*s in the Konkan celebrated their *urs* on the full-moon night of the Māgh month, further fuelling the visual of a Konkani-Sufi region interrelated through brother-ships. The *mujāwar* at Bhatye told me that most ancient *dargah*s in the Konkan were built during the *shivakālīn* period,[27] even though subsequent renovations provided many newcomers with a false impression of these *dargah*s being more recent. The *mujāwar* said that he had been ritually initiated by the Bābā Karāmuddīn in a *bashārat* (divine vision), and he now received regular *bashārat* from the latter who was said to be meditating inside his grave.

I proceeded to Shirgaon from Bhatye to the *dargah* of Pīr Jawān Shāh Walī. The *mujāwar* at Jawān Shāh's shrine was unclear about the *pīr*'s identity and hagiographical details, though he knew that the Bhatye Bābā was one of Jawān Shāh's brothers. He lamented over how worship (*ibādat*) was missing at the shrine in current times and described how Jawān Shāh, when present, could walk over water. It seemed the latter often walked over water, crossing the backwaters (*khāḍī*) of Shirgaon to meet his other Sufi brother, Hasan Pīr at Kalba Devi, whenever bored. He described how the Sufi brothers between Shirgaon and Kalba Devi helped to moor fishing boats and trading ships that were caught in storms, assisting them to dock at the old Shirgaon harbour, conveniently located between the two *dargah*s. One could see Hasan Pīr's *dargah* from Jawān Shāh's across the arching coast of the old harbour, now silted over with a sand-bar. Pointing to the *khāḍī*, the *mujāwar* told me how ships would earlier dock here, when trade between Konkani Muslims and *Arabastān* was active and not considered illegal. According to the *mujāwar*, Pīr Jawān Shāh Walī's *dargāh* was magical. It had never suffered damage, despite being stuck many times by lightning during storms. The *dargah* also had an Alphonso Mango tree with very sweet fruit in its courtyard. This fruit, however, had turned bitter after the 1947 Hindu-Muslim riots at Shirgaon. (*Jaisā jaisā mohobbat khallās huā, vaisā vaisā pīr-sāheb ke pattāngaṇ kā āpūs-āmbā kaḍū ho gayā*! – 'As the love receded, so, did the Alphonso mango in the Pīr's courtyard turn bitter'!) According to the *mujāwar*, there was a piquant reason for the increasing popularity of Jawān Shāh's *dargāh* at Shirgaon, despite many Muslims departing from the Konkan, or turning anti-Sufi. Legend has it that there was a curse on Shirgaon. Hindu temples built here during the day would break in the night. It was only after the Sufi arrived here and established his *dargah* that Hindu temples also began surviving. This benefice was considered a result of the Sufi's blessing. Hindus, therefore, provided enormous patronage to the *dargah*, and the *mujāwar* was certain that Hindus in Shirgaon could not live without Muslims. However, the *mujāwar* also felt that Hindus in the village did not respect the purity of the Sufi and the morality of Sufi-Islam, since they came to the *dargah* and wished for boons that would help to hide their wrongdoings from the police. They utilized the *dargah* as a protective shield instead of turning over a new leaf, taking the Sufi for granted by bribing the *dargah* with gifts in return for unlawful protection. This created misapprehension among Muslims, especially those who were against Sufi-Islam, and who charged the *dargah* with sheltering Hindu criminals. But the Sufi changed that soon enough. Nowadays, immoral wishes were no longer fulfilled at the *dargah*, and many criminals had been arrested for their misdemeanours, notwithstanding their ritual promises made to the Sufi, the *mujāwar* claimed. This did not mean that the Sufi power of effecting miracles was not real as claimed by rationalists and reformists, or that the Sufi only helped Muslims, as claimed by right-wing Hindus. It meant that the Sufi no longer harboured criminals.

The *dargah* of Hasan Pīr at Kalba Devi, just across the backwater from Jawān Shāh's, had a modern-looking, Portuguese-style frontal façade that gave way to the inner sanctum, resembling a Hindu temple. There was a cremation ground directly adjoining the *dargah*, and the rest of the surrounding area, I was told by a local respondent, was largely populated by affluent local fishermen. The *dargah* seemed to have been claimed by local Hindu groups too, since there was a saffron flag planted in front of it.[28] The hagiography of Hasan Pīr was virtually unknown, apart from his brother-ship with Jawān Shāh. The *mujāwar* at Jawān Shāh's *dargah* recounted similarities between the two Sufis by describing how Hasan Pīr's *dargah* survived lightning attacks but diverted the light from the lightning into the sea, to show ships and boats their navigational path. There was an interesting story about the Sufi brothers that the *mujāwar* from Jawān Shāh's *dargah* told me: Jawān Shāh, arriving from Arabia to the Konkan coast at Shirgaon, encountered a Hindu magician who lived at the cremation grounds of Kalba Devi. This magician possessed an enormous army of evil spirits at his command, who helped him operate a flourishing illicit-liquor trade. The magician secretly tapped toddy (*tāḍi-māḍi*) from adjoining coconut and palm trees and sold this liquor made illicitly to nearby fishermen. Receiving complaints about this magician, Jawān Shāh defeated the latter in a dramatic battle that ruined his liquor business and disbanded his army of evil spirits. He then initiated the magician into Sufi-Islam and turned him into his *murīd*, renaming him Hasan Pīr. And this purified Kalba Devi. Hasan Pīr, thereafter, used his miraculous powers to intercede with Allah on behalf of sufferers in the village. And he also dug a sweet-water well near the sea-front for local fishermen, to whom he had earlier sold illicitly made toddy. At the *dargah* of Hasan Pīr at Kalba Devi, I found an early twentieth-century inscription that reveals the present structure to have already been in ruins in 1906. I have made and provided a translation of this dedicatory *nāgarī*-Marathi inscription below:

> *Hail to the holy structure!*
>
> *Kalba Devi, village Pusāḷe, the dargah of Hasan Pīr Sāheb was earlier in ruins. This dargah was repaired and rebuilt, according to memory, from its foundations, insides, and to its dome by late Rao Gobal Shivaji Mayekar Khot Tanaji with his own money. All the labour for this task was explained to us, and carried out under the instructions of Rao Ramji Gopal Mayekar Nagji Khot. January 10th, Wednesday 1906. Paush Shukla 15th, Shak Saṁvat 1827.* [His wife's dedication below the main inscription, adds:] *Whatever destruction took place at the dargah in the year 1931 due to destruction caused by sea-water was repaired by Chimābāī in the memory of her husband.*

This inscription demonstrates the significance of Hasan Pīr's *dargah* to non-Muslim and local land-owning dominant-caste clans from Kalba Devi. Evidently, the *dargah* was important for Khot-Tanaji, Nagji Khot, their clan, the village members to whom financial arrangements were explained and even to a surviving wife, Chimābāī, who repaired the *dargah* after her husband passed away. The Khots were obviously influential and affluent enough to not just repair the *dargah* repeatedly but to claim ownership over a public, religious structure. The inscription claims that the *dargah* was almost completely rebuilt in 1906. And there is no reason to doubt that the structure and grave were already present before 1906, when repairs were first made and documented by the Khots. Since modest narratives of praising new ownership are often displaced by disparaging the earlier conditions of that property, it is unclear whether the *dargah* was truly dilapidated or whether the narrative uses 'dilapidation' as indirect references to the grandeur of the Khots (a *praśastī*). The inscription does suggest the acquisition of the land connected to the *dargah* by the Khots – agrarian property, whose borders were perhaps marked by the *dargah* – and reiterates their political claims to this ownership by repeating renovations in 1931.

From Shirgaon and Kalba Devi, I progressed to Hatis and Lanja. Pīr Bābar Sheikh's *dargah* at Hatis was entirely controlled by Hindus belonging to a specific clan called Nagvekar, who formed the village's demographic majority. The Nagvekars conceptualized the *dargah* as a grave, and the shrine as that of a Muslim deity and not a Sufi, who was veiled but alive inside his grave. The present-day village of Hatis has no Muslims, and the *dargah* has no *mujāwar*. The Sufi's story is printed and sold in the form of slim booklets that mostly describe the Nagvekar-narrative about other Hindu village deities, the village administration, information about Hindu village festivals, and self-appreciation for rural-development activities at Hatis. The 16-page booklet titled 'Pīr Bābar Sheikh's *dargah* at Hatis' contains only three pages about the Sufi, mostly describing his present-day rituals and *urs*. The booklet describes Bābar Sheikh as an interstitial being, who arrived in the village by sailing miraculously up the Kajali River (against the current) towards the hinterland in a boat. Some respondents in the village described him to have arrived in a coffin. The confusion between the boat and coffin, implying confusions between the live and dead saint, went unnoticed at Hatis as my respondents continued to recount how Bābā, existing between being dead and alive, served people at the village and cured them of illnesses. He was buried along with those who accompanied him, and their house and graves became collectively revered as the *dargah*. It is an ambivalent structure at Hatis today,[29] with its dome already altered and coloured yellowish-saffron to make the structure look like a Hindu temple. Due to this Hindu layering at Hatis, the graves of Pīr Bābar Sheikh's *murīd* at the *dargah* are also considered demonic or *khavīs* employed in the service of the saint, who are ritually deployed by the village like policemen to detect wrongdoings. The ritual process of making offerings, called *hukmāchā-ikkā* (the ruling ace in a pack) is said to transform the Sufi and the *dargah* into a Muslim village deity that exorcises a Hindu village of evil and witchcraft. My interlocutors at Hatis did not even know of the existence of seven Sufi brother-ships, and denied that Bābar Sheikh was ever anyone's brother, though they confirmed that his *urs* took place on the full-moon night in Māgh. However, despite the Nagvekars co-opting the Sufi and *dargah* as a village deity temple, Bābar Sheikh's original identity as Muslim continued to be capitalized. The Nagvekars sold the booklet titled 'Pīr Bābar Sheikh's *dargah* at Hatis' to attract Muslim tourists during the saint's *urs* to the village, even though there was very little about the saint printed in it. Konkani Muslims from neighbouring areas still visited Hatis to pay the Sufi their respects.

The last *dargah* from the Bhatye trajectory was Chānd Shāh Bukhāri's *dargah* at Lanja. The *mujāwar* confirmed Chānd Shāh's brother-ship with Hatis and Bhatye, but not with Shirgaon and Kalba Devi. According to the *mujāwar* at Lanja, who was joined by the head of a local Muslim school for the meeting I had organized with them, the village was segregated between Muslims and Hindus. While Chānd Shāh looked after the Muslim part of the village, other Hindu village deities Kolteshwar and Kedarlinga, who were also each other's brothers, helped to keep the Hindu parts intact. Many in the village had claimed to have witnessed Kolteshwar, Kedarlinga and Chānd Shāh Bukhāri riding around the village at night astride their horses. The three deities kept order in the village, tightly surveying all villagers and ensuring that no one crossed the religious boundaries between Hindu-Muslim segregated zones. Festivals at the *dargah* were likewise celebrated by keeping this religious segregation in mind. Rituals were performed at the *dargah* by all communities, but respect for religious differences was also strictly adhered to. Muslims and Hindus did not perform rituals together. However, Sufi miracles took place for both Hindus and Muslims here, subject to devotees maintaining strict religious separation. Although the legal ownership (*sanad*) of the *dargah* was a pending court matter (at Bangalore), problems of witchcraft-solving took place through divine visions or *bashārat* received by the *mujāwar* at the *dargah*. The *mujāwar* told me that Chānd Shāh Bukhāri and his brothers from Hatis, Bhatye and a few other neighbouring villages, arrived in Lanja together during the *shivakālin* period and civilized the forests of Ratnagiri. I found the hagiographies of Lanja and Hatis similar, though the Lanja *dargah* narrative was a level above the Hindu predominance encountered at Hatis; Lanja was also Brahminical in addition, as rituals at the *dargah* involved ideas about ritual pollution and untouchability. As evident from the hagiography, Muslims at Lanja were treated as a separate and untouchable caste (*jāt*) and village deities here that included the Sufi played an important role in segregating castes, predicated on the experience of blessings and miracles.

Quotidian Muslim religiosity in rural Konkan

In conclusion, I would highlight two issues: one concerning the discursive production of vernacular Sufi-Islam in the Konkan and, second, the quotidian framework of Sufi-Islam that is provided by vernacular hagiographies. However, intrinsic to these concerns is the encapsulation of Sufi-Islam as historically and culturally contextual, without falling into the puritanical trap of viewing all Sufi-Islam as universally Quranic, or conversely as un-Islamic, if expressed in the vernacular. Sufi-Islam in Western Maharashtra or the Konkan is, therefore, a valid spatially and temporally specific expression of vernacular Islam. This Konkani Sufi-Islam is differentiated from Sufism in the Deccan or North India; though by saying this, I do not rule out the historical existence of vibrant contact between Sufis of different regions. Postcolonial transformations within Konkani Sufi-Islam are specific to postcolonial transformations in the Konkan as a whole and cannot be analysed as corruptions within any universal discourse about Sufism. Postcolonial transformation in the Konkan has impressed religiosity in general, and Muslims and Sufi-Islam as part of it. Differences and disagreements between Konkani Sufi-Islam and other varieties of vernacular Sufi-Islam in South Asia cannot, therefore, be treated as hierarchical: non-acceptance of difference as an instrument that denigrates vernacular Sufism as lower, un-Islamic, and requiring of Islamic reform. Islamic reform is a different cultural and historical idea, linked with the rise of nineteenth-century Muslim modernity in North India, or with Salafi or Wahhabi reformist activism in eighteenth-century Saudi Arabia that has influenced the Konkan. This cannot be necessarily linked with current-day Konkani Sufi-Islam that engages deeply with the Indian nation-state, Hindu nationalism, and the subsidiary formation of an ethnic-Marathi identity. Neither can Konkani Sufism be explained as a single and unbroken trajectory. Its origins in the transcultural trading and travelling nexus of Indian Ocean trade, and the diaspora it created between the Mediterranean and Java since the tenth century,[30] cannot be compared to its nature in nationalist Hindu Maharashtra that labels transcultural Muslim contacts as infiltration. But this does not make twenty-first-century vernacular Sufism in the Konkan less Islamic than Sufism in the tenth century, or less Islamic than twenty-first-century Sufism in other regions.

Coming to the first concern, it is already obvious that Konkani vernacular Sufi-Islam became transformed from its tenth-century avatar in postcolonial times. This transformation, mediated by the birth of the Hindu majoritarian Indian nation state, reconfigures Sufism as a variety of Muslim religiosity that is discursively differentiated from Islam, as the latter is increasingly relegated to neighbouring Muslim nations, but this does not excise Sufism from Islam either. As already discussed, while transformations refashion and rearticulate *bayat* and the transfer of *baraka* as ritualistic healing, this transformation also rearticulates ideas about *tarīqa* and brotherhood as seven brother conglomerates and brother-ships. These transformations are not due to Konkani Sufi-Islam becoming non-Islamic or more Hindu but because *dargah*s in the Konkan interact more deeply with Hindu devotees and Hindutva politics in India. The recounted oral hagiographies demonstrate tremendous political negotiation, revealing the *dargah* at the epicentre of Konkani Sufi-Muslim attempts at being counted as ancient and autochthonous inhabitants of the Konkan and Maharashtra. On the other hand, the *dargah* is also utilized by Hindus as a boundary-marker of agrarian castes-clan property and as a village deity, who not only reforms magicians, but is a demon-catching magician himself, enlisted to serve Hindu villages.[31] Sufis are also revered as policemen, segregating religious groups on the lines of Hindu castes.

Any disregard and violence transforms the Sufi's blessing into a curse, by turning the sweet mango bitter after Partition Hindu-Muslim riots in the village. While rearticulating *bayat* as healing teaches Hindus about the Sufi's love, it also conserves *dargahs* in the Konkan that suffer from regular abandonment. For example, the only shrine of Khwāja Khizr in Western India is abandoned, overgrown and dilapidated today, as it lies on the outskirts of Dabhol, on the Raigarh coastline.[32] It is an enormous shrine reminiscent of the contacts between Konkan, Sindh, the estuaries of the Indus River and Khizr's *Uwaisi tarīqa* that once enjoyed powerful initiates such as Makhdoom Ali Mahimi in Mumbai.[33] My argument here seeks to highlight the political breakdown between classical associations that relate Sufism with Islam in specific ways, which define Muslim religiosity as prescriptive and universal. Resisting this view, I contend that one of the more important components within Sufism and its present-day postcolonial transformations in Maharashtra includes delinking it from a reformist approach that considers un-Islamic all that is outside the classical association between Sufism and Islam and in contrast, calls for an acceptance of difference while considering vernacular linkages between Sufism and Islam.

The most interesting example of such postcolonial transformations in the Konkan lies in the alterity between brotherhoods or *tarīqa* and seven brother-ships or *sāt-bhāū*. This alterity, conjoined with the increasing transformation of *dargahs* into village deity shrines, views Sufis as reformed demigods, who in their benign form identify wrongdoers in the village. The visual-spatial relationship between seven Sufi brothers, moreover, almost mirrors ritualistic relationships between seven village-goddesses bound together as sisters, whose shrines mark and protect agrarian rural boundaries in Maharashtra.[34] Just like seven village-goddesses or seven sisters produce an affiliated micro-region of semi-endogamous agrarian Hindu clans, seven Sufis, tied-together as brothers, also produce a Sufi-Muslim micro-region of interrelated adherent Hindu and Muslim clans. The shift from brotherhood to brother-ship constitutes a piquant example of everyday rural Konkani religiosity, wherein Sufi *dargahs* accompany village-goddess temples as representatives of a mixed religious, albeit caste-segregated society. This participation on the lines of seven sister-goddesses does not make Sufis or *dargahs* less Islamic; it only refashions the experience of Sufism, and Islam in rural Konkani society, in present times.

In terms of my second concern, I propose that the above-recounted oral hagiographies are constitutive of a quotidian framework for emerging and present-day *dargah* literature and Muslim religiosity in postcolonial Maharashtra. While there are two identifiable streams within *dargah* literature in Western India, the first stream originated in Bombay's Sufi-Muslim print culture, in the eighteenth and nineteenth century. This has already been substantially explored by Green, who contextualizes early Muslim print culture within the framework of religious 'firms', and the existence of cosmopolitan Sufi-Muslim trading groups in Mumbai.[35] This corpus becomes significantly transformed in postcolonial times with the departure and general absence of Konkani Muslims, as a result of the partition in 1947. The postcolonial Sufi stream in Konkan, on the other hand, is fragmented and characterized by a differentiated Muslim religiosity that is often lauded as Marathi and Indian.[36] But the alleged schism between Sufism and Islam, threatened by Muslim-reformist critiques that brand Konkani *dargah*s as un-Islamic, has led to the impossibility of developing any independent postcolonial literary style for *dargah* hagiographies and miracle stories. Modern *dargah* literature in India and especially Maharashtra, therefore, inhabits an anxious and thin boundary-line of being condemned as corrupt by Muslim reformists and accused of spreading Islam by Hindu nationalists. On the other hand, modern *dargah* narratives are further transformed into audio-video recordings and locally printed booklets about the devotion and *bhakti* of Sufism and *dargah*s that resemble devotional literature from temples to ward off Hindu criticism. These new and postcolonial variety of hagiographical materials, written in the Devanagari script, and in a mix of languages using idioms from Marathi, Dakhini and Hindi are mostly based on oral narratives and suffused with *bhakti-bhāv*, sold outside *dargah*s or encountered within private collections. The *dargah* administration members whom I interviewed were not keen to develop this shrine literature any further. According to them, apart from the fear of being attacked by reformist rationalists, and Hindus, most *dargah*-goers in Maharashtra were also poor, rural and uneducated. They enjoyed oral hagiographies and audio-video tapes more and their devotion for the saint was predicated on songs recounting the saint's stories of miracles, curses and punishment, in keeping with religious formats suggested by local village deity-worship.

Most academics of Islam and enthusiasts of Sufism have lost interest in postcolonial and vernacular *dargah* literature, since these don't reflect traditional relationships between Sufism and Islam or inform the history of local Muslim empires or Sultanates. This disinterest, that is in tacit alliance with Konkani Muslims, reformists, rationalists and Hindu nationalists today, unfortunately endangers the institution of the *dargah*. Viewing Sufism within the binaries of literary and philosophical profundity, linked with Sultanate or Mughal practices on the one hand, and the parameters of Islamic reform on the other, has the potential of destroying an academic examination of rural and oral-vernacular Sufism that constitutes quotidian and everyday Islamic religiosity in Maharashtra and the Konkan. I borrow and extend Novetzke's powerful concept of the quotidian revolution[37] here to propose an affirmative framing of everyday religiosity and emerging literary culture, when arguing for oral hagiographies constituting the quotidian framework for postcolonial *dargah* literature in Maharashtra today. Novetzke argues persuasively for the existence of an everyday, public and quotidian democracy during the Yadava-century that spawned the vernacular revolution represented by the first Marathi texts, the *Līḷācharitra* and the *Jñāneshvarī*. Using Novetzke's framework, I extend the argument to posit oral Sufi and *dargah* hagiographies as constituting the quotidian and everyday framework for postcolonial *dargahs* and Konkani Muslim identity politics, based on miracle stories and songs. This quotidian framework of Sufi Islam is, finally, what is projected as secular and tolerant in postcolonial Maharashtra, while encapsulating positive Hindu-Muslim relationships in the coastal region.

Notes

1 *Dargah* is a Persian word that connotes a threshold or doorway. It has been used to describe a Sufi's abode and is a common term used for Sufi burials and Sufi shrines in South Asia. Cf. Michel Boivin, 'Authority, Shrines and Spaces: Scrutinizing Devotional Islam from South Asia', in Michel Bovin and Rémy Delage (eds.), *Devotional Islam in Contemporary South Asia: Shrines, Journeys and Wanderers*, Oxon: Routledge, 2016, pp. 1–12.
2 I conducted fieldwork with Konkani Muslims around Mumbai, Raigarh, Ratnagiri and Sindhudurg districts of Konkan.
3 Nile Green, *Bombay Islam. The Religious Economy of the West Indian Ocean, 1840–1915*, Cambridge: Cambridge University Press, 2011, pp. 90–117.
4 Nile Green, *Sufism: A Global History*, Chichester: Wiley-Blackwell, 2012, pp. 1–14.
5 Cf. John Renard, *Friends of God: Islamic Images of Piety, Commitment, and Servanthood*, Oakland: University of California Press, 2008.
6 Cf. Ian Richard Netton, *Sufi Ritual*, Oxon: Routledge, 2013.
7 Nile Green, *Sufism: A Global History*, Chichester: Wiley-Blackwell, 2012, pp. 71–124.
8 For brotherhoods in Islam; cf. Spencer, J. Trimmingham, *The Sufi Orders in Islam*, Oxford: Clarendon Press, 1971. Also, for the limited use of the term 'brotherhood' to exclusively refer to Sufi *ṭarīqas* that prohibit followers from being simultaneously part of different *ṭarīqas*, cf. Abubn-Nasr, Jamil M, *Muslim Communities of Grace: The Sufi Brotherhoods in Islamic Religious Life*, New York: Columbia University Press, 2007, pp. 127–132.
9 This is a common belief, cf. Jane Idleman Smith, and Yazbeck Yvonne Haddad, *The Islamic Understanding of Death and Resurrection*, New York: Oxford University Press, 2002 [1981], p. 183.
10 Cf. Annemarie Schimmel, *Mystical Dimensions of Islam*, Chapel Hill: The University of North Carolina Press, 1975.
11 Annemarie Schimmel, *Islam in the Indian Subcontinent*, Leiden, Koln: E. J. Brill, 1980.
12 Cf. Mohiuddin Momin, *Muslim Communities in Medieval Konkan (610–1900 A.D.)*, New Delhi: Sundeep Prakashan, 2002.
13 Malfuzat-i-Naqshbandiyya Simon Digby, *Sufis and Soldiers in Awrangzeb's Deccan*, New Delhi: Oxford University Press, 2001.
14 Cf. Simon Digby, 'The Sufi Shaikh as a Source of Authority in Medieval India', in M. Gaborieau (ed.), *Islam et Societe en Asie du Sud*, Paris: École des Hautes Études en Sciences Sociales, 1986, pp. 57–77.

15 Nile Green, 'Stories of Saints and Sultans: Remembering History at the Sufi Shrines of Aurangabad', *Modern Asian Studies*, 2004, 38(2): 419–446.
16 For more on Shivaji as a Hindu ruler, cf. James W. Laine, *Shivaji: Hindu King in Islamic India*, New Delhi: Oxford University Press, 2003.
17 Cf. Carl W. Ernst, *Eternal Garden: Mysticism, History, and Politics at a South Asian Sufi Center*, New Delhi: Oxford University Press, 2004. For an exposition on *Chistis* in the Deccan, cf. Carl W. Ernst, and Lawrence B. Bruce, *Sufi Martyrs of Love: The Chishti Order in South Asia and Beyond*, New York: Palgrave Macmillan, 2002. For *Junaydi* Sufis in the Deccan, cf. Mohammed Suleman Siddiqi, *The Junaydī Sufis of the Deccan: Discovery of a Seventeenth Century Scroll*, New Delhi: Primus Books, 2014.
18 Cf. Deepra Dandekar, 'Margins or Centre? Konkani Sufis, India and "Arabastan"', in K. Mielke and A.-K. Hornidge (eds.), *Area Studies at the Crossroads. Knowledge Production after the Mobility Turn*, New York: Palgrave Macmillan, 2017, pp. 141–156. Also cf. Vaibhav Purandare, *Bal Thackerey and the Rise of the Shiv Sena*, New Delhi: Roli Books, 2012.
19 Cf. Elizabeth Sirriyeh, *Sufis and Anti-Sufis: The Defense, Rethinking and Rejection of Sufism in the Modern World*, London: RoutledgeCurzon, 1999.
20 Pu. Nā Oak [Ōk], 2001, *Samast itihāskārānnā niṣprabh karṇārā śodh: Tājmahāl he tejomahālay āhe* (A Disappointing Discovery for Historians: Taj Mahal is Tejo-Mahalay). Pune: Ravirāj Prakāśan, 1989.
21 Deepra Dandekar, 'Abdul Kader Mukadam: Political Opinions and a genealogy of Marathi Intellectual and Muslim Progressivism', in Deepra Dandekar and Torsten Tschacher (eds.), *Islam, Sufism and Everyday Politics of Belonging in South Asia*, Oxon: Routledge, 2016c, pp. 177–195.
22 For information for Sufism contextualized within the Bijapuri Sultane, cf. Richard Maxwell Eaton, *The Sufis of Bijapur, 1300–1700: Social Roles of Sufis in Medieval India*, Princeton: Princeton University Press, 1978.
23 Deepra Dandekar, 'Grey Literature at the Dargāh of Pīr Bābar Sheikh at Hātis', *Pantheon: Journal for the Study of Religions*, 2016b, 11(1): 121–135.
24 For more on the question of British interference in Indian religious matters, cf. Gauri Viswanathan, *Outside the Fold: Conversion, Modernity, and Belief*, Princeton: Princeton University Press, 1998, pp. 3–43.
25 For Quranic methods of exorcism, cf. Joyce B. Flueckiger, *In Amma's Healing Room: Gender and Vernacular Islam in South India*, Bloomington: Indiana University Press, 2006.
26 For the symbolic number of 1,24,000 prophets in Islam, cf. Annemarie Schimmel, *Deciphering the Signs of God: A Phenomenological Approach to Islam*, Albany: State University of New York Press, 1994, p. 188. There is a parallel drawn here between the Prophet Muhammad, prophets in Islam, and Bābā Karāmuddīn.
27 Most Konkani Muslims referred to the past in two ways: by *Shivakālīn* they referred to Shivaji's times, and by *Pandavkālīn*, they referred to the time of the Mahabharata epic.
28 Cf. Robert M. Hayden, 'Antagonistic Tolerance, Competitive Sharing of Religious Sites in South Asia and the Balkans', *Current Anthropology*, 43, 2002: 205–231.
29 Cf. Deepra Dandekar, 'Grey Literature at the Dargāh of Pīr Bābar Sheikh at Hātis', *Pantheon: Journal for the Study of Religions*, 2016b, 11(1): 121–135.
30 André Wink, Early Medieval India and the Expansion of Islam 7th–11th Centuries (volume I), *Al-Hind: The Making of the Indo-Islamic World*, Leiden: E.J. Brill, 1996.

31 Cf. Carla Bellamy, *The Powerful Ephemeral: Everyday Healing in an Ambiguously Islamic Place*, Ranikhet: Permanent Black, 2011.

32 Geographically speaking, Khwāja Khizr is traditionally associated with the Sindh region and the estuaries of the River Indus. The proximity between Sindh and Konkan, common activities such as sailing the seas through estuaries have also produced Khwāja Khizr as important for coastal Maharashtra. Cf. Brannon Wheeler, *Prophets in the Quran: An Introduction to the Quran and Muslim Exegesis*, New York: Bloomsbury Publishing, 2002.

33 Deepra Dandekar, 'Muṃbaī ke Aulīyā: The Sufi Saints Makhdoom Ali Mahimi (Mumbai) and Hajji Malang (Mumbai-Kalyan) in Songs and Hagiography', *Zeitschrift für Indologie und Südasienstudien*, 2015/16, 32/33: 233–255.

34 Deepra Dandekar, *Boundaries and Motherhood: Ritual and Reproduction in Rural Maharashtra*, New Delhi: Zubaan, 2016a.

35 Nile Green, *Bombay Islam. The Religious Economy of the West Indian Ocean, 1840–1915*, Cambridge: Cambridge University Press, 2011, pp. 90–117.

36 Deepra Dandekar, and Torsten Tschacher, 'Introduction: Framing Sufism in South Asian Muslim Politics and Belonging', in Deepra Dandekar and Torsten Tschacher (eds.), *Islam, Sufism and Everyday Politics of Belonging in South Asia*, Oxon: Routledge, 2016c, pp. 1–15.

37 Christian Lee Novetzke, *The Quotidian Revolution: Vernacularization, Religion, and the Premodern Public Sphere in India*, New York: Columbia University Press, 2016.

References

Abubn-Nasr, Jamil M. *Muslim Communities of Grace: The Sufi Brotherhoods in Islamic Religious Life*. New York: Columbia University Press, 2007.

Bellamy, Carla. *The Powerful Ephemeral: Everyday Healing in an Ambiguously Islamic Place*. Ranikhet: Permanent Black, 2011.

Boivin, Michel. 'Authority, Shrines and Spaces: Scrutinizing Devotional Islam from South Asia'. *Devotional Islam in Contemporary South Asia: Shrines, Journeys and Wanderers*. Ed. Michel Bovin and Rémy Delage. Oxon: Routledge, 2016.

Dandekar, Deepra. 'Abdul Kader Mukadam: Political Opinions and a genealogy of Marathi Intellectual and Muslim Progressivism'. *Islam, Sufism and Everyday Politics of Belonging in South Asia*. Ed. Deepra Dandekar and Torsten Tschacher. Oxon: Routledge, 2016, pp. 177–195.

Dandekar, Deepra. *Boundaries and Motherhood: Ritual and Reproduction in Rural Maharashtra*. New Delhi: Zubaan, 2016.

Dandekar, Deepra, 'Grey Literature at the Dargāh of Pīr Bābar Sheikh at Hātis'. *Pantheon: Journal for the Study of Religions*, 2016, 11(1): 121–135.

Dandekar, Deepra. 'Margins or Centre? Konkani Sufis, India and "Arabastan"'. *Area Studies at the Crossroads. Knowledge Production after the Mobility Turn*. Ed. K. Mielke and A.-K. Hornidge. New York: Palgrave Macmillan, 2017.

Dandekar, Deepra. 'Muṃbaī ke Aulīyā: The Sufi Saints Makhdoom Ali Mahimi (Mumbai) and Hajji Malang (Mumbai-Kalyan) in Songs and Hagiography'. *Zeitschrift für Indologie und Südasienstudien*, 2015/2016, 32/33: 233–255.

Dandekar, Deepra and Torsten Tschacher. 'Introduction: Framing Sufism in South Asian Muslim Politics and Belonging'. *Islam, Sufism and Everyday Politics of Belonging in South Asia*. Ed. Deepra Dandekar and Torsten Tschacher. Oxon: Routledge, 2016, pp. 1–15.

Digby, Simon. 'The Sufi Shaikh as a Source of Authority in Medieval India'. *Islam et Societe en Asie du Sud*. Ed. M. Gaborieau. Paris: École des Hautes Études en Sciences Sociales, 1986.

Digby, Simon. *Sufis and Soldiers in Awrangzeb's Deccan*. New Delhi: Oxford University Press, 2001.

Eaton, Richard Maxwell. *The Sufis of Bijapur, 1300–1700: Social Roles of Sufis in Medieval India*. Princeton: Princeton University Press, 1978.

Ernst, Carl W. *Eternal Garden: Mysticism, History, and Politics at a South Asian Sufi Center*. New Delhi: Oxford University Press, 2004.

Ernst, Carl W. and Lawrence B. Bruce. *Sufi Martyrs of Love: The Chishti Order in South Asia and Beyond*. New York: Palgrave Macmillan, 2002.

Flueckiger, Joyce B. *In Amma's Healing Room: Gender and Vernacular Islam in South India*. Bloomington: Indiana University Press, 2006.

Green, Nile, *Bombay Islam. The Religious Economy of the West Indian Ocean, 1840–1915*. Cambridge: Cambridge University Press, 2011, pp. 90–117.

Green, Nile. 'Stories of Saints and Sultans: Remembering History at the Sufi Shrines of Aurangabad'. *Modern Asian Studies*, 2004, 38(2): 419–446.

Green, Nile. *Sufism: A Global History*. Chichester: Wiley-Blackwell, 2012.

Hayden, Robert M. 'Antagonistic Tolerance, Competitive Sharing of Religious Sites in South Asia and the Balkans'. *Current Anthropology*, 2002, 43: 205–231.

Laine, James W. *Shivaji: Hindu King in Islamic India*. New Delhi: Oxford University Press, 2003.

Momin, Mohiuddin. *Muslim Communities in Medieval Konkan (610–1900 A.D.)* New Delhi: Sundeep Prakashan, 2002.

Netton, Ian Richard. *Sufi Ritual*. Oxon: Routledge, 2013.

Novetzke, Christian Lee. *The Quotidian Revolution: Vernacularization, Religion, and the Premodern Public Sphere in India*. New York: Columbia University Press, 2016.

Oak [Ōk], Pu. Nā, 2001. *Samast itihāskārānnā niṣprabh karṇārā śodh: Tājmahāl he tejomahālay āhe* (A Disappointing Discovery for Historians: Taj Mahal is Tejo-Mahalay). Pune: Ravirāj Prakāśan, 1989.

Purandare, Vaibhav. *Bal Thackerey and the Rise of the Shiv Sena*. New Delhi: Roli Books, 2012.

Renard, John. *Friends of God: Islamic Images of Piety, Commitment, and Servanthood*. Oakland: University of California Press, 2008.

Schimmel, Annemarie. *Deciphering the Signs of God: A Phenomenological Approach to Islam*. Albany: State University of New York Press, 1994.

Schimmel, Annemarie. *Islam in the Indian Subcontinent*. Leiden: E.J. Brill, 1980.

Schimmel, Annemarie. *Mystical Dimensions of Islam*. Chapel Hill: The University of North Carolina Press, 1975.

Siddiqi, Mohammed Suleman. *The Junaydī Sufis of the Deccan: Discovery of a Seventeenth Century Scroll*. New Delhi: Primus Books, 2014.

Sirriyeh, Elizabeth. *Sufis and Anti-Sufis: The Defense, Rethinking and Rejection of Sufism in the Modern World*. London: Routledge Curzon, 1999.

Smith, Jane Idleman and Yazbeck Yvonne Haddad. *The Islamic Understanding of Death and Resurrection*. New York: Oxford University Press, 2002 [1981].

Trimmingham, J. Spencer. *The Sufi Orders in Islam*. Oxford: Clarendon Press, 1971.

Viswanathan, Gauri. *Outside the Fold: Conversion, Modernity, and Belief*. Princeton: Princeton University Press, 1998.

Wheeler, Brannon. *Prophets in the Quran: An Introduction to the Quran and Muslim Exegesis*. New York: Bloomsbury Publishing, 2002.

Wink, André. *Al-Hind: The Making of the Indo-Islamic World*. Vol. 1, *Early Medieval India and the Expansion of Islam 7th–11th Centuries*. Leiden: E.J. Brill, 1996.

Chapter 11

Emplacing holiness

The local religiosity between Vaishnavas, Sufis and demons

Dušan Deák

Recent studies discussing South Asian holy men share one important observation. It is the holy men's devotees and a plethora of interpreters – from the local expounders of their glory up to academics – that to a considerable degree create who the holy men are understood to be. Holy men are credited with an active role in shaping people's religiosity, setting the moral principles of correct behaviour and forming examples of the ways that humans can pierce the layers of the experienced realities of life. Comprehending holy men thus takes a route that starts from them and leads to the forming of others. Yet the mechanics of the holy men's engaging with other people's worlds articulate through the observation of people's diverse engagements with the holy men rather than the other way round. For instance, Christian Novetzke, in a study of Namdev that placed his analysis under the umbrella rubric of public religion, showed us not one but several "Namdevs" depending on the materials that have produced Namdev's identity, be they texts attributed to (the most probably illiterate) Namdev, oral sources, hagiographies or movies.[1] Nile Green exposed the commercial firm-like character of people devoted to Bombay's Muslim saints, launching the branches of their devotional enterprises within, but also outside, South Asia across the territories of the Indian Ocean.[2] Richard Eaton emphasized Tukaram's role in laying the foundations of the social movement of the commoner Varkaris, triggered by the vernacular vehicle of social protest,[3] and recently Timothy Dobe unsettled the holy men from the constraints of the petrifying societal traditions of the sacred and identitarian in order to discuss the holy men's active re-production of shared religious visions.[4]

This is not mere engagement with social constructivism in academic praxis. It is giving credit to, recognizing and organizing the sources of our knowledge about people who may be invoked for social good as well as be seen as the backbone of social unrest, past or present.[5] For indeed, these people do appear as 'polivestiary' – many clothed, to borrow a term from Nile Green[6]; because of this and in order to describe them at least with some erudition, several types of materials must inevitably be consulted. These may range from written evidence, as varied as land grants, histories, saint-poetry, hagiographies or academic writings, to orally transmitted narratives, if only the domain of the word is observed. If attention is also paid to the people's agency, practices and creativity, then the materials swell to ethnographic data about rituals, periodic festivals, pilgrimages, social activism, visual data such as pictures and paintings, or objects embodying the holiness of the sanctified people as well as their memory, such as shrines, graves, but also different objects of their daily use and so on. This list is by far not exhaustive.

Thus there is a valid reason why paying more attention to 'people-derived holy men' may reveal something about people, holy men not excluded. In what follows, I will be addressing the community of holy men's devotees, particularly the devotees of Sheikh Muhammad Baba from Shrigonda (ca. 1560–1660), who live in greater density in the Ahmadnagar district of the Indian state of Maharashtra, but are represented in other parts of this Western Indian state and even beyond it. It is a multifarious folk – a characteristic that has been epitomized in the colloquial term used by the Sheikh's devotees describing him as a saint 'of all castes' (*sarvajātice sant*). In academic parlance, this would mean not only a holy man revered by all people across social hierarchies but also across the modern religious labels of the devotees as Hindus and Muslims.[7] Argued ideologically and certainly practically, given the threats and memory of communal animosity, the Sheikh has also been seen as bringing both religious communities together.[8] However, I will argue that this broad religious division of South Asians into Hindus and Muslims plays a much lesser role in the divisions that are observable among the devotees of Sheikh.

To my eyes, what brings the devotees together primarily is their devotional allegiance to the Sheikh, which already has a history of several centuries. What divides them is the form through which they choose to practice their devotion and the narratives through which the devotion is explained: in other words, the history of constructing the Sheikh's holiness. In order to demonstrate this claim, I will first briefly introduce the Sheikh and the complex legacy that he left for others to decipher and follow. Second, I will discuss how this legacy was narratively appropriated and what the appropriation meant in terms of the tradition of the Sheikh's veneration. Third, I will explore how the places that the different strands of the Sheikh's devotees associate with the Sheikh enable them to produce 'their own' Sheikh. Indeed, the places of Muslim holy men, in particular their graves, are known to embody the powers that the holy men are believed to possess and share even after their demise.[9] These powers may be beneficial for some and malleable for others, but they are one of the crucial reasons why many people seek out holy men. The places associated with holy men and their ability to intervene in one's life then understandably become social centres and focal points for gatherings of the communities associated with them. Therefore, by discussing both the people whose religious devotion has been focused on Sheikh Muhammad and the Sheikh's emplacement, I would like to argue that, contrary to the popular and politically endorsed majoritarian idealization of social collectivity that crosses the religious boundaries of Hinduism and Islam, what is in fact to be observed is a placial drama between different claimants that construct the world of the sacred and venerated.

Discussing the importance of places in constructing and construing traditions is not new to academic discourse. Some scholars have spoken about the importance of analysing places within the current 'spatial turn' in the human sciences,[10] and, within the broader framework of religious geography, the role of places in forming religious traditions has been usefully summarized.[11] In my own take on the subject, I partly draw on the observations that emphasize experience of the place. For instance, Edward Casey highlighted places' dual quality as at once cultural/tame and on their own (natural or wild).[12] Indeed, the power believed to intervene in the devotees' lives and to be accumulated in the worshipped graves may serve as an example of placial wildness, whereas the narratives and practices engaged during people's interaction with the grave would speak for its cultural aspect. Furthermore, Jeff Malpas' claim that 'place is integral to the very structure and possibility of experience'[13] allows an observation of the processes of how a holy man's followers argue the possession of a place that their narratives and practices are connected to. Hence, my aim is not to discuss the quality of the experiences conveyed by the interaction with holy places. Neither is my goal to explore the placially coded rituals enhancing a holy man's charisma.[14] Rather, I will look at the process that preconditions the narratives and practices, and particularly at how emplacing the historically conceived narratives shape both the community of the Sheikh's followers and more particularly their internal disputes. Hence, in this chapter, I will focus on the cluster of place, narrative and practice articulated through people's interactions that enable the community of the Sheikh's devotees to persist.

Sheikh Muhammad Baba

The religious life of Maharashtrians has been formed and inspired by a plethora of holy figures. Many of them are known also as saint-poets, which has been already highlighted by several important studies.[15] The historical process of creating a discourse around holy figures, which has been accompanied by the practices of their worship, also helped cluster them early on into networks of preceptors and followers (*sampradāy*; such as Varkari, Nath, Datta or even Sufi), and later classify them under the rubric of world religions. Both the networks with their agendas, narratives and praxis, as well as modern religious labelling, necessarily participate in providing the venerated and venerating people with their own sectarian identity, which has been recently and productively seen in terms of vernacular, lived and localized religiosity.[16] Hence we find Shaiva Nath connections to Varkari Vaishnava devotionalism, or Muslim holy men present literally in all major and historical Hindu sampradays in Maharashtra.[17] Among these, Muhammad Baba, as the Sheikh is colloquially known, along with his multifarious followers, could be a telling example (Figure 11.1).

Figure 11.1 A picture of Sheikh Muhammad near his shrine.
Source: Photo by Dušan Deák.

According to tradition, Sheikh Muhammad was born and spent most of his life in the region that today corresponds to the Ahmadnagar, Beed and Aurangabad districts of Maharashtra. By the end of the sixteenth century, he settled in the town of Shrigonda, which was patronized by the grandfather of Maratha king Shivaji, Maloji Bhosle, who respected the Sheikh as his preceptor.[18] This suggests that his followers, since the inception of his public recognition, were more characterized by their devotion to him than by the sectarian traditions to which they belonged.[19] Sheikh Muhammad has been ranked among the most influential Muslim saint-poets whose vehicle of literary communication was Marathi (‘*musalmān marāṭhī santakavī*’ [Muslim Marathi saint-poets], a term coined by Dhere, an acknowledgement of which should be seen in the inclusion of some of his poems in the collection of prevalently Vaishnava poetical compositions ‘*Sakalasantagāthā*’).[20] The Sheikh’s literary legacy, which is the only primary source through which his historical self is approachable, is embodied mainly in his chief work, '*Yogasangrām*' (War of Yoga), a couple of other texts and a plethora of shorter poems.[21] On the one hand, the majority of these texts convey his deep sympathy for Varkari-Vaishnavas, the mainstream Vaishnava network in Maharashtra, past and present. He is familiar with their devotional philosophy, saints and myths but also with yogic practices and experiences that extend beyond the Vaishnava world.[22] On the other hand, his firm claims of being Muslim, and his familiarity with basic Islamic (and possibly also Sufi) theology, certainly pose a problem for those who have chosen to see him exclusively through Vaishnava eyes. Perhaps, similarly to what Stewart suggests,[23] the Sheikh's texts could be efforts in translating Islamic monotheistic ideas (… *tuṭe dvaitācā ṣram bodha lāgoniyā* [gaining wisdom breaks the toil of seeing the world through the philosophy of dualism]) for a local audience. Such an interpretation, however, very much depends on the one who accesses and interprets the Sheikh's texts, because not everybody concerned is willing to admit that '*advaita*' (non-duality) could be, for instance, read as '*tawḥīd*' (oneness of God). What then is it possible to say about how the community venerating the Sheikh historically originated?

How the Sheikh's followers framed the Sheikh

Similarly, as the Sheikh's own beliefs and practices were formed by learning through interactions with the local society, the community of followers that first arose under his guidance and later developed into a community of several tens of thousands of currently active devotees has also been formed in an interactive process. What appears as a unified body of followers of a holy man can well be also a forum for often differing interests. Bhakti – under which the Sheikh's legacy has been classified–involves both personal devotion, often described as love for the deity by an earlier generation of scholars of bhakti,[24] and public participatory activities that necessarily must happen somewhere and somehow.[25]

Part of the evidence about the Sheikh's followers comes from legal documents related to possession of land by his descendants.[26] However, despite their importance for reconstructing the family history, given their administrative form, they allow only for concluding that worship and its supervision by the family continues most probably from the time of the Sheikh's death. Another early source is an anonymous text of '*Sijrā jadi Qādirī*', written most probably during the lifetime of the third generation of the Sheikh's descendants. It places the Sheikh into a Qadiri Sufi lineage, thus creating a narrative that accounts for the Qadiri Sufi tradition being upheld by the Sheikh and followed by his family.[27] But it should be said that this tradition has been completely lost during the centuries since the Sheikh's demise. None from the current descendants claims himself to be a part of Qadiri Sufism[28] nor among the Sheikh's other Muslim devotees is any emphasis on Sijra's narrative observable. Muslims have always formed an obvious part of the community of devotees, including a few wandering faqirs who attend his annual festival, but currently the local Muslims tend to see the Sheikh rather as an extraordinary holy man than as a concretely historicized Qadiri Sufi.[29]

Another window into seeing how the Sheikh was understood is provided by numerous Marathi materials. In their folk-originated stories, the Sheikh is said to cure a man mutilated by thieves, save a ship from sinking, save a fellow saint from a fatal incident, kill a people-eating demon and prove his authority on religious matters vis-à-vis Brahmans, Kazi or even the Emperor, etc.[30] Similar to several other early authors (all listed and their poems published by Bendre),[31] Mahipati, the prominent hagiographer of Marathi Varkari saints in the second half of eighteenth century, decisively includes the Sheikh among the Vaishnavas. Apart from narratively connecting the Sheikh with Tukaram, whom the former helped during troubles, Mahipati also places Baba among the saintly pilgrims visiting the sacred city of the Varkaris – Pandharpur.[32] The source of the Sheikh's inclusion among the Vaishnavas by Marathi authors can be traced to the Sheikh's works, and particularly to his shorter poems (*abhanga*), heavily conforming to Vaishnava, and particularly Marathi Vaishnava-Varkari, devotional discourse. Indeed, the most famous verse attributed to the Sheikh runs, '*Although Sheikh Muhammad is a Muslim (avindha), in his heart dwells Govinda*'.

Later, the inclusion was retold in a short but anonymous and undated hagiographical text,[33] possibly from the nineteenth century, that classifies the Sheikh as an incarnation of Kabir, another Vaishnavized saint, which resembles a well-known oral saying of the Varkaris: '*Eka is like/of Dnyanadev, Tuka is like/of Nama and the Sheikh is like/of Kabir*' and firmly establishes the Sheikh in the company of the most famous Maharashtrian Varkari saints. The text also retells the story of the writings of saints that can't be destroyed, even when thrown into a river, which is known also with respect to Varkaris Eknath and Tukaram, just referred to above. This time it is the *Yogasangram* (thus homologized with the texts of Eknath's Bhagavat and Tukaram's Gatha) that comes undamaged out of a water ordeal performed in Varanasi. The caritra also narratively connecteds the Sheikh with other Maharashtrian Vaishnavas, namely Jayram Swami and Samartha Ramdas, both seventeenth-century figures.

A peculiarly Vaishnava touch to narratives capturing the personality of the Sheikh comes from an earlier oral narrative[34] popularized by another well-known Maharashtrian hagiographer – Dasganu. The Sheikh, whose family is said to practice the business of butchers, rejects such a way of living.[35] Dasganu also clearly neglects any narrative that pronounces the Sheikh's Islamic learning and connection to Sufis, by depicting his family as opposing and even ridiculing the Sheikh's decision.

The story has become so prominent in defining the Sheikh's personality that it found its firm place also in the only extant traditionally styled account of Shrigonda, '*Śrīpura Mahātmya*', to which I will soon turn.[36] Finally, the Vaishnavization of the Sheikh, or if you like his firm establishment in the Maharashtrian Vaishnava discourse, culminates in claiming him to be a convert to Hinduism by Dasganu and none else than that prominent Maharashtrian political figure and lawyer, Mahadev Govind Ranade (Figure 11.2).[37]

The narrativization, oral or textual, appears to be woven through two recognizable discursive spaces. On the one hand, it stemmed from the vernacular, locally derived and framed memory of Muhammad Baba, where he appears as a yogi, bhakta or siddha, the one who, due to his supernatural abilities, helps people in need and enforces his own authority. Seeing him in terms of Vaishnava or Sufi traditions, on the other hand, discursively connected the Sheikh to pan-Indian and cosmopolitan frameworks. However, with respect to the community of Baba's followers, the Sufi narrative has remained apparently historically underdeveloped. Also, the Vaishnava referents in the Sheikh's works, along with the conceptual world of the renouncer's practice, have been reduced by both local upholders of tradition and academics only to illustrate an example of integration between Hindu and Muslim traditions.[38] It was the involvement of local Shrigonda Brahmans, who freely move across and embody both the local

Figure 11.2 Vaishnava performers in front of Sheikh's dargah-samadhi.
Source: Photo by Dušan Deák.

and pan-Indian discourses, that allowed the Vaishnava narrative to be fruitfully elaborated.

The first visible effort of such an elaboration may be seen in publishing *Yogasangram* under the supervision of Brahman scholars, its first publication dated to 1889.[39] However, Eknath Joshi's *Shripura Mahatmya*, written in the first half of the twentieth century but published only in 2004, and classified under the '*sthaḷa-mahātmya*' genre (a narrative serving glorification of a locality), brings a peculiar account of the town, its deities and venerated holy people. Written by the local scholar from Shrigonda, it strives to explain why Shrigonda is a holy town – 'Shripura'. There's no space here to further discuss the particulars, but *Shripura Mahatmya* brings to the public and, by Brahmanic authority, legitimizes two claims that are important in the context of this study. First, via the myth of a certain Pandu bhakta who is seen as Panduranga (another name of Pandharpur's Viththal), it establishes a peculiar mythical connection between Shrigonda and Pandharpur that already resonates in calling Shrigonda a second Pandharpur (Prati Pandharpur).[40] Second, similar to Pandharpur, it is a city with its own circle of saints: the mythical, such as Pandharpur's Pundalik, and historical, whose dwellings are still to be seen in the town, such as Sheikh Muhammad and his saintly friends Prahlad, Godad and Raul. These claims accommodate the '*avindha*' but Govinda-loving Sheikh Muhammad in the local environment and at the same time link the location's glory with Pandharpur's, which, in the region where the Varkaris form the mainstream devotional community, certainly sets conditions for claiming prestige. Shrigonda and its honoured representatives, gods as well as holy men, have been homologized by the local Brahman scholars with Pandharpur and its myths.[41] However, as will be seen below, the homologizing symbols have been fairly well emplaced and with all probability prior to *Shripura Mahatmya*. Thus the efforts of the learned Shrigonda Brahmans discursively organize the beliefs that speak through places.[42]

How the Sheikh was framed by places

Apart from the personality of the Sheikh, his composite teachings, and broader narratives articulating his inclusion in different religious traditions, the places associated with the Sheikh's life and afterlife intrinsically code the process of creating the community of his devotees. Among these places, the most prominent are those where he lived (Shrigonda), where he is said to have visited (Pandharpur), and particularly the site of his grave, where his powers are believed to be accumulated and where he has become the object of worship. All of them are needed for his community to maintain the tradition of its devotional allegiance to the Sheikh. Without having him visit the Vaishnava-Varkari centre of Pandharpur, seeing him as a prominent historical person of Shrigonda, keeping his memory and accessing his blessings via his grave, which serves as the focal point of the community's gathering, one can hardly understand the community itself. As Ethington, while discussing the role of places in people's understanding of the occurrence of past events in time has insightfully put it, 'experiential, memorial time ... takes place',[43] and especially the time of those who guide and protect contemporary people.

As it appears problematic to claim only one identity and narrative for Muhammad Baba and his followers, similarly the places where he gets embodied have been contested by upholders of particular narratives and identities. There certainly might be different dimensions to analysing several places associated with the Sheikh, but I have chosen to discuss particularly those that symbolize the contest and inner dynamics of maintaining the tradition of his worship. It should be clear by now that in the historical process of constructing the Sheikh's holiness, which has been accompanied by his narrativization and emplacement, it was not only one, but a few communities that evolved and got involved. This is manifested in several ways, but the most important one is that there exists yet another grave of the Sheikh, as well as one more grave, where the Sheikh's memory is publicly articulated. Let me discuss them in greater detail below.

Shrigonda

Shrigonda[44] is currently a regional administrative centre (*tālukā*) of Ahmadnagar district, with more than 30,000 inhabitants prevalently classified as Hindus. Out of all Shrigondians, Muslims form just a tiny minority of around 2,500 people.[45] Sheikh Muhammad is considered the town's patron saint or rather a patron divine being (*grāmadevatā*). Over the years of visiting Shrigonda, I have hardly met with anybody, irrespective of his/her religion, who would deny visiting the Sheikh's tomb at least sometimes. The tomb/dargah of the Sheikh was built over the cave where he, similar to the Varkaris Dnyanadev and Nivrittinath, is said to eternally meditate. Therefore, the place is considered to be a '*jīvanta samādhi*' (living samadhi) and the source of the saint's beneficial powers. The tomb and those graves with a classic south-north orientation were constructed most probably at the time of the Sheikh's grandson Balbava, in the eighteenth century, whose smaller tomb nearby stylistically corresponds with the original Sheikh's tomb. There are three steps leading inside. The last of them is the place of samadhi of Modoba, the oilmen (*telī*), a devotee of Baba. Anybody conversant with Varkari tradition will immediately recognize here a pattern similar to Namdev's step in front of Pandharpur's temple (Figure 11.3).

The whole place was once enclosed by walls from all sides, to which the interiors of the houses of the dargah's current residents, Baba's descendants, have been attached. On the eastern side of the Sheikh's tomb, Balbava's tomb and a couple of other graves of the family members are located. On

Figure 11.3 Devotees during the first day of Sheikh's utsava.
Source: Photo by Dušan Deák.

its western side is the grave of Chand Bodhle, guru/*pīr* of the Sheikh.[46] At the southern back of the walled space is a roofed platform. On its wall from left to right the chaknama linking the Sheikh to Maloji Bhosle is displayed, along with information on the Sheikh and his fellow Shrigondian saints. Further, in a small niche is a picture of the Sheikh, which serves as a temple murti (idol), suggested also by the small bell hanging in front of it. The niche apparently serves also as a shrine. Near it there are also other pictures, namely of Viththala (Vishnu of Varkaris), Dnyanadev, Shirdi Sai Baba, again Sheikh Muhammad, but also Muslim children reading from the Qur'an, the Kaaba, the great mosque of Mecca, as well as Husayn's horse Zuljanah.[47] Finally, the niche shelters the old '*pālkhī*' – the palanquin used for carrying the Sheikh's '*pādukā*' (literally shoe or slipper of a holy person, but also an impression of the feet of a holy being). On the tomb's northern side a square-shaped black slab usually adorned by flowers marks the original entrance to the cave below. The entrance, according to the locals, has been sealed after the last man who entered it lost his mental health.

The devotional service in Baba's tomb is run by his descendants, which come from three distant lineages of cousins. The participation of Vaishnavas (Brahmans, Telis and several other groups, out of which many are also Varkaris)[48] in the process is equally prominent and tangible, given that the majority of visitors are local Hindus either from Shrigonda itself or from the villages and towns around it. But the situation with regard to the process of the emplacement of the Sheikh is hardly as serene as it may seem, because of the different groups involved having different interests. The problem becomes apparent as soon as some devotional practices espoused by a particular group are preferred to others. The practices, in turn, are vitally linked to narratives that explain them via historically argued current concerns, as well as to places where the practices are performed. All this pertains to the current polemic about the right of taking care of the grave (*mujāwarī*) by Baba's descendants, which transpires also in claims contesting each other's relation to the Sheikh. To one of the three families, the mujawari was denied some time ago, despite its members being direct descendants of the last mujawar. This family prefers the Vaishnava narrative of the Sheikh's legacy and is backed by the Vaishnavas. The other two prefer the Sufi narrative, both parties accusing each other of misunderstanding the family tradition (narrative-practice). This affects the ways of worship and claims to possession of the place and escalates in the calls of the more numerous Vaishnava-cum-Muslim party to displace the current mujawars from service, as well as from the tomb. This situation is also reflected by outwardly marking the place as '*mandir*' and not as '*dargāh*', which matches the efforts to promote the majoritarian narrative by its upholders. It is quite possible, as I have tried to argue,[49] that sticking to a Sufi narrative that has been historically lost or marginalized, and to gradually developing Sufi practices, speak for the Sufism of the social option as opposed to the Sufism of the continuous tradition. Illustratively, since the last two years, '*qawwālī*' (a Sufi musical performance) has been held during the '*utsava*' (the annual festival in honour of the Sheikh). Hence in the conflict the contested mujawari apparently serves as an instrument through which authority over the disputed tradition and place can be gained and the preferred narrative enforced. Whose is the place if the Sheikh is said to belong to all (*sarvajāti*)?

To some extent, it is certainly misleading to see 'Hindus' and 'Muslims' as meaningful descriptive categories when addressing the Sheikh's devotees. The devotees' internal divisions, however, should also not be overrated. The different roles played by different groups in the Sheikh's veneration certainly make them appear as one community living through the Sheikh's legacy, and his emplaced symbols the 'total, symbolic reality', as Werbner and Basu insightfully note.[50] Depending on their employment, the symbols may lead to conflicting claims, as well as fruitful collaboration. Such ambiguity is well illustrated by the annual utsava. During the ritual adoration of the grave, each group has its own share. Before the event, one of the descendants recites a part of the *Yogasangram*,[51] a local Muslim cleric recites the Quran's '*fateha*', the Brahmans perform the puja and recite Sanskrit mantras, and the representative of the Telis is the first to apply the sandal paste to the graves (which is his privilege, i.e. *mān*), later followed by the others. Another example could be the puja closing the utsava. Started by the Brahmans' ritual, the puja culminates in worshipping the *Yogasangram*[52] with representatives of the Brahmans, the Sheikh's family, and the family of Prahlad Maharaj, apparently the most important saint from among the Sheikh's associate saints, equally participating. The puja culminates in congregational singing (*ārtī*), where literally everybody present participates and the three main actors symbolically hold their hands together at the ceremonial plate (Figure 11.4).

However, the symbolic action may also take a different turn. During the puja of 2017, the opposing party of Baba's descendants performed their own ritual of applying sandal to the grave. I have also witnessed how a group of youngsters, shouting slogans of Victory to Islam ('*Islām zindābād*') and God is great ('*Allāhu Akbar*'), suddenly appeared at the site of the concluding puja carrying a '*chādar*' (decorative sheet) to put on the Sheikh's grave. Apparently, the tension arising from the disputed mujawari has a local public following. Fortunately, the participants in the puja, among whom were several Muslims, did not get distracted in any way. The youngsters covered Sheikh's grave and went away shouting as they had come. The whole incident suggests how shaky the symbolic reality may become when the cluster of 'place-narrative-practice' gets disputed.

Figure 11.4 Paying respect to Yogasangram.
Source: Photo by Dušan Deák.

Vahira

Vahira in Ashti taluka, district Beed (sometimes written as Rui-Vahire or Pundi-Vahira) lies some fifty-five kilometres north-east of Shrigonda and contains another grave of Sheikh Muhammad. It is a little village of around 1,500 inhabitants and is also a place tied to the memory of Muhammad Baba. The latter is said to have visited it as well as resided there,[53] but local devotees firmly believe that he spent a considerable part of his life in Vahira before moving to Shrigonda.[54] A folk etymology of the village's name ('*vā hirā*!' What a diamond!) attempts to convey his shining presence there. From all that we know, it seems that there is some historicity to these claims; however, they are too few to say anything with certainty. The earliest known historical reference to the Sheikh's family residing in Vahira is a land grant to them by a certain Istril Khan, dated ca. 1860–1861.[55] What transpires prominently in our context is the claim that the actual place of the Sheikh's last residence is Vahira and not Shrigonda, which brings another narrative dispute to the already complex legacy of the Sheikh. The locals believe that, after his burial in Shrigonda, using yogic powers, Baba transferred himself to Vahira and so it is here where the living samadhi emplaces his powers and provides devotees with a place of worship and gathering. According to them, his grave, which is the most prominent one among several others at the village's cemetery, located at its north-west outskirts, serves as a place where local disputes are decided (Figure 11.5).

Figure 11.5 Devotees encircling Sheikh Muhammad's grave in Vahira.
Source: Photo by Dušan Deák.

Another significant context to the discussed 'place-narrative-practice' cluster is that the families of yet another three cousins – descendants of Sheikh Muhammad, who are also distant cousins of the Shrigondian family – are closely connected to Vahira. All three of their main representatives are known under the appellative '*mahārāj*' and actively participate at Vaishnava devotional gatherings where the Yogasangram is ritually read (*parāyaṇ*), devotional songs sung, stories told and philosophy of devotion explained (*bhajan, kīrtan*). Along with their fellow villagers they conduct their own pilgrimage, carrying the paduka of the Sheikh, to places sacred to the Varkaris – Alandi, associated with Dnyanadev, Paithan, associated with Eknath, and Pandharpur. Being born Muslims, which is in fact more of a social and genealogical than a religious referent in their case, these cousins are clearly Muslim Varkaris.[56] Unsurprisingly, they prefer and by their practice promote the Vaishnava narrative extolling the Sheikh's greatness.

However, theirs are quite different concerns than those of the Shrigondians. Here it is not the social choice of Sufism that provides ground for the dispute, for Sufism is simply out of the question. Rather, it is the concern with the fact that Vahira is a place that is second only to Shrigonda. This problematizes the Vahirans' claim that they are the rightful upholders of what they think is a correct (Vaishnava) family tradition believed to have been started by their saintly ancestor. So again, but in a different setting, the family tradition is disputed. Clearly, it is the location of the Sheikh's grave which offers the chance of social prestige that, in contrast to the mujawari, becomes instrumental in claiming authority over the disputed role of the Sheikh's family in the tradition of his worship and identitarian interpretation. Hence, similarly, as Shrigonda's tomb has been homologized with the Vaishnava narrative centred on Pandharpur, Vahira's cemetery has been homologized with Shrigonda's tomb. It is a jivant samadhi, and down in the village is a sealed place leading to the cave of the Sheikh's eternal meditation. Overall, the place of 'second rank' causes an alienation of Vahira's cousins from the mainstream Vaishnava appropriation of Sheikh Muhammad. They neglect the Shrigonda festivities and prefer their own ways of being Vaishnavas.

Pisore Khand

Approximately between both Shrigonda and Vahira, down one of the offshoots belonging to the mountain range of the Western Ghats, lies the little village of Pisore Khand. Just north of Pisore is the dargah sheltering the grave of Khaki Buva (Old Man of Ashes), a peculiar symbolic representation of the Sheikh and a striking example of the vicissitudes the cluster of 'place-narrative-practice' may take. Khaki Buva's is a remote, lonely place, located at a broad pass between the Ghats' hillocks that in older times could have been considered dangerous. Apparently, the youngest of the three – the dargah being built in 1940 according to the date inscribed on its walls – this place is under custody of a local Muslim family unrelated to the Sheikh. They started their service some time before the dargah was built by their ancestors.[57] But this fact does not mean that Khaki Buva wasn't worshipped there before the existence of the dargah. Visitors of Khaki Buva are generally but not exclusively followers of the Sheikh. In comparison with Shrigonda, they are indeed few, most of the devotions being performed by the locals of Pisore Khand, where Muslims, including the family of custodians, form a tiny minority of a few families settled on the outskirts of the village. The only considerable number, a few hundred, gather at the time of the annual festival (Figure 11.6).

There is hardly any known history to the place, but there is a lot told about it. Most common is the story that vaguely identifies the Sheikh with Khaki Buva. Once Aurangzeb's army travelled near to the current dargah. Soldiers carrying a heavy load saw a strong looking Muslim who, however, was engrossed in repeating God's names. It was Sheikh Muhammad. They placed on his head some of the luggage, but it flew about a metre above his head, and in this manner, he carried it until told to put it down. Then the luggage turned to ashes whereupon the soldiers realized that this was

Figure 11.6 Khaki Buva's dargah.
Source: Photo by Dušan Deák.

a holy man. Today, the spot is marked by the grave of Khaki Buva, we are told by the narrator, but he does not tell us who the Buva was.[58] Another story, which I have heard but could not find written, explains that in fact Khaki Buva was a demon (*rākṣas*). He used to block the pass with his huge body and eat anybody who happened to be nearby. Once the Sheikh came to the spot and challenged the demon to fight. After the demon realized that he would face a yogi, he asked the Sheikh to ensure that he would be remembered and provided with food even if he lost. The Sheikh granted the request, burned him to ashes and his holy touch purified the demon's vile nature. Later, the demon started to be worshipped as Khaki Buva and fed with sacrificed goats. A third story, provided by the custodians, who also knew the other two, is that Khaki Buva is in fact Khaki Shah, Sufi and a brother of the Sheikh, the second of the three Sufi brothers, the third being Sayyid Badshah, buried in the nearby village of Akadi Van.[59]

These three stories provide another angle on how the holiness of the Sheikh can be emplaced. Khaki Buva's place may symbolize the powers of the Sheikh, enabling him to face and impress even the Emperor's army as well as mark Baba's memory, so dear to the inhabitants of the region where the Sheikh was made holy. This is how the Shrigonda Vaishnavas would see it,[60] and therefore, this story is the most popular. A much different context is provided in the demon's story, which displays the inclusion of a narrative not originating in the Vaishnava environment. Indeed, turning a demon into a deity is a common folk narrative of pastoral groups across the Deccan.[61] Since Dhangars, Maharashtrian pastoralists, visit Khaki Buva and offer their goats and sheep in exchange for granted wishes, the story possibly captures the fact of the Sheikh's fame spreading among the pastoral visitors of the region in a way familiar to them. Finally, the narrative of the three Sufi brothers, although without support of any historical evidence – for there is no trace of any brothers of the Sheikh in the materials concerning him – offered yet another local Muslim family a way to benefit from the regional popularity of Muhammad Baba as well as participate in sharing the benefits of his worship. Perhaps due to the remoteness of Khaki Buva's place and its lesser attractiveness in terms of local prestige, Khaki Buva – whomever the person in the grave was – has been able to accommodate several of the locally popular narratives that, in contrast to Shrigonda and Vahira, however, did not create space for conflict. Khaki Buva may be avoided by the staunchly vegetarian Muslim Vaishnavas of Vahira and neglected by seekers of Sufism from Shrigonda, but it is precisely the enigma of the place, the undecidedness of the Buva's narrative emplacement with respect to the Sheikh, as well as the non-restrictive practice (one may not necessarily offer meat) unconnected to any popular network of devotees (*sampradāy*), that allows in one place not only the inclusion of other people like dhangars but also the coexistence of all who deem Khaki Buva beneficial for their lives.

Instead of a conclusion...

Making one holy appears, in my eyes, to be an interactive social and historical process. It is accompanied by narrative interpretations of the places associated with a holy person. These places are consummated through ritually coded worship. Possessing places, populating them with narratives and guiding them through practices allows the creation of a space where ideals can be turned into social facts. This is what I have chosen to see in terms of emplacement. Even if holiness and holy men may today often be seen in identitarian terms of belonging to unified religious collectives or traditions, I have attempted to show that there is much more at stake, because the motivations of people to become part of any societally produced whole vary, as do the ways different groups employ the different places. These variations also participate in imagining who is worshipped, why and in what form. Hence, we met with the Vaishnava-Varkari sant Sheikh Muhammad, who could variously be seen as a Sufi with his brothers, within a prestigious Qadiri Sufi lineage, or as a powerful yogi who could turn to ashes a bloodthirsty demon or a load of goods placed on him by a royal army. Overall then, my material shows that the legacy of holy men has great potential to divide as well as to unite; in any case our analytic categories pertaining to 'world religions' (Hindus, Muslims) or 'religious groups' (Vaishnavas, Sufis) hardly fit the observed current or historical realities. Similarly, the ethical ideals of communal harmony, even if they are in today's world more than necessary, are rather misplaced if they neglect people's concern with the practicalities of their religious convictions. Places connected to narratives and practices are obviously only one way of exploring what in fact takes place in making and remaking one holy. Economies of emplacement could be, for instance, another.

***

Sakharam Paithanpagar, a local Dalit Marathi author, narrates yet another story about Sheikh Muhammad.[62] Near Vahira lived two brothers, Sada and Bodha. One day, Sada finds an antinomian chillum-smoking faqir, who speaks Hindustani instead of local Marathi, appearing near his home. He smokes with the faqir, who in turn asks him not tell anybody about their meeting. But that does not happen. After Sada shared his experience with a friend, Sada gets ill and dies, later followed by Bodha, who died from the shock of his brother's death. Hence, Sada's own place, despite the holy man whose powers are said to sanctify places, has not been so lucky. Indeed, behind Paithanpagar's narrative there might be an agenda reflecting the modernist criticism of blind beliefs, or the pains of Dalits seeking their own religious place, and yet a different one behind employing the trope of the well-known local holy man, who unfortunately scored so poorly in the story. But the story certainly reminds us how the narrative and ideals of the holiness emplaced by some may get a completely different meaning when seen through different eyes. This is, perhaps, what should concern us when considering the processes of upgrading any narrative to a collective conviction that has all too often been named as tradition. For the question always remains, whose tradition and why?

Notes

1 Christian L. Novetzke, *Religion and Public Memory: A Cultural History of Sant Namdev in India*, New York: Columbia University Press, 2008.
2 Nile Green, *Bombay Islam: The Religious Economy of the West Indian Ocean 1840–1915*, Cambridge: Cambridge University Press, 2011.
3 Richard M. Eaton, *A Social History of the Deccan 1300–1761 (The New Cambridge History of India)*, Cambridge: Cambridge University Press, 2005 (Chapter 6, pp. 129–154).
4 Timothy S. Dobe, *Hindu Christian Faqir: Modern Monks, Global Christianity and Indian Sainthood*, Oxford: Oxford University Press, 2015.
5 The recent violent events following the detention of a Punjabi guru Gurmeet Ram Rahim Singh make another telling example.
6 Nile Green, 'The Faqir and the Subalterns: Mapping the Holy Man in Colonial South Asia', *Journal of Asian History*, 2007, 4 (1): 59–60.
7 Charlotte Vaudeville, 'Sant Mat: Santism as the Universal Path to Sanctity', in Karin Schomer and William H. McLeod (eds.), *The Sants (Studies in Devotional Tradition in India)*, Delhi: Motilal Banarsidass, 1987, p. 21.
8 Ramachandra Ch. Dhere, *Ekātmatece Śilpakār*, Pune: Manjul Prakāśan, 1994, p. 77, pp. 83–85, Narayan S. Gavli and Lanka N. Gavli, *Śrī Sant Śekh Mahaṃmad Mahārāj*, Aurangabad: Kailās Publications, 2011, p. 39, pp. 42–44.
9 Vernon J. Schubel, 'Dargāh' and 'Pīr', and Richard Kurin, 'Saints', in Margaret A. Mills, Peter J. Claus, and Sarah Diamond (eds.), *South Asian Folklore: An Encyclopedia*, New York: Routledge, 2003, pp. 140–141, p. 478, pp. 531–533.
10 Phillip. J. Ethington, 'Placing the Past: "Groundwork" for a Spatial Theory of History', *Rethinking History*, 2007, 11 (4): 465–493.
11 Chris C. Park, *Sacred Worlds: An Introduction to Geography and Religion*, London: Routledge, 1994, pp. 245–284.
12 Edward Casey, 'How to Get from Space to Place in a Fairly Short Stretch of Time: Phenomenological Prolegomena', in Steven Feld and Keith Basso (eds.), *Senses of Place*, Santa Fe: School of American Research Press, 1996, pp. 33–36.
13 Jeff Malpas, 'Finding Place: Spatiality, Locality and Subjectivity', in Andrew Light and Jonathan M. Smith (eds.), *Philosophy and Geography III. Philosophies of Place*, Lanham: Rowman & Litllefield Publishers, 1998, p. 33.
14 Cf. Pnina Werbner and Helene Basu (eds.), *Embodying Charisma: Modernity, Locality and the Performance of Emotion in Sufi cults*, London: Routledge, 1998.
15 Mahadev G. Ranade, *Rise of the Maratha Power*, Delhi: Publication Divisions, Ministry of Information and Broadcasting, Government of India, [1900] 1974, Ramachandra D. Ranade, *Mysticism in Maharashtra*, Delhi: Munshiram Manoharlal, [1933] 1982, G. B. Sardar, *The Saint Poets of Maharashtra (Their impact on Society)*, translated and edited by Kumud Mehta. Pune: Orient Longmans Limited, 1969, Charlotte Vaudeville, *Myths, Saints and Legends in Medieval India*, Delhi: Oxford University Press, 1996.
16 Cf. Imtiaz Ahmad and Helmut Reifeld (eds.), *Lived Islam in South Asia – Adaptation, Accommodation and Conflict*, Delhi: Social Science Press, 2004,

Pushkar Sohoni, 'Vernacular as a Space: Writing in the Deccan', *South Asian History and Culture*, 2016, 7 (3): 258–270, or Afsar Mohammad, *The Festival of Pirs: Popular Islam and Shared Devotion in South India*, New York: Oxford University Press, 2013. My use of the term 'religiosity' corresponds to its widely used academic meaning as an individual approach to religious matters, and particularly divinity, which can take multifarious forms. However, I recognize the social context of these forms that complicate the solely individual agency of a religious person.

17 Cf. Bhalchandra P. Bahirath and Padmanabha J. Bhalerav, *Vārkarī sampradāy uday va vikās*, Pune: Vhīnas Prakāśan, [1972] 1988, Dhere, *Ekātmatece Śilpakār*, and Yusuf, M. Pathan, *Musalmān (Sūphī) Santānce Marāṭhī Sāhitya*. Mumbai: Mahārāṣṭra Rājya Sāhitya āṇi Sanskṛti Manḍaḷ, 2011.

18 Vasudev S. Bendre, *Tukārām mahārāj yānce santasangatī*, Mumbai: Mauj Prakāśan, 1957, pp. 69–70.

19 Respect for holy people irrespective of their particular identity is not at all exceptional to the South Asian religious environment. Yet there is also the possibility of viewing such a preceptor-devotee constellation as the conscious choice of some Maratha nobles to participate in a different and politically interesting, non-Brahmanic, even if not necessarily freer, space of devotion. The relation of Mansur Shah with the great Maratha warrior Mahadaji Shinde – who is another famous Shrigonda figure – immediately comes to mind as another fitting example.

20 Ramachandra Ch. Dhere, *Musalmān Marāṭhī Santkavī*, Pune: Dnyānarāj Prakāśan, 1967. R. Ra. Gosavi (ed.), *Śrīsakalasantagāthā*, Pune: Sārthī Prakāśan, 2000, pp. 911–917.

21 Discussion of his compositions is found in Achyut Na. Deshpande, *Prācīn Marāṭhī Vānmayācā Itihās*, Vol. 2, Pune: Vhīnas Prakāśan, 1973, pp. 124–136.

22 Dhere, for instance, discusses how the Sheikh's writings are influenced by the founder of the Varkari literary tradition – Dnyanadev. Dhere, *Ekātmatece Śilpakār*, pp. 100–104.

23 Tony K. Stewart, 'In Search of Equivalence: Conceiving Muslim-Hindu Encounter through Translation Theory', *History of Religions*, 2001, 40 (3): 261–288.

24 E.g. Ramachandra D. Ranade, *Mysticism in Maharashtra*, Delhi: Munshiram Manoharlal, [1933] 1982, or Charlotte Vaudeville, 'Sant Mat: Santism as the Universal Path to Sanctity', in Karin Schomer and Hew, W. McLeod (eds.), *The Sants (Studies in Devotional Tradition in India)*, Delhi: Motilal Banarsidass, 1987, pp. 21–40.

25 Cf. Christian L. Novetzke, 'Bhakti and Its Public', *International Journal of Hindu Studies*, 2007, 11 (3): 255–272.

26 These are mainly the noted chaknama of Maloji Bhosle, dated to 1592–1596 depending on the version, the petition by Baba's descendant to Peshwa, dated ca. 1775 (Naveena Naqvi, personal communication, March 2017), a confirmation of yet another land grant by a certain Istril Khan from ca. 1860–1861, and a few others referred to by Bendre, *Tukārām mahārāj yānce santasangatī*, pp. 63–82 and Narayan S. Gavli, S. '*Vārsā Māhitī Kendrācyā Ubhārṇīcā Pathadarśī Prakalpa Ārākhaḍā Tayār Karṇe: Viśeṣ Saṃdarbha Śrīgonde Śāhar, Ji. Ahmadnagar, Mahārāṣṭra*', unpublished Ph.D. dissertation, Sāvitrībāī Phule Puṇe Vidyāpīṭh, 2015, p. 329.

27 Vasudev S. Bendre (ed.), *Śekh Mahammadbābā yāncā kavitāsangraha*. Mumbai: P. P. H. Bookstall, 1961, pp. 123–124. The association of the Sheikh with organized Sufism is problematic. Although in one of the recently discovered manuscripts of Maloji's land grant to the Sheikh the latter is clearly called 'darwesh Qadiri', the question is not only why the other three manuscripts of the grant call him differently but also why the Sheikh himself does not clearly

confirm his belonging to the Qadiri Sufis, or why he is not mentioned among then contemporary Qadiris by other Sufis, or why none of his descendants admits, or is recorded to admit, any association with Qadiri Sufism. Answering these questions needs much deeper discussion and rethinking, which I am unable to offer in the present study, but there certainly is space for seeing the problem in terms of the marginalization of the Sheikh's Islamic roots by the later Vaishnava tradition. I thank Naveena Naqvi, Miklós Sárközy and Pushkar Sohoni for their help with the Persian version of the Maloji's grant and Girish Mandke for helping with reading the modi script.

28 Dušan Deák, 'Making Sufism Popular: A Few Notes on the Case from the Marathi Deccan', *Deccan Studies*, 2013, 11 (2): 13–19.

29 Fieldwork observation and interview with Shrigonda resident and primary schoolteacher, Haji Ismail Mohinuddin Hakim, January 2014.

30 Cf. B. N. Shinde, *Śrī Śekh Mahammad Śrīgonde yānce stotra va caritra*, Shrigonda: Vimal Prakāśan, 1987, pp. 1–7, pp. 17–27, Gavli and Gavli, *Śrī Sant Śekh Mahammad Mahārāj*, pp. 48–55.

31 Bendre, *Śekh Mahammadbābā yāncā kavitāsangraha*, pp. 124–130.

32 S. R. Devle (ed.), *Śrībhaktavijaya*, Pune: Sarasvatī grantha bhanḍār, 2002, 51: p. 85, 52: pp. 87–119.

33 Bendre, *Śekh Mahammadbābā yāncā kavitāsangraha*, pp. 119–123 (*caritra*).

34 There exists also a poem attributed to the Sheikh recounting his experience with the pain of animals. Bendre, *Śekh Mahammadbābā yāncā kavitāsangraha*, poem no. 30.

35 Shankar N. Joshi (ed.), *Dāsgaṇūmahārājkrut Ākhyān Samuccaya*, Pune: Shankar N. Joshi Citraśāḷā Press, 1932, pp. 71–75.

36 Eknath, S. Joshi, *Śrīpura Mahātmya*, Shrigonda: Purushottam Eknath Joshi via Shri Printers, 2004.

37 Joshi, *Dāsgaṇūmahārājkrut Ākhyān Samuccaya*, p. 83, Ranade, *Rise of the Maratha Power*, p. 75.

38 Dhere, *Ekātmatece Śilpakār*, p. 77, Shankar G. Tulpule, *Classical Marāṭhī Literature*, Wiesbaden: Otto Harrassowitz, 1979, pp. 377–378, Gavli and Gavli, *Śrī Sant Śekh Mahammad Mahārāj*, p. 39.

39 All of them are listed in Ramachandra Ch. Dhere (ed.), *Yogasangrām*, Pune: Varda Books, 1981, pp. 7–8.

40 Gavli and Gavli, *Śrī Sant Śekh Mahammad Mahārāj*, pp. 60–61.

41 For instance, I was told in Shrigonda that the local Varkaris do not necessarily need to go to Pandharpur, even if many of them certainly do, because Viththal also comes to Shrigonda to meet Sheikh Muhammad.

42 The vaishnavization of the Sheikh articulates in many other ways. For instance, the great rally of Vaishnavas gathers a week prior to the annual festival for ritual reading (*parāyaṇ*) of Dnyanadev's Dnyaneshvari – the sacred book of the Varkaris. Another angle of the process can be seen in following the Hindu Shaka calendar for determining all festivals of the Sheikh.

43 Ethington, 'Placing the Past: "Groundwork" for a Spatial Theory of History', p. 466.

44 If not given otherwise, most of the presented information comes from the fieldwork in Shrigonda that I have been conducting since 2005.

45 For details consult http://censusindia.gov.in/ (accessed on 28 September 2017).

46 Discussion of the enigmatic figure of Chand Bodhle has been left out of this study. However, note that Bodhle's more prominent grave is located opposite to the main gate of Daulatabad Fort, near the royal baths.

47 Sandria Freitag observes that their 'visual vocabulary' provides Muslims with a 'notion of shared membership' within the religious group. Sandria B. Freitag,

'South Asian Ways of Seeing, Muslim Ways of Knowing: The Indian Muslim Niche Market in Posters', *The Indian Economic and Social History Review*, 2007, 44 (3): 301.

48 The visits of the tomb of various hosts of the Varkaris is summarized in Gavli and Gavli, *Śrī Sant Śekh Mahaṃmad Mahārāj*, pp. 60–61.

49 Dušan Deák, 'Making Sufism popular'.

50 Werbner and Basu, *Embodying Charisma*, p. 4.

51 Dhere, *Yogasangrām*, 18: 51–66.

52 Ceremonial carrying of the *Yogasangram* on the head of a chosen descendant of the Sheikh, when contextualized with the similar practice of Sikhs carrying on their head the Guru Granth Sahib, displays yet another and cosmopolitan layer to this local, or vernacular, practice.

53 Sheikh's visit is suggested in one of the poems collected by Bendre. Bendre, *Śekh Mahaṃmadbābā yāncā kavitāsangraha*, p. 124, poem 323. Sheikh's residence in Wahira has been mentioned by Priyolkar. See Shankar G. Tulpule, 'Purvaṇī', in V. L. Bhave (ed.), *Mahārāṣṭra Sārasvat*, Mumbai: Popular Prakāśan, 1983, p. 831.

54 Interview with Sheikh Abdul Maharaj, descendant of Sheikh Muhammad residing in Vahira.

55 Bhima V. Modle, '*Sant Kavī Śekh Mahaṃmad: Ek Cikitsak Abhyās*', unpublished Ph.D. dissertation, Puṇe Vidyāpīṭh, 1998, p. 296.

56 More details on their Vaishnava proclivities and practices can be found in my forthcoming study 'Communicating Devotion, Sharing Experience and Calling for Participation among the Muslim Varkaris' in the volume *Religion and Advertising: Less Traditional Means of Religious Communication*, edited by Miloš Hubina.

57 Interview with the current custodian Suleiman Sheikh, July 2005.

58 Shinde, *Śrī Śekh Mahaṃmad Śrīgonde yānce stotra va caritra*, pp. 13–14.

59 I am unsure about the spelling of this name, because the recording is unclear when it was mentioned by Suleiman Shekh.

60 Gavli and Gavli narrate yet another story connecting Shrigondians and Khaki Buva. Gavli and Gavli, *Śrī Sant Śekh Mahaṃmad Mahārāj*, p. 62.

61 Günther-Dietz Sontheimer, 'Between Ghost and God: A Folk Deity of Deccan', in Alf Hiltebeitel (ed.), *Criminal Gods and Demon Devotees: Essays on the Guardians of Popular Hinduism*, Albany: State University of New York Press, 1989, pp. 299–302; Günther-Dietz Sontheimer, *Pastoral Deities in Western India*, Translated by Anne Feldhaus, Delhi: Oxford University Press, 1993, pp. 22–26, John M. Stanley, 'The Capitulation of Maṇi: A Conversion Myth in the Cult of Khaṇḍobā', in Alf Hiltebeitel (ed.), *Criminal Gods and Demon Devotees: Essays on the Guardians of Popular Hinduism*, pp. 271–298.

62 Sakharam Paithanpagar, '*Pūrvicī vatandārī va Śekh Mahaṃmadbābā*', photocopy of the short story from Paithanpagar's book, Archive of Abdul Maharaj, Vahira, n.d., pp. 26–33.

References

Ahmad, Imtiaz and Helmut Reifeld, Eds. *Lived Islam in South Asia – Adaptation, Accommodation and Conflict*. Delhi: Social Science Press, 2004.

Bahirath, Bhalchandra P. and Padmanabha J. Bhalerav. *Vārkarī sampradāy uday va vikās*. Pune: Vhīnas Prakāśan, (1972) 1988.

Bendre, Vasudev S., Ed. *Śekh Mahaṃmadbābā yāncā kavitāsangraha*. Mumbai: P. P. H. Bookstall, 1961.

Bendre, Vasudev S. *Tukārām mahārāj yānce santasangatī*. Mumbai: Mauj Prakāśan, 1957.

Casey, Edward. 'How to Get from Space to Place in a Fairly Short Stretch of Time: Phenomenological Prolegomena'. In *Senses of Place*. Steven Field and Keith Basso, Eds. Santa Fe: School of American Research Press, 1996, pp. 13–52.

Deák, Dušan. 'Making Sufism Popular: A Few Notes on the Case from the Marathi Deccan'. *Deccan Studies*, 2013, 11 (2): 5–24.

Deshpande, Achyut Na. *Prācīn Marāṭhī Vānmayācā Itihās*. Vol. 2, Pune: Vhīnas Prakāśan, 1973.

Devle, S. R, Ed. *Śrībhaktavijaya*. Pune: Sarasvatī grantha bhanḍār.

Dhere, Ramachandra Ch., Ed. *Yogasangrām*. Pune: Varda Books, 1981.

Dhere, Ramachandra Ch. *Ekātmatece Śilpakār*, Pune: Manjul Prakāśan, 1994.

Dhere, Ramachandra Ch. *Musalmān Marāṭhī Santkavī*. Pune: Dnyānarāj Prakāśan, 1967.

Dobe, Timothy S. *Hindu Christian Faqir: Modern Monks, Global Christianity and Indian Sainthood*. Oxford: Oxford University Press, 2015.

Eaton, Richard M. *A Social History of the Deccan 1300–1761 (The New Cambridge History of India)*. Cambridge: Cambridge University Press, 2005.

Ethington Phillip. J. 'Placing the Past: 'Groundwork' for a Spatial Theory of History'. *Rethinking History*, 2007, 11 (4): 465–493.

Freitag, Sandria B. 'South Asian Ways of Seeing, Muslim Ways of Knowing: The Indian Muslim Niche Market in Posters'. *The Indian Economic and Social History Review*, 2007, 44 (3): 297–331.

Gavli, Narayan S. and Lanka N. Gavli. *Śrī Sant Śekh Mahaṃmad Mahārāj*. Aurangabad: Kailas Publication, 2011.

Gavli, Narayan S. '*Vārsā Māhitī Kendrācyā Ubhārṇīcā Pathadarśī Prakalpa Ārākhaḍā Tayār Karṇe: Viśeṣ Saṃdarbha Śrīgonde Śāhar, Ji. Ahmadnagar, Mahārāṣṭra*'. Unpublished Ph.D. dissertation, Sāvitrībāī Phule Puṇe Vidyāpīṭh, 2015.

Gosavi, R. Ra, Ed. *Śrīsakalasantagāthā*. Pune: Sārthī Prakāśan, 2000.

Green, Nile. 'The Faqir and the Subalterns: Mapping the Holy Man in Colonial South Asia'. *Journal of Asian History*, 2007, 4 (1): 57–84.

Green, Nile. *Bombay Islam. The Religious Economy of the West Indian Ocean 1840–1915*. Cambridge: Cambridge University Press, 2011.

Joshi, Eknath, S. *Śrīpura Mahātmya*. Shrigonda: Purushottam Eknath Joshi via Shri Printers, 2004.

Joshi, Shankar N, Ed. *Dāsgaṇūmahārājkrut Ākhyān Samuccaya*. Pune: Shankar N. Joshi Chitrashala Press, 1932.

Kurin, Richard. 'Saints'. In *South Asian Folklore. An Encyclopedia*. Margaret A. Mills, Peter J. Claus, and Sarah Diamond, Eds. New York: Routledge, 2003, pp. 531–533.

Malpas, Jeff. 'Finding Place: Spatiality, Locality and Subjectivity'. In *Philosophy and Geography III. Philosophies of Place*. Andrew Light and Jonathan M. Smith, Eds. Lanham: Rowman & Littlefield Publishers, 1998, pp. 21–43.

Modle, Bhima V. '*Sant Kavī Śekh Mahammad: Ek Cikitsak Abhyās*'. Unpublished Ph.D. dissertation, Puṇe: Puṇe Vidyāpīṭh, 1998.

Mohammad, Afsar. *The Festival of Pirs: Popular Islam and Shared Devotion in South India*. New York: Oxford University Press, 2013.

Novetzke, Christian L. *Religion and Public Memory: A Cultural History of Sant Namdev in India*. New York: Columbia University Press, 2008.

Novetzke, Christian L. 'Bhakti and Its Public'. *International Journal of Hindu Studies*, 2007, 11 (3): 255–272.

Office of the Registrar General & Census Commissioner, India. http://censusindia.gov.in. (Accessed 28 September 2017).

Paithanpagar, Sakharam. '*Pūrvicī vatandārī* va *Śekh Mahammadbābā*'. Photocopy of the short story from Paithanpagar's book, Archive of Abdul Maharaj, Vahira, nd. pp. 26–33.

Park, Chris C. *Sacred Worlds. An Introduction to Geography and Religion*. London: Routledge, 1994.

Pathan, Yusuf, M. *Musalmān (Sūphī) Santānce Marāṭhī Sāhitya*. Mumbai: Mahārāṣṭra Rājya Sāhitya āṇi Sanskṛti Manḍaḷ, 2011.

Ranade, Mahadev G. *Rise of the Maratha Power*. Delhi: Publication Divisions, Ministry of Information and Broadcasting, Government of India, [1900] 1974.

Ranade, Ramachandra D. *Mysticism in Maharashtra*. Delhi: Munshiram Manoharlal, [1933] 1982.

Sardar, G. B. *The Saint Poets of Maharashtra (Their Impact on Society)*. Translated and edited by Kumud Mehta. Pune: Orient Longmans Limited, 1969.

Schubel, Vernon J. 'Dargāh'. In *South Asian Folklore. An Encyclopedia*. Margaret A. Mills, Peter J. Claus, and Sarah Diamond, Eds. New York: Routledge, 2003, pp. 140–141.

Schubel, Vernon J. 'Pīr'. In *South Asian Folklore. An Encyclopedia*. Margaret A. Mills, Peter J. Claus, and Sarah Diamond, Eds. New York: Routledge, 2003, p. 478.

Shinde, B. N. *Śrī Śekh Mahammad Śrīgonde yānce stotra va caritra*. Shrigonda: Vimal Prakāśan, 1987.

Sohoni, Pushkar. 'Vernacular as a Space: Writing in the Deccan'. *South Asian History and Culture*, 2016, 7 (3): 258–270.

Sontheimer, Günther-Dietz. 'Between Ghost and God: A Folk Deity of Deccan'. In *Criminal Gods and Demon Devotees: Essays on the Guardians of Popular Hinduism*. Alf Hiltebeitel, Ed. Albany: State University of New York, 1989, pp. 299–337.

Sontheimer, Günther-Dietz. *Pastoral Deities in Western India*. Translated by Anne Feldhaus. Delhi: Oxford University Press, 1993.

Stanley, John M. 'The Capitulation of Maṇi: A Conversion Myth in the Cult of Khaṇḍobā'. In *Criminal Gods and Demon Devotees: Essays on the Guardians of Popular Hinduism*. Alf Hiltebeitel, Ed. Albany: State University of New York Press, 1989, pp. 271–298.

Stewart, Tony K. 'In Search of Equivalence: Conceiving Muslim-Hindu Encounter through Translation Theory'. *History of Religions*, 2001, 40 (3): 261–288.

Tulpule, Shankar G. *Classical Marāṭhī Literature*. Wiesbaden: Otto Harrassowitz, 1979.

Tulpule, Shankar G. 'Purvaṇī'. In *Mahārāṣṭra Sārasvat*. V. L. Bhave, Ed. Mumbai: Popular Prakāśan, 1983, pp. 639–1113.

Vaudeville, Charlotte. 'Sant Mat: Santism as the Universal Path to Sanctity'. In *The Sants (Studies in Devotional Tradition in India)*. Karin Schomer and William H. McLeod, Eds. Delhi: Motilal Banarsidass, 1987, pp. 21–40.

Vaudeville, Charlotte. *Myths, Saints and Legends in Medieval India*. Delhi: Oxford University Press, 1996.

Werbner, Pnina and Helene Basu, Eds. *Embodying Charisma: Modernity, Locality and the Performance of Emotion in Sufi Cults*. London: Routledge, 1998.

Chapter 12

Dakhani Sikh identity and the religious space(s) in Nanded (Maharashtra)

Birinder Pal Singh

> Space is a social morphology: it is to lived experience what form itself is to the living organism, and just as intimately bound up with function and structure.
>
> ... [S]pace is neither a 'subject' nor an 'object', but rather a social reality – that is to say, a set of relations and forms ....
>
> Henri Lefebvre, The Production of Space[1]

I

The followers of the Sikh religion and males among them are manifestly conspicuous people due to the religious form prescribed in their code of conduct, *rehatnama*. They are scattered all over the country and in the Deccan too, including Maharashtra. They appear to be homogeneous to non-Sikhs and to those among them who do 'Sikh politics'. The latter type sees them in opposition to other religious communities like the Hindus or Muslims. In reality, Sikhs are very heterogeneous people in terms of caste, class and other sociological parameters of social stratification. Broadly speaking, there are three main types of Sikhs in the Hyderabad Deccan as also in Maharashtra. The Dakhani Sikhs claim to be the largest and the oldest amongst them. There are tribal Sikhs also, such as the Sikligars and Banjara or Labana/Lambada Sikhs. The third type, called the Punjabi Sikhs, includes relatively recent migrants who moved there for business. They are further of two types belonging to two castes. The Khatris are a trading caste who came largely after the partition of India in 1947. They are engaged in the wholesale and retail trade of a variety of commodities, from cloth to grain and steel to furniture. The Jutts, on the other hand, are peasants, agriculturalists who migrated yet more recently following the development of road and transport services. They control and manage surface transport from cabs to trucks and tankers including passenger buses.

The present chapter focuses on the issues of identity of the Dakhani Sikhs only, especially in the context of a religious space, the famous gurdwara Sach Khand Hazoor Sahib Abchalnagar at Nanded in Maharashtra. It is one of the five *takhts* (throne) of the Sikh religion in the country, and the only one in south India.[2] Its significance may be gauged from the identity the Sikhs gave to the place called Nanded, referring to it as Sri Hazoor Sahib. Sikhs all over the globe know Nanded by this name. It is a large town with 550,439 persons in 2011, situated in the Marathwada region in south-eastern Maharashtra bordering Telengana on the northern bank of Godavari river. It acquired its name from Nandi (Lord Shiva's bull) who had done *tapasaya* (penance) on the river bank, hence Nandi-tat. Its existence goes back to the fifth century BCE, though its present status owes largely to its being a seat of Sikh religious authority, *takht* second in command or significance to Harmandar Sahib at Amritsar.

The significance this place had for Sikhs in the Deccan historically is due to patronage from the Nizam of Hyderabad and Maharaja Diwan Chandu Lal in particular. Its importance has grown manifold in the recent past due to enhanced religious tourism over the last two decades. It helps foster Sikh religious identity among followers and encourages others to come into its fold. It is suggested that the perceived, conceived and lived spaces à la Henri Lefebvre are cementing the Sikh identity so much that the Dakhani Sikhs believe themselves to be the saviours of *Sikhi* that they feel is waning in Punjab, the cradle of Sikhism. The dakhani identity of these Sikhs is of relatively recent origin that emerged from their encounter with the Punjabi Sikhs; until then they were known as Sikhs only. Their unit in the irregular troops was called the Sikh Force under the department Nazim-i-Jami'at-i-Sikhan.

II

The Dakhani Sikhs derive their name and fame from their ancestors being the employees of the erstwhile state of Hyderabad Deccan. Oral tradition maintains that they are the descendants of the Sikh soldiers dispatched there by Maharaja Ranjit Singh from Punjab. Each Dakhani Sikh narrates the story that his ancestor was sent there to maintain law and order in the disturbed state of Hyderabad.[3] The security of dignitaries and the collection of revenue were their main duties. A contingent of fourteen Risalas, each consisting of one hundred soldiers, reached there in 1832 and got stationed at Barambala, called Sikh Chhawniat (cantonment) in Kishan Bagh (Attapur), now a buzzing suburb of Hyderabad. An internet source says: '1500 Lahori soldiers in the supervision of 14 Risaldars was sent to Hyderabad State and Maharaja Ranjit Singh ji announced that the salaries and basic equipments for this Lahori Force will be sent from Punjab. 200 acres of land...was given to Lahori Force for their cantonment'.[4] But according to the journalist Nanak Singh Nishter:

> In 1830, after completing four months of arduous journey, the Sikh army arrived from Lahore in Hyderabad. The army consisted of twelve *Risalas* – army units, each comprising of a 100 personnel and each

> *Risala* headed by a Risaldar. ... They were first stationed outside the walled city of Hyderabad near the Mir Alam Tank on Rajinder Nagar road from Bahadar Pura, which place till today is famously known as the *Braham Bala Sikh Chhawni – the Sikh Cantonment, and the army was called Jamiyat-i-Lahori* (Army of Lahore). Their salaries and expenses for maintenance of equipment etc., used to come from the treasury of Maharaja Ranjit Singh as they were here on a goodwill mission from Punjab.[5]

Some of these people, however, do not appreciate their characterization as Dakhani Sikhs vis-à-vis other Sikhs. A senior respondent argues: 'A Sikh is a Sikh. Why are we called Dakhani? It smells discrimination'. Nishter, a journalist amongst them writes: 'Deccani is not a word for segregation from the mainstream Sikhs, but it is a geographical identity which was attributed to the North Indians settled in Hyderabad Deccan such as Deccani Pathan, etc'.[6] It is pertinent to note that the Hyderabad Deccan is so qualified since there is another Hyderabad in Sind in what is now west Punjab in Pakistan. H.K. Sherwani, a noted historian, suggests this about the Dakhani nomenclature:

> The scions of the dynasty (Qutb Shahis) formed a connection link between the Bahmanis and the Asaf Jahis, and they were also promoters of that peculiar culture which is sometimes dubbed as Dakhani culture, itself the result of the synthesis of cultures from particularly all parts of the country as well as from overseas, which came face to face in the great table land of which the Qutbshahi dominions formed a significant part.[7]

The Deccan in brief refers to the state of Hyderabad under nizams of Asaf Jah dynasty from eighteenth to the middle of the twentieth century (1720–1951). It comprised erstwhile sixteen districts (cf. *Imperial Gazetteer of Hyderabad 1909*) now distributed over three states, namely Andhra Pradesh (now Telengana) with the largest share followed by Maharashtra and Karnataka. Each has its own city of concentration of Dakhani Sikhs viz. Hyderabad, Nanded and Bidar, respectively, though they are present in all district headquarters in some numbers. Besides Nanded, Aurangabad, Parbani, Beed and Osmanabad are all places of significant Sikh presence in the erstwhile Deccan that now fall in Maharashtra. All these places belonged to the former division of Aurangabad of the Deccan state.

The Dakhani Sikhs are primarily urban dwellers and non-agricultural by occupation who prefer employment to any other occupation. The socio-economic profile of these Sikhs does not place them on a high pedestal since the majority of them are engaged in self-dependent occupations or low-level positions in the public and private sectors.[8] There are a few officers and rich people too who may be counted on one's fingertips. The majority of them claim general caste status, though some also call themselves Other Backward Classes (OBCs). A feature that distinguishes them from other Sikhs in Punjab is their appearance, as they appear to be a mix of north and south Indian facial features since the erstwhile Sikh soldiers married local women. Another conspicuous characteristic is their ignorance of Punjabi language, for which they are ridiculed and called 'duplicate' Sikhs by Punjabi Sikhs.[9]

III

The Dakhani Sikhs have carved their distinct identity in the social spaces of Maharashtrian towns and cities as a consequence of their employment in the irregular forces of the Hyderabad Deccan. There was a separate state department – Nazim-i-Jami'at-i-Sikhan – that looked into their employment, deployment and service records. No doubt, the historians of Punjab and the Sikhs, namely J.S. Grewal and Himadri Banerjee, contest the Dakhani Sikhs' belief that their ancestors were dispatched from Punjab, but each Dakhani Sikh, high or low, rich or poor, believes otherwise.[10] Each one of them narrates the story verbatim that Raja Chandu Lal, then diwan of Hyderabad, was instrumental in soliciting support from Punjab. They 'remember' that before seeking the Maharaja's favour, an emissary of the Nizam was sent to the Lahore Darbar to present a shawl embroidered with silver. The Maharaja accepted it but offered the same to the Guru at Harmandar Sahib, the Golden Temple, as *chandoya*, a canopy over the Guru Granth, saying that such a precious gift suits there only. They add that that gift was destroyed during the Operation Bluestar in June 1984 when the Indian armed forces moved there for the eviction of Sikh militants. It is interesting to note that all these incidents are vividly narrated and with such confidence as if the informants had witnessed these happenings. The reference to Operation Bluestar is made again to reinforce their Sikh identity. The targeting of Sikhs as objects of hate crime happened in November 1984, immediately following the assassination of the Prime Minister Indira Gandhi. It was an all-India phenomenon. During those days when many Sikhs were shearing off their religious symbols, the Dakhani Sikhs not only preserved but displayed these manifestly. They keep loose beards and wear *kirpan* (short sword) over their shirts.

IV

Contrary to popular perception, it is probable that under the turbulent conditions prevailing then, Chandu Lal would have liked to strengthen himself by having a contingent of fiery soldiers on his side. Wood notes: '[G]iven the frayed nature of Hyderabadi politics in the first half of the nineteenth century, and given the almost total absence of any rule of law, Chandu Lal's private army of Sikhs was simply another aspect of his genius for self-preservation'.[11] Although this must be substantiated by further research, it is plausible that the Sikhs already present there in the Deccan and around were made into Jami'at-i-Sikhan. Once organized into a force, it did not take them long to establish their supremacy over the Arab and Rohilla troops and other miscreants.

The ancestors of Dakhani Sikhs, if believed to be *nihangs* (the blue-robed soldiers of the Guru's army) accompanying Guru Gobind Singh from Punjab to Nanded, also called Hazoori Singhs;[12] or as soldiers of the Lahori Fauj dispatched from Punjab by Ranjit Singh; or even as Sikhs scattered already in the Deccan and organized into Jami'at-i-Sikhan; all of them have one streak in common, that they were soldiers primarily. Thus, it gives credence to their belief that they are the progeny of Sikh soldiers. The notion of a 'martial race' had not developed then, but the qualities of bravery and obedience, among others, were part of their identity.[13] The personnel of the Sikh Force, as it was called then, was deployed at strategic positions like guarding palaces and royal processions; they also collected revenue from the districts and deposited that in the treasury. Their success in containing Arab and Rohilla criminals and establishing law and order in the state was a major task. No doubt, Maharaja Chandu Lal was their patron, but they excelled in the tasks assigned to them. The Sikh Force emerged as peace keepers, which enhanced their respect in the eyes of the administration and the people at large.

This also magnified their self-perception, enlarging their perceived space à la Lefebvre of being great warriors and the saviours of people fighting against evil; in this way, they lived up to the purported image of the Khalsa, their conceived space, who is ordained by the Guru to fight for the righteous cause. The Dakhani Sikhs boast of Sikh chivalry in one voice, claiming that the presence of not only a soldier but an ordinary Sikh in the village was enough to deter any miscreant or criminal.[14] Further, many claimed that a Sikh paying a social visit to a house would make news in the village, and people would surmise what wrong had been done by the family that a Sikh [Sikh Force] had come to them. They often boost their self-image by comparing this perception among the local people with Hari Singh Nalwa, a general in Ranjit Singh's army.[15] That the political and economic conditions of the Hyderabad state were disturbed and stressed is well borne out by certain documents. In the words of an Englishman: 'Despite British influence, the administration was appallingly bad. Finance was hopelessly muddled. The countryside for half a century was dominated by Arabs and Rohillas, mostly disbanded mercenaries from the Maratha and Pindari armies. At one period the Arabs practically over shadowed the government'.[16]

Another significant component of the Dakhani Sikhs' perceived space is the self-esteem of their ancestors. Once again, one respondent's comments were echoed by others:

> Our fore-fathers were so concerned about self-esteem that when Nizam gave them the *jagir* [fief] of Nirmal for their excellent services, they rolled the said *farman,* Nizam's order, inserted into the muzzle of a gun and blew that off, saying: 'We get salary from our Maharaja. He is our lord. Who is he [the Nizam] to give us *jagir*?'[17]

It is maintained by the respondents that until the death of Maharaja Ranjit Singh, the salary of the Sikh Force was paid from the Punjab treasury since 'the economic condition of the Nizam was not sound'.[18] It is interesting to note that today Dakhani Sikhs remain proud of this history, even if most of them are poor and not doing 'status' jobs. Their self-perception of being descendants of the Lahori Fauj, reinforced by the achievements of the Sikh Force in containing the mercenaries, the collection of revenue and guarding the royal processions and ceremonies, all inflate their self-image of bravery and chivalry. It also confirms their sense of being natives who made the Deccan their home.

The perceived space of the Dakhani Sikhs is further constituted by their ancestors' defiance of the authority of Nizam or his officers if they did not behave 'properly'. These instances are fondly remembered and reiterated with pride.[19] It is much in tune with what Guru Nanak, the founder of Sikhism, preached for believing in one God, the almighty True Lord (*sachcha patshah*) as against the worldly false lords, *chuthhe patshah.* One among them, Asa Singh, revolted against the Nizam and challenged the state forces when the salaries of his men were not disbursed for some months. Despite numerous casualties, he did not yield. There now stands a gurdwara in the memory of martyrs called Puratan Gurdwara Asa Singh Bagh Singh Shaheedan in the Sikh Chhawniat at Hyderabad. A mortal being, a *risaldar* has been elevated to the status of a religious icon for the community.[20]

The case of Narayan Singh Mortad, a soldier of the Sikh Force, also reveals a figure who rebelled against the Nizam and started 'Robin Hooding'. Mortad is about fifty kilometres from Nizamabad on the state highway. It is a large village that was once the area of his operations. He looted the wealthy and helped the poor and the needy. A nearby hillock where he camped is named Narayan Singh Pahar. There are stories about his strength and chivalry. People hold that he lived among tigers and that one of their dens was his resting place. The state police was terribly scared of him. Many expeditions were sent to arrest or kill him but in vain. Finally, he was poisoned through a lady to whose house he used to visit sometimes for food. It is said that when he was poisoned he came to know of it.

First, he killed her and later shot himself, taking a *chadar* (sheet) on him as his *kaphan* (coffin). People narrate that the dead Mortad was fired upon for an hour before 'capture'. It is said that he infused terror to such a degree that when the *chadar* fluttered in the wind, policemen would run for their lives. Interestingly, the Maoist (Naxalite) guerrillas of the region have kept him alive in their songs.

The above-mentioned self-perception of the Dakhani Sikhs is not imaginary. It had the recognition of the State. The Sikh soldier's son was given a stipend and free education in the police school on attaining the age of five years. At eighteen years, he was inducted into regular employment in Jami'at-i-Sikhan. The respondents maintain that one reason they never bothered about modern education and other occupations was because of this state facility (of guaranteed job) available to them. Because their sons were ensured employment, they did not look towards alternative occupations like trade and agriculture. The respondents reiterate: '*naukari hamare khoon mein hai, hum wahi kar sakte hain*': 'Service is in our blood, and we can do that only'.[21]

V

In his classic discussion of religion and cultural symbols, Clifford Geertz has argued that: 'Religion is a system of symbols which acts to establish powerful, pervasive and long-lasting moods and motivations in men by formulating conceptions of a general order of existence and clothing these conceptions with such an aura of factuality that the moods and motivations seem uniquely realistic'.[22] Religious symbols play a significant role in the lives of Dakhani Sikhs. The conceived religious space in Gurdwara Sach Khand at Nanded produces and reinforces not only Sikh religious identity but contributes to constructing their social identity as well – not only of the devotees but of the very place called Nanded. The religious space has become so significant and imposing that it has given Nanded a new name, Sri Hazoor Sahib. Sikhs all over the globe know Nanded by this name; the place of Nanded has been transformed into a sacred space, Sri Hazoor Sahib.[23] Indeed, for Sikhs there is no such entity called Nanded but Sri Hazoor Sahib. Even Nanded is called Nanded Sahib.

Sach Khand Hazoor Sahib at Nanded is a distinctly conceived space conspicuously different not only from other religious spaces around but from other Sikh religious spaces anywhere as well, including the Harmandar Sahib at Amritsar. It also does not conform to the prescriptions of the Shiromani Gurdwara Parbandhak Committee (SGPC).[24] It differs in two ways: One, keeping the two Granths – *Dasam Granth and Guru Granth* – together in the sanctum sanctorum gives them equal respect.[25] Two, different ritual practices are undertaken there, including sacrificing a ram within the gurdwara premises, and others such as a distinct way of reciting *ardas* (the Sikh prayer), *aarti* (showing of the lamps) and the display of weapons. Interestingly, the weapons at this site do not belong to the Guru only. It is also a rule here that the *takht jathedar* (chief of Sri Hazoor Sahib gurdwara) has to be a bachelor, a condition that does not apply to other takhts in the country. According to Gyani Mohan Singh: 'You will find in every Gurdwara except here that highest seat is given to Sri Guru Granth Sahib ji, But [sic] the highest seat is given to "shastars" (weapons)'.[26]

With an increasing influx of pilgrims following religious tourism over the last two decades, the relatively open religious space at Sri Hazoor Sahib has been increasingly fortified. Structurally speaking, the sanctum sanctorum is enclosed by five large iron gates between three-storey guest rooms (*sarais*) on its three sides, which encircle a large marble compound with shrubs and colourful fountains. The gates are guarded by *sewadars* (security guards) holding large spears as well as swords, short (*kirpan*) or large, the regular outfit of an *amritdhari* Sikh. The site resembles a guarded fort, as it is the seat or throne (*takht*) of the eternal guru. Each Sikh is expected to fight for its sovereignty, and those who have sacrificed themselves for its sake are the revered ones who are remembered in *ardas*, the Sikh prayer, always.

The enlargement and beautification of this prime religious space owes much to the manifold increase in the number of pilgrims and donations flowing in abundance from across the globe. The central Indian government also made a massive grant of about Rs. 300 crores for the celebrations of the 300th *gurtagaddi divas* in 2008.[27] A Non-Resident Indian (NRI) guest house has been opened besides other *sarais* (resting places) and guest houses for pilgrims. A museum named after the tenth guru is also in progress. The rise in Sikh pilgrims' number from abroad has connected this relatively small town with air to Delhi and Mumbai, besides the enhanced express rail and road connectivity. The airport is named after Guru Gobind Singh. The place called Nanded has now acquired a global reach as Sikhs pour in from all over. The Sach Khand Express train carries hundreds of pilgrims from Punjab everyday besides the chartered tours.[28] This has resulted in manifold magnification of the conceived space called Sach Khand Hazoor Sahib, now a preserve of the Dakhani Sikhs, distinct from the north Indian and other Sikhs. Earlier the tours were taken especially on festive occasions, but now it is a year-round business. Besides the main gurdwara, a dozen more sacred spaces have assumed importance in the city that also are associated either directly with the Guru or with his associates such as Banda Bahadur and Mai Bhago. At Banda Ghat, a Sikh seminary teaches recitation and singing of *gurbani* (the text of the Guru Granth Sahib) to the tribal Banjaras and others from places as far as Bihar. The Banjara Sikhs excel in this pursuit so much so that out of seven *raagi jathas* (bands of hymn singers) with the main gurdwara, four belong to them.

VI

The prime religious space, Sri Hazoor Sahib, is not a mere mental construct or conceived space but constitutes a concrete lived space with active dialectics between the perceived and conceived spaces à la Henri Lefebvre. This is also akin to 'betweenness of places' suggested by Entrikin, a meeting point for subjective and objective spaces where subjective meanings and objective reality come together.[29] Gurdwara Sach Khand not only provides free food and shelter to pilgrims but also employment to local Sikhs. It has about 800 employees on a regular basis, providing ample opportunity for voluntary services or *sewa* of various types to them and the pilgrims. The Banjara and Sikligar Sikhs too are gainfully employed. The increasing number of pilgrims has also given impetus to numerous ancillary services to cater to their needs, thus generating self-employment for Dakhani Sikhs and others in Nanded.

The lived space of the Sikhs is thus expanding and becoming concretized. It has become an interacting space between regions and cultures. The pilgrims from the north and abroad are overwhelmed by the Sikh spirit and *shardha* (faith) of the Dakhani and the tribal Sikhs. They, on the other hand, notice that the Sikh form (*sikhi*) is losing space in the Punjab as they encounter *mona* (with head hair shorn) Sikh pilgrims.[30] Films and television programmes also attest to this observation. A dialectic between subjective and objective reality enhances Dakhani Sikhs' self-estimation of being better Sikhs, which is why they mince no words in claiming: '*Hamney sikhi ko sambhala hai, Punjab mein to bura haal hai*', literally, 'we have conserved the Sikh religion (in form and content) that is in ruins in Punjab'. Moreover, while historians debate interpretations of the Guru's southward journey, Dakhani Sikhs have a definite answer to this riddle. A retired police inspector with family links in Punjab, remarks: '*Guru sahib jaani-jaan thhe. Voh Dakhan mein isi liye aaye thhe ki sikhi to vahin bachegi, Punjab mein nahin*': literally, 'the Guru had a grand intuition. He knew too well that the Sikh religion (*sikhi*) would be saved in the Deccan not in Punjab, which is why he traveled southwards'.[31]

The spurt in religious fervour over these years has marked increased participation of people in religious festivals since the opening up of the Indian economy and the policy of liberalization, privatization and globalization (LPG). On *gurpurabs* (days associated with the birth or death of gurus) and other days of religious celebration, Gurdwara Sach Khand looks like a Sikh *chhauni* (cantonment). The pomp and show of *nagar kirtan jaloos* (religious procession in the city) carrying Granth Sahib in a large decorated motor vehicle with armed *panj piyaras* (five beloved ones) in the front along with a band of fire brand *gatka* (Sikh martial art) players make the procession an intensely involved affair of chivalry and service (*sewa*). All along the procession, *langar* (free food) of snacks and tea or cold drinks, depending on the season is served. The participants brandishing kirpans in the procession frequently reverberate *jaikaras* (war cries) at a loud pitch like *Jo bole so nihal, Sat Sri Akal; Waheguru ji ka Khalsa, Waheguru ji ki Fateh; Degh Tegh Fateh; Panth ki Jeet;* and *Raj Karega Khalsa.* (Blessed is the one who says the Timeless only is true; The Khalsa belongs to God and God is ever victorious; Victory to the kettle and the Sword; The Sikh community shall be ever victorious; and The Khalsa shall ever rule.)

On Hola Mahalla in mid-March, the procession starts from the main gurdwara. Not far from there is a wide crossing in the market area called Halla Bol Chowk, so named because at that very place the enactment of offence and defence between the charged camps is carried out to celebrate a practice initiated by the last guru at Anandpur Sahib (Punjab) for celebrating Holi, the festival of colours.[32] It involves intense physical activity on the part of participants, each of which carries a weapon and charges towards the opponent. A senior respondent at Nizamabad informs: '*Jab 300 sala divas manaya to kayi parivar darr ke Nanded chhod kar yahan aa gaye*'; literally, 'When the 300th anniversary of *gurtagaddi divas* was celebrated, many non-Sikh families left Nanded for Nizamabad out of fear'.

The prime religious space, the Hazoor Sahib (in Nanded) has contributed significantly in entrenching and authenticating the religious identity of the Dakhani Sikhs. The religious sanctity of this conceived space owes to the 'presence' of Guru Gobind Singh. People believe that the Guru is present there and those who enjoy the grace of Waheguru do 'see' him around. A descendant of the Guru's horse that makes a part of the religious procession is also groomed there, and observers notice that the Guru himself is seated on the stallion. His gait makes it clear that a rider is on him. The Guru's presence is also believed as he has ordained none to enter the enclosure and search his funeral pyre (*angeetha*). When it was searched, there were no remains (*phull*) but a mini-kirpan. And, some attendants had seen him going to the heavens on his horse. Thus, people believe that the Guru is very much there.

Two events in the Guru's life have enhanced the religious sanctity of Hazoor Sahib. First, the Guru passed away there in 1708, and it was not a normal natural death. Rather, he was stabbed by two Pathans, one of whom he killed before dying. Second, he bestowed gurudom/guruship to Guru Granth Sahib. He ordained: *Sab Sikhan ko hukam hai Guru maniyo Granth* – All Sikhs are ordained to accept the Granth Sahib as the living guru. This prescription is so significant that it is inscribed boldly on the face of the double storey gurdwara. The pilgrim's perceived space is constituted of such memories: the Guru is not only a martyr himself but sacrificed his family members from father to sons, his lineage hence addressed as *sarbansdani.* Such an awe grips the mind of a pilgrim who goes there to pay homage to such a martyr.

VII

The question of consolidation of the Sikh identity of the Dakhani Sikhs is a consequence of the dialectic of the lived space that has grown more intense in the recent past. Richard Jenkins defines identity minimally: 'Identity is our understanding of who we are and who other people are, and, reciprocally, other people's understanding of themselves and of others (which includes us). It is a very practical matter, synthesising relationships of similarity and difference'.[33] Social practices in this space of interaction have seemingly fixed the responsibility of maintaining the Sikh form and the Sikh spirit on the Dakhani Sikhs: they have assumed the role of maintaining the legacy of Guru Gobind Singh and have historically carried out practices at Hazoor Sahib purportedly ordained by him.

The manifest identity of Dakhani Sikhs has two striking characteristics – their physical features and their religious symbols. In terms of the former, they are different from other Sikhs (say in Punjab or even elsewhere) and with respect to latter, they are distinct from non-Sikhs at a place where they are a minority. Ethnically, they make a different stock owing to the marriage of their ancestors to local women.

The person of the last Sikh guru is also significant. He was no pacifist but a militant who gave a distinct form and content to his followers, so distinct that his Sikhs would stand out from the crowd prominently. He gave them, men and women both, a conspicuously manifest identity. Over the years, Sikh women have merged into the crowd but Sikh males stand out still, given their beard and turban if not other identity markers, the five symbols of Sikhism called *kakar* or simply the Five Ks (in English). A Sikh who has taken *amrit* is bound to support *kesh* (uncut hair), *kanga* (comb), *kirpan* (sword), *kada* (steel bracelet) and *kachha* (long breeches).

The Dakhani Sikhs have not failed Sikhism but rather nurtured it in a way different from its northern counterpart. It is constitutive of Dakhani identity. They fought against the local lords, taking support from the rulers and people (*sangat*) in the north but kept the flame glowing. They maintain the Sikh form (*sikhi saroop*). They do not tolerate the cutting of hair. Uberoi writes that 'the custom of wearing long and unshorn hair (*kes*) is among the most cherished and distinctive signs of an individual's membership of the Sikh Panth, and it seems always to have been so'.[34] The turban and *kara* (steel bracelet) are distinctly visible. Most of them wear *kirpan* manifestly. Ravinder Kaur also notes in the case of Jat Sikhs of Punjab: 'Most Sikhs wear at least two of these overt symbols – the turban signifying uncut hair and *kara* or the steel bracelet. Most non-Sikhs identify Sikhs by these symbols'.[35]

The Dakhani Sikhs' religious practices are in consonance with their past as members of the Sikh Force, and this keeps their militant image alive and fearsome. Their love for *shastars* (weapons) as also religious symbols adds to their chivalrous image, besides legends mentioned above. The case of Gurdwara Maal Tekdi and subsequent communal riots with Muslims in the late 1920s also increased their self-perception as a 'martial' people who can challenge anyone.[36] In a phrase that displays his own values, Major Macready, who was in Nanded around 1820, maintained that that Sikhs were 'the only part of the population whose appearance and demeanour were at all respectable'. He describes their 'martial and manly contour of countenance, which, set off by their picturesque turbans, their black curling beards and whiskers, and their warlike appointments, forms a brigandish and interesting picture. They have more of the independent, self-confiding military look than any Easterners I have seen'.[37]

The patronage of the Nizam and Maharaja Chandu Lal in particular and the Sikhs' ensured employment in the Sikh Force must have made them adhere to the principles of Sikh religion. Chandu Lal, who was a *sehajdhari* Sikh – someone who believed in the Sikh gurus and the scripture but without the Sikh form – not only took initiative in building gurdwaras but also managed to get liberal grants and land to Gurdwara Sach Khand at Nanded. Nihang and Singh note that of the three major sources of income to the *pujaris* of gurdwara at Nanded, 'The second source was Maharaja Chandu Lal who often made rich offerings to the shrine and looked to the general interest of the Sikhs in the colony'.[38]After his demise, some land granted to the gurdwara was withdrawn, but that was restored later at the instance of the Nizam's daughter.

VIII

The Dakhani Sikhs are fully entrenched in their social space – perceived, conceived and lived spaces – and have carved a niche for themselves with a distinct identity. There is also a correspondence in their levels of identity formation at what Jenkins calls individual, interactional and institutional orders.[39] Barth argues in this context: 'we give primary emphasis to the fact that ethnic groups are categories of ascription and identification by the actors themselves, and thus have the characteristic of organizing interaction between people'.[40] By so doing they create boundaries around themselves and tend to sustain these. The Dakhani Sikhs' ancestors married local women after making them take *amrit*, thus a Sikh married a Sikh (*anand karaj*) as prescribed in *rehat maryada*, the Sikh code. The Dakhani Sikhs marry within their own community from anywhere in the erstwhile state of Deccan that now cuts across barriers of the present territorial states and the linguistic boundaries as well. Their kinship network cuts across three states namely Telengana, Karnataka and Maharashtra.

Harold Garfinkel suggests the notion of identity constancy when he asks, 'What are the conditions under which the person's interpreter regards the person as the same'.[41] I suggest that the Dakhani Sikhs have maintained a continuity with their past identity that remains functional and becomes concretized in the lived space at Hazoor Sahib. Each Dakhani Sikh is spiritually connected to this space. Like their ancestors, they still enjoy social esteem from the local people. They maintain religious markers, especially the flowing beard and turban. In this way, with the Dakhani Sikhs, the social and the religious are inseparable. Niharranjan Ray once wrote: 'History … taught the Punjab and her people one very important lesson, namely, not to forget or be oblivious of temporal or secular situations of any given time'.[42] As I have argued elsewhere, 'I would rather re-verse Niharranjan Ray, saying that however engrossed a Sikh may find oneself in matters of day-to-day life in the present-day market society, s/he is never oblivious of the "religious", hence the primacy of the sacred space in their lives'.[43]

Notes

1 Henri Lefebvre, *The Production of Space*, Oxford: Blackwell, 1991, p. 94, p. 116.
2 Three takhts are in Punjab and one in Bihar, Patna Sahib. Interestingly, all but one are directly associated with Guru Gobind Singh.
3 Respondents were interviewed by the author during the fieldwork conducted thrice in 2012 during the months of March, May–June and December.
4 *Puratan Gurudwara Sahib Asha Singh Bagh Shaheedan Singh Asthan* www.sikhmatrimonials.com/sikhnet/directory.nsf (date accessed: 2 August 2013).
5 Nanak Singh Nishter, *Babri Masjid vs Gurdwara Maal Tekdi*, Hyderabad: International Sikh Centre for Interfaith Relations, 2011, pp. 15–16.
6 Ibid., p. 15.
7 H. K. Sherwani, *The Bahmanis of the Deccan*, Delhi: Munshiram Manoharlal, 1985, p. ix.
8 For details on the socio-economic profile of Dakhani and other Sikhs in the Deccan including Nanded, see Birinder Pal Singh, 'Sikhs of the Hyderabad Deccan', *Economic and Political Weekly*, July 26, Vol. XLIX, No. 30, 2014, pp. 163–170. Given the homogeneity of the universe/sample, there are hardly significant variations among Dakhani Sikhs at different places. The Sikligar Sikhs, however, are most poor.
9 The term 'duplicate Sikhs' is also used for the Axomiya Sikhs who have settled in the Nagaon district of Assam for the past 200 years. (Birinder Pal Singh, *Sikhs in the Deccan and North-East India*, London and New York: Routledge,2018.) It is also true of the Bihari or Agarahari Sikhs in Kolkata. (Himadri Banerjee, *The Other Sikhs: A View from Eastern India*, Volume 1. Delhi: Manohar, 2007. Also see Najnin Islam 2012).
10 The historians of Punjab, Himadri Banerjee (2007, 61) and Grewal, not only doubt but reject the possibility of Ranjit Singh sending troops to the Deccan following the Treaty of Amritsar (1809) and the rules of British paramountcy. Grewal notes that it was a matter of foreign relations between the Indian states, hence no king could send military support without their permission. Moreover, such support would have had to pass through the British territory. He said: 'I have not seen any such entry in the British records to the best of my information. The same is the case of records at Lahore darbar'. (Personal interview on 26 May 2013 at Chandigarh.) But *The Encyclopaedia of Sikhism* argues that 'In order not to arouse British suspicions these soldiers travelled to Hyderabad in small batches' (1998, Vol. IV, p. 160).
11 Peter Wood, *Vassal State in the Shadow of Empire: Palmer's Hyderabad, 1799–1867* (Ph.D. thesis, University of Wisconsin). Michigan: UMI Dissertation Services, 1981, p. 375.

12 See Nidar Singh Nihang and Paramjit Singh, *In the Master's Presence: The Sikhs of Hazoor Sahib, Volume 1. History*, London: Kashi Publishing House, 2008.
13 Richard Fox quotes R.W. Falcon, an officer in the British army: 'The Sikh is a fighting man and his fine qualities are best shown in the army, which is his natural profession. Hardy, brave, and of intelligence; too slow to understand when he is beaten; obedient to discipline; attached to his officers; and careless of caste prohibitions, he is unsurpassed as a soldier in the East ... The Sikh is always the same, ever genial, good-tempered and uncomplaining; as steady under fire as he is eager for a charge'. *Lions of the Punjab: Culture in the Making*, Delhi: Archives Publishers, 1987, p. 144.
14 A number of respondents made similar statements to this effect. These are summaries based on interviews conducted in March, May–June and December of 2012.
15 Hari Singh Nalwa was a celebrated general in the army of Ranjit Singh posted at the western frontiers for the security of the kingdom. Mothers, it is chronicled, would scare their crying children by saying that Nalwa would come if they did not stop. They were also threatened similarly if they would not take food.
16 Sir William Barton, *The Princes of India with a Chapter on Nepal*, London: Nisbet & Co., 1934, p. 197.
17 Personal interview, ibid.
18 Personal interview, ibid.
19 Personal interview, ibid.
20 Besides the Sikh form, the tenth guru infused in the Sikhs' militancy against tyranny and injustice. His conception of the Khalsa embodies ever readiness to fight against any domination and oppression. His confrontation against the Dilli darbar and other regional lords is well documented in literature. The Sikh Forces of the Nizam, whether from Punjab or organized locally, must have been inspired by the last guru's exemplary sacrifice of the whole family for *panth*, the community hence called *sarbansdani*.
21 Personal interviews at Sikh Chhawniat, Hyderabad and at Nanded.
22 Clifford Geertz, 'Religion as a Cultural System', *The Interpretation of Cultures: Selected Essays*. Fontana Press: London, 1993, p. 90.
23 Respectfully honouring a place of religious significance is common in Sikhism and Islam such as Sri Amritsar Sahib, Sri Anandpur Sahib, Sri Patna Sahib and others for Sikhs and Ajmer Sharif, Mecca Sharif, etc. for Muslims.
24 This is the highest body that looks into the working of the gurdwaras and other Sikh institutions; it was established in 1920 with headquarters at Amritsar (Punjab).
25 Dasam Granth is also placed at another Takht Patna Sahib, which is also associated with the birth of Guru Gobind Singh. The SGPC and many others scholars believe that Dasam Granth is not wholly the Guru's writing; hence, it cannot be treated at par with the Granth Sahib. Moreover, it is also noted that when the question of the Dasam Granth's status was posed to the Guru himself, he remarked: 'This one is Adi Guru Granth, the root book; that one (refers to Dasam Granth) is only for my diversion. Let this be kept in mind and let the two stay separate'. (*The Encyclopaedia of Sikhism*, Vol. I, Patiala: Punjabi University, 1995).
26 Gyani Mohan Singh, *Tawarikh Sachkand: A Correct History of Gurdwara Saheb*, Nanded: n.d., p. 2.
27 *Gurtagaddi divas* refers to the day gurudom was conferred on *Guru Granth Sahib* by Guru Gobind Singh in 1708.
28 A superfast weekly train also connects Amritsar with Nanded.
29 J. Nicholas Etrikin, *The Betweenness of Place: Towards a Geography of Modernity*, Baltimore: John Hopkins University Press, 1990.

30 *Mona* means clean shaven but with Sikhs it refers to a person without turban and who has a trimmed beard or is clean shaven. This trend is more common among the peasantry in Punjab and elsewhere. See McLeod (1989).
31 Interview with a retired police inspector at Sikh Chhawniat, Hyderabad on 13 May 2012.
32 According to *The Encyclopaedia of Sikhism*:

> Holla Mohalla or simply Hola, a Sikh festival, takes place on the first of the lunar month of Chet which usually falls in March. This follows the Hindu festival of Holi. The name Hola is the masculine form of the feminine sounding Holi. *Mohalla*, derived from the Arabic root *hal* (alighting, descending), is a Punjabi word signifying an organized procession in the form of an army column accompanied by war-drums and standard-bearers ... The custom originated in the time of Guru Gobind Singh (1666–1708) who held first such march at Anandpur on ... 22 February 1701 ... Unlike Holi ... the Guru made it an occasion for the Sikhs to demonstrate their martial skills in simulated battles ... at Takht Sri Abchalnagar Hazur Sahib, Nanded ... the procession is led by a white horse believed to be a scion of the favourite blue-black stallion of Guru Gobind Singh.
>
> (pp. 282–283)

33 Richard Jenkins, *Social Identity* (Third edition), London and New York: Routledge, 2012, p. 18.
34 Jit Pal Singh Uberoi, *Religion, Civil Society and the State: A Study of Sikhism*, Delhi: Oxford University Press, 1996, p. 1.
35 Ravinder Kaur, 'Jat Sikhs: A Question of Identity', *Contributions to Indian Sociology* (n.s.), Vol. 20, No. 2 (1986), p. 222. For further details see Birinder Pal Singh, *Sikhs in the Deccan and North-East India*, London and New York: Routledge, 2018.
36 For details see Nishter (2011). The high-power committee constituted by the Nizam decided in favour of the Sikhs. This not only boosted their morale but also justified their sense that they fought for a just cause.
37 Qtd. in Nidar Singh Nihang and Paramjit Singh, *In the Master's Presence: The Sikhs of Hazoor Sahib, Volume 1. History*, London: Kashi Publishing House, 2008, p. 98.
38 Ibid., p. 146.
39 Jenkins, (Ed.), *Ethnic Groups and Boundaries: The Social Organisation of Culture Difference*. London: George Allen and Unwin, 1969, pp. 40–45.
40 Fredrik Barth,1969, p. 10.
41 Harold Garfinkel, *Seeing Sociologically: The Routine Grounds of Social Action*, edited and introduced by A.W. Rawls, London: Paradigm Publishers, 2006, p. 151.
42 Niharranjan Ray, *The Sikh Gurus and the Sikh Society: A Study in Social Analysis*, Delhi: Munshiram Manoharlal, 1975, p. 105.
43 Birinder Pal Singh, *Sikhs in the Deccan and North-East India*, London and New York: Routledge, 2018, p. 208.

References

Bannerjee, Himadri, *The Other Sikhs: A View from Eastern India*. Volume 1. Delhi: Manohar, 2007.

Barth, Fredrik, Ed. *Ethnic Groups and Boundaries: The Social Organisation of Culture Difference*. London: George Allen and Unwin, 1969.

Barton, Sir William. *The Princes of India with a Chapter on Nepal*. London: Nisbet & Co., 1934.
Entrikin, J. Nicholas. *The Betweenness of Place: Towards a Geography of Modernity*. Baltimore: John Hopkins University Press, 1990.
Fox, Richard Gabriel. *Lions of the Punjab: Culture in the Making*. Delhi: Archives Publishers, 1987.
Garfinkel, Harold. *Seeing Sociologically: The Routine Grounds of Social Action*, edited and introduced by A.W. Rawls. London: Paradigm Publishers, 2006.
Geertz, Clifford. *The Interpretation of Cultures: Selected Essays*. Fontana Press, London, 1993.
Islam, Najnin. 'Negotiating Borders: Community and the Dynamics of Punjabi and Bihari-Sikh Relations in Kolkata', *Man in India*, 92 (1), 2012, pp. 55–76.
Jenkins, Richard. *Social Identity* (Third edition). London and New York: Routledge, 2012.
Kaur, Ravinder. 'Jat Sikhs: A Question of Identity', *Contributions to Indian Sociology* (n.s.), 20 (2), 1986, pp. 221–239.
Lefebvre, Henri. *The Production of Space*. Oxford: Blackwell, 1991.
McLeod, William Hewat. *Who Is a Sikh? The Problem of Sikh Identity*. New Delhi: Oxford University Press, 1989.
Nihang, Nidar Singh and Paramjit Singh. *In the Master's Presence: The Sikhs of Hazoor Sahib. Volume 1. History*. London: Kashi Publishing House, 2008.
Nishter, Nanak Singh. *Babri Masjid vs Gurdwara Maal Tekdi*. Hyderabad: International Sikh Centre for Interfaith Relations, 2011.
Puratan Gurudwara Sahib Asha Singh Bagh Shaheedan Singh Asthan www.sikhmatrimonials.com/sikhnet/directory.nsf (date accessed: 2 August 2013).
Ray, Niharranjan. *The Sikh Gurus and the Sikh Society: A Study in Social Analysis*. Delhi: Munshiram Manoharlal, 1975.
Sherwani, H.K. *The Bahmanis of the Deccan*. Delhi: Munshiram Manoharlal, 1985.
Singh, Birinder Pal. *Sikhs in the Deccan and North-East India*, London and New York: Routledge, 2018.
Singh, Gyani Mohan. *Tawarikh Sachkand: A Correct History of Gurdwara Saheb*. Nanded, n.d.
The Encyclopaedia of Sikhism, editor-in-chief Harbans Singh. Vols. I-IV. Patiala: Punjabi University, Patiala, 1995–1998.
Uberoi, Jit Pal Singh. *Religion, Civil Society and the State: A Study of Sikhism*. Delhi: Oxford University Press, 1996.
Wood, Peter. *Vassal State in the Shadow of Empire: Palmer's Hyderabad, 1799–1867*. (Ph.D. thesis submitted to the University of Wisconsin) Michigan: UMI Dissertation Services, 1981.

Appendix 1

A locality-wise distribution of Sahukars (bankers) in Pune city, c. 1750–1850

Shukrawar Peth

1. Murar Naik Dev 2. Jeevandas Govardhandas Wanawle 3. Trimbakrao Naik Yerande

Raviwar Peth

1. Wisoba Naik Saraf 2. Jiuba Naik Wakde 3. Krishnaji Bahirav Thate 4. Rangoba Naik Wanawle 5. The house of Haribhakti 6. Mankoji Naik Gogle 6. Gopal Naik Tambwekar

Mangalwar (Astapur) Peth

1. Mahadeo Naik Mayenkar 2. Trimbak Naik Harbhare 3. Sadoba Naik Dandekar 4. Sitaram Naik Chikte 5. Bapuji Naik Chikte 6. Sadoba Naik Labhare

Budhwar Peth

1. Krishnaji Naik Thate 2. Ragho Sadashiv Thate Pedhiwale 3. Ramchandra Naik Paranjape 4. The house of Tambwekar – Narsoba Naik Tambwekar, Prahlad Witthal Naik Tambwekar 5. Wasudeo Naik Datar 6. Bhikaji Naik Bhide 7. Ganeshpant Gokhle 8. Dullabh Shet 9. Harbaji Naik Chabookswar 10. Rangoba Naik Wanawle 11. Babuji Naik Datar 12. Krishnaji Naik Wakde 13. Balaji Naik Awchat 13. Neelkanth Aburao Baramatikar 14. Abaji Naik Kabras 15. Bhikaji Naik Kolatkar

Sadashiv Peth

1. Raghoji Naik Salunkhe

Shaniwar Peth

1. Bapuji Naik Marathe 2. Chimaji Naik Bhakre 3. Balaji Naik Joshi

Kasba Peth

1. Balaji Naik Bhide 2. Bhikaji Naik Bhide 3. Sadashiv Naik Tambwekar

Mentioned without specifying location

1. Baloba Naik Potdar 2. Krishnaji Naik Bhave 3. Dadaji Naik Sorte 4. Malhar Naik Kanere

Appendix 2

Two entries in the Tulshibagwale papers of the year AD 1758

1 Remark for income of 644.5 rupees:

जमा ६४४।।· मुधोजी भोसले तुम्ही श्रीमंतांवर वराता दिल्या रुपये ६६५०० पों आमचे रोकडे येणे रुपये २५००० त्याची वरात वजा रुपये ४१६६६ बाकी रुपये २४८३४ यापैंकी राघोबाबाजी यास वरात देविले रुपये ५००० बाकी रुपये १९८३४ सदर्हूस दरबारखर्च दरशेंकडा ३।· प्रों श्रीमंतांनी वजा केला तो तुमचें नावें सबब वरात बरह्या ऐवज तुम्हांस मजुरा देणे त्यास खर्च झाला तो नावें लिहून

2 Remark for expenditure of 64338.75 rupees:

खर्च ६४३३८।।।· हंसपुरी गोसावी तुम्हांकडे हवालाराजश्री पंतप्रधान यांचा ह्या जानोजी भोसले मिाा श्रावण शुाा १३ शके १६८० रुपये आर्कटी औरंगाबादेस द्यायचा करार त्यापैंकी श्रीमंतांनी आम्हांस देविले बाा वरात मुधोजी भोसले रु. ६६५०० पैकी दरबारखर्च दर शेंकडा ३।· प्रों रुपये २१६१।· घेऊन तुम्हावर वराता दिल्या

Appendix 3

Commission per cent while changing one kind of rupees to another (Chapekar, 33)

Malkapuri to Chandwad – 25
Mirji to Rahimatpuri – 25
Farshi to Malkapuri – 25
Arkat to Surati – 3.5
Arkat to Ingraji – 5
Sikka to Chandwad – 5
Trishuli to Nagache – 12.5
Bawadi to Nagache – 25
Bhatodi to Chandwad – 1
Belapuri to Chandwad – 7.5
Chandwad to Shahu Shikka – 37
Halli Sikka to Chandwad – 8.25

Index

Note: Page numbers followed by "n" denote endnotes.

Adilabad 60, 63–67, 73–75
Āditya temples 156, 159n20, 159n21
agrarian 30, 34–35, 50, 170, 173, 174
Ahmadnagar 6, 9, 107, 110–111, 182, 184, 189
Ambedkar, Dr. Bhimrao (Babasaheb) 77, 79–81, 127, 128, 137–140; Ambedkarite 80–81, 82n2; Broken Men 138
Ambedkar Buddhists 126–7, 128, 137–140
Ambedkarite movement 80
Ambedkarite songs 81
Andhra Pradesh 52, 56, 60, 67–68, 160, 206
Appadurai, Arjun 106
Arabia 164, 169, 173
Architecture 8, 107–113, 155, 159n19
Asafjahi 52, 60
ascetics and asceticism 147, 161
Asifabad 63, 64, 66, 75, 76
Assistant Collector 47
Aurangabad, Auraṅgābād 67, 92, 100, 101, 155, 156, 157, 179, 184, 202, 206
Aurangzeb 59, 108–110, 112, 162, 195

Baba, Sheikh Muhammad 9, 182, 183, 190, 196
Bajirao 20, 31n21, 46, 50n29
Bakht Buland 59
Balaghat 59
Ballarshah 58
Banjara 204, 211–212
baraka 161–162, 165–166, 173
bashārat 166, 168, 172
bayat 162, 165, 166, 173, 174
Beed 184, 193, 206
Berar 6, 59, 60, 64, 68
Bhakti 152, 175, 185, 203, 221
Bhandara 59, 61, 62
Bhavani, Bhavani (Tulja Bhavani) 24, 26, 133, 135–137
Bhikkhus (Buddhist monks) 129–133
Bhil 63
Bhim Ballal 58
Bhima (River), Bhima 36, 40
Bhonsale (Shivaji), Bhosle (Shivaji) 8, 19, 21, 91, 107–112, 115–123, 124n13, 124n15, 137, 162, 170, 184
Bhonsla, Bhonsle 36, 52, 60–62, 91, 92, 101, 199n26
Bhopal 15, 61
Bijapur 6, 103, 107–108, 110–112, 163–164, 177n22
Bombay Presidency 36, 38, 48, 50, 96
Brahmanism 139
Brahmans 129, 138, 186–188, 190–192
British protection 23
British Raj 115
brother-ship 166, 169, 171, 173–174
brotherhood 9, 161–166, 173–174, 176n8
Buddha 77, 130, 133, 138–140
Buddhism (ancient, contemporary), Buddhists 6, 129, 131, 137–140, 142n17, 143n35
Buddhist leni [caves] 8, 126–141

Cakradhar 147, 149, 150–157, 158n1
Cartography 17–18
Caste (castes) 9, 55, 60, 62, 70n42, 77, 78, 80–82, 82n2, 108, 113n3, 115,

136–139, 170, 172–175, 182, 204, 207, 217n13
chaitya 80, 126, 128, 130, 132, 134, 139, 140, 141n3
Chamunda 15, 24, 25
Chanda 57–62, 64–67
Chandrapur 57, 60, 63, 64, 66, 67
Chandraseniya Kayastha Prabhu caste (CKP) 136, 137
Chandwad 92, 95
Chhatrapati Shivaji see Bhonsle, Shivaji
Chhatrapati Shahu 108
Chinnur 65
chronology, pegged to geography 150
Clunes, Captain John 96, 97
Cohen, Benjamin 106
Coins, currency 8, 87–105
commemoration 115, 121

Dalit 77–82, 82n2, 138, 197
Dargah 9, 161–176, 176n1, 189, 191, 194–195
D. D. Kosambi 131–133, 136, 141n3, 142n25
Dakhani identity 205, 214
Dakhani Sikhs 204–219
Dasganu 186, 187
Dattātreya 149
Dattatreya, Datta 183
Daulatabad 92, 95, 110
Deogadh 60
dependence on the Mahānubhāv biographies 149, 154
Desh 1, 6, 18
deshmukh 37, 41, 50n3, 65
Dewas Junior 17, 24, 27, 30
Dewas Senior 15–17, 21, 24
digital divide 79
Diwan Chandu Lal 205
Dnyanadev/Jnanadev 186, 189–190, 194, 199n22, 200n42

ecological (spheres, cultures) 53–55
Eknath 186, 188, 194
Ekvira temple 8–9, 126–127, 129, 131–2, 134, 138–140, 143n36
Ekvira, Ekvera 9, 126, 128, 131–141
Ellora 109–110
English East India Company 46
equestrian statues 116, 120, 121, 122–124, 124n12

Facebook 80
Fergusson, James 128, 133–134, 136, 142n19, 142n26
'financescape,' finanscape' 89
funerary structures (*chhatri*) 110

"geography of money" 8, 87–89
Ghrishneshwar/Ghrishneshwara 110
Godāvarī river/valley 56, 58, 65, 92, 147, 151, 155, 157, 158n5, 158n11, 205
goddess, goddesses 15, 25–26, 126, 128–129, 131–137, 140, 142n17, 143n28
Golconda 6, 107–108, 112
Gond State 7, 12, 59, 62, 68
Graham, Maria 133, 142n20
graves 163, 165, 171, 182, 183, 189, 192
Gujarat 5, 20, 50n3, 123n4, 147, 158n1, 162
Guṇḍam Rāüḷ 147, 149, 151, 154–155, 157, 159n28
Guru Gobind Singh 208, 211, 213–216, 217n2, 217n25, 218n32
Guru Granth Sahib 211, 213, 217n27

hagiography 167, 169, 172, 178
healing 164–167, 173, 174
Hill of Devi (The) 15, 17
Hindu 59, 65, 108, 112–113, 134, 137–141, 153, 156–157, 159n24, 159n28, 162–167, 169, 171–176, 182, 183
Hindu temples 112, 128, 169
Hinduism 3, 139, 182, 187, 201, 203
Historiography 82, 118; Academic, cloistered, scientific, professional history 118–119, 122; Popular, public 118–120
holy man/holy men 181–183, 188, 197
Horse, horses 24, 37, 40–48, 101, 120, 121–122, 190, 213, 218
Hundi (bills of exchange) 100–101

Inam 37
Indapur Pargana 35–50
Indian Ocean 164, 173, 176, 178, 179, 181, 198, 202
Indian Union 5, 67
indigenous concepts 9, 19, 59
Islam 59, 64, 124, 130, 161, 164, 166, 167, 173–176, 183, 185, 217n23, 219

Jadhav, Jadhavrao 109, 110–112
jagir 36–48, 48n3, 49n6, 49n7, 66, 92

Kabir 186
Kala Godha 121–123
Kamavisdar 37, 39, 40, 42, 46, 47
Kānaḍā land 147
Karle (Karli, Carli) 126–141
Khaki Buva 194–196, 201
Khaṇḍobā 134, 140
Kherla 57, 59, 60
Kinwat 63–67, 71n77
Kirpan 207, 211, 213–214
Konkan 1, 6, 9, 161–169, 171–175
Kṛṣṇa 157
Kumaram Bhimu, Kumra Bhimu 66

Lahori Fauj/Force 205, 208, 209
Līḷācaritra 147, 149, 150, 156, 158n6
Līḷācharitra 176

Madras Presidency 47, 57
Mahadev Koli 136
Mahānubhāv theology (See also: theological explanations) 9, 148
Mahānubhāv, Mahānubhāvs I, 9, 147–149, 151–157, 159n28
Mahānubhāv Monks 152
Mahar 41, 49n16
Maharaja Ranjit Singh 205, 206, 209
Maharashtra State Archives 38, 40, 49n9
Mahur 63, 65, 149
malguzar 61–62
Maloji Bhosle 184
Malwa 18–22, 27, 33n49, 61
Mang, Mangs 41, 49n16
Mankeshwar, Sadashiv 47, 50, 50n29, 97
Maratha Confederacy 16, 18–22, 31n14, 36, 60, 109
Maratha kingdom 7, 36, 107
Marathi language 19, 47
Marathi, ethnic identity 173
Marathi-Gondi 67
Marāṭhvāḍā, Marathwada 6, 59, 67, 91, 155, 205
Marlavai 66–67, 72n97
memorial, memorials 8, 23, 32n36, 72, 72n97, 110–117, 124n13, 137, 189
mints 90–92, 95–97, 99, 103n3, 104, 105n9
miracles 161–162, 164–165, 169, 172, 175
Mirji 101, 102, 224
money 87–106
moṅglāī 18, 19
Mortad, Narayan Singh 209
mother goddess 128, 131–133, 135–136, 141, 142n3
Mughal 6, 7, 20, 36, 43, 52, 55, 57, 58, 59, 60–63, 71n74, 90, 92, 99, 103n1, 107–113, 175
Mughal empire 36, 43, 57, 59, 90
Mughal rupee 90
mujāwar (*mujāwari*) 166–169, 171, 172, 191, 192, 194
Mumbai/Bombay 80, 101, 116, 121, 122, 123, 124n13
Muslim 59, 108, 110, 112, 139, 161–176, 180–197, 200n47, 201n56, 204, 214, 217n23
Mysore 43

Nāgdev 147, 151, 153
Nagpur 52, 59, 60, 61, 62, 65, 67, 91, 92, 101, 140, 147
Naik, Bapujirao 44–45
Namdev 181, 189
Nanded 10, 63, 67, 71n77, 149, 204–215, 216n8, 218n32
Narasiṃha temples 157, 159n25
Narayan, Madhavrao 43
Naths 183
Nationalism 5, 138–139, 173
Nationalists 163, 164, 175
Nazim-i-Jami'at-i-Sikhan 205
Nira River 36, 40, 46
Nirmal 64–65, 209
Nizam, Nizam of Hyderabad 6, 7, 51–52, 55, 57, 60, 63, 64, 65, 66, 91n71, 90, 91, 92, 205, 206, 207, 209, 215, 217n20, 218n36
Nizam Shah, Nizamshah 8, 19, 107–111

oṭās 151–154, 156–157

Pagaḍī, Setumādhavrāv 155–157, 159n20
Paiṭhaṇ 100, 101, 150, 151, 157, 194
Paloncha 65
Pandharpur 156, 186, 188, 189, 194, 200n41

Pandurang Naik 44–46
pargana 7, 27, 35–48, 49n5, 49n6, 50n29
Pāṭhak, Aruṇcandra 155–157, 159
patil 37, 41
Patwardhan, Patwardhan family 39, 47, 49n5, 91, 101
pavitra, places as 152
Periphery, peripharal 54, 57
Peshwa, Peshwas 7, 20, 22, 31n21, 35, 36, 39, 42, 43, 45, 46, 49n5, 61, 91, 92, 95–100, 135–136, 199n26
Phadnis, Nana 43
Phulgaon 96, 97, 98
pilgrimage and pilgrims 3, 136, 149, 151, 152, 153, 154, 155, 158n5, 164, 182, 194
Prabhakar 92
Puars / Ponwars / Pawars 19–22, 32n27
Pune 18, 22, 21–22, 30n8, 36–40, 43, 46–48, 92–93, 96–102, 124n15
Punjabi (language) 198, 204, 205, 207, 218n32, 219

Qadiri, *Qādiriyya* 162, 163, 167, 185–186, 197, 199–200n27
Quotidian/quotidian 161, 172, 174, 175, 176

Raghunathrao 39
Rahimatpuri 101–102, 224
Raigad 108–109, 112, 167
Raigarh 163, 167, 174, 176n2
Raj-Gond 62
Rājmaḍh/Rājmaṭh 157, 159n25
Rajura 64–65
Ramdas, Samarth 186
Ratnagiri 50n31, 161, 163, 167, 172
Ṛddhipur 147, 148, 149, 151, 152, 154, 157, 158n4, 158n15, 159n19
Ṛddhipurcaritra (The Deeds of God in Ṛddhipur) 149, 154
Reformist 169, 173, 174, 175
rehat (rehatnama, rehatmaryada) 204, 215
riots 80, 81, 82, 169, 174, 214
Rompa 66
Rupee; *Ankushi* 93, 95–100, 103; *Furshee* 93–94, 100; *Hali Sikka* 92–93, 95; *Hubshee* 98; *Potechal* 95, 104; Surti rupee 92
Rural 6, 13, 53, 55, 67, 69n23, 115, 171, 172, 174, 175, 178n34
Ryotwari Settlement 35–36, 42, 47, 48, 49n1

Sach Khand Hazoor Sahib 204, 210–212, 215
saint-poets 183, 184
Śakti 152
samadhi 112, 187, 189, 193, 194
sampraday 183, 196
sannidhān (presence) 152
Sarangpur 20, 23, 24, 26
sarañjām 18, 20–22, 48n3
Satara (Satara Subha) 20, 39, 91, 92, 100, 101
scaffolding 7, 52, 54, 59, 67, 68
Seoni 59
Shiv Sena 137, 163, 179
Shiva, Shaivite, Śiva 128, 133, 134, 155–157, 159n20, 160
Shiva temple 128
Shivalinga, Shiva lingam 133, 135, 140
Shrigonda 9, 182, 184, 187, 188, 189, 191, 193, 194, 195, 196, 199n19, 199n41, 199n44
shrines 3, 152, 154, 157, 174, 176n1, 182
Shripura Mahatmya 188
Shroff 91, 95, 98
Sikh Chhawniat 205, 209, 217n21, 218n31
silsila 162
Sindkhed Raja 109–111
smaraṇ (recollection) 152–154
smṛtisthaḷ 147, 151, 153
social media 4, 81, 84, 117, 120
Soja, Edward 6, 126
Son Koli 128, 136, 137, 142n7, 143n35
sovereignty 17, 18, 22, 30n8, n31, 51, 52–56, 59, 63, 67, 109, 211
spatial lexemes 19
statues 8, 115–123, 123n4, 124n13
Sthānpothī 151–157, 159n21, 159n23
sthāns, Mahānubhāv 151, 153, 154
Stupa 126, 128, 130, 132–137, 140–141
Stupa-worship 130

Sufi, Sufism, Sufis 6, 9, 110–114, 161–200
Sūtrapāṭh 147, 152
svarājya 18, 19
Swayambu 132, 133, 135

takht 20, 205, 211, 216n2, 217n25, 218n32
taluqdar 65, 66, 71n86
tariqa, tarīqas 162–167, 173–174, 176n8
Telangana 5, 8, 52, 56–58, 63, 66–68, 69n25
Telugu land 147
territory 17–19, 21, 23–24, 27–30
Thackeray, (Bal), (Udhav) 137
tombs 110–111
translocal 53, 165
tribal Sikhs 204, 212
Tryambakeśvar 149, 158n5
Tukaram 77, 83n4, 181, 186
twin states ('both' oddity) (two states) 15, 23, 27, 28

Untouchables 82n2, 138
urs 168, 171

Vahira 193, 194, 196, 197, 201n62
Vaishnava, Vaishnavas 9, 183–191, 194, 196–197, 200n42, 201n56
Varkari, Varkaris 6, 159, 181, 183, 185, 186, 188–190, 194, 197, 199n22, 200n41, 200n42, 201n48, 200n56
Veherai 126, 136
Verardi, Giovanni 138, 139
Vidarbha 6, 59, 67, 91–92, 147, 155
Vihara 130, 132–134, 136
Viśṇu temples 155, 156
Viṭhobā 156

Wadepuri 39
Wahhabi/Wahhabism 163–165, 173
Wai 97, 100, 103
Watan, watandar, watandari 41, 61, 65
Whatsapp 80–81

Yogasangram 185, 186, 188, 191, 192, 194
yogi 187, 196, 197
YouTube 80

Zamindar, *zamindari* 58, 61

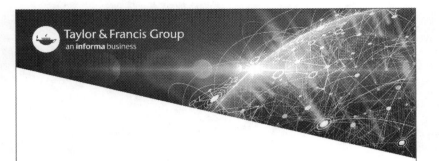